CATHOLIC
IMMIGRANT ADJUSTMENT

BY THE SAME AUTHOR

CATHOLIC IMMIGRANT ADJUSTMENT

Burton Confrey

EXPOSITION PRESS • **NEW YORK**

Exposition Press Inc., 386 Park Avenue So., New York 10016

FIRST EDITION

© 1966 by Burton Confrey. *All rights reserved, including the right of reproduction in whole or in part in any form, except for short quotations in critical essays and reviews.* Manufactured in the United States of America.

IN MEMORY OF

MISS BRIDGET MULLEN

—"Aunt Bix"—

Contents

Preliminary

In *Catholic Educational Heritage From Abroad*, we considered three overarching movements instead of divisions into ancient, medieval, and modern. "Achieving Our Catholic Heritage" brought us up to "Integrating Life Through the Liturgy," and what historians call "modern times" we designated "Inculcating a Catholic Sense."

Now we shall explore American educational development of intrinsic interest to Catholics. Here only those factors, institutions, and events as offset United States citizens who are Catholic merit discussion. We shall consider the relation of geographical surroundings to frontiers. The American heritage as a frontier of European culture, religion, language, and customs, and the relation of a knowledge of geography and past history to future planning and operation. We shall regard appreciatively why our ancestors came to America and where they settled, and these people as individuals and groups in regard to physique and growth in numbers, intelligence, soul life, and emotions.

The daily life of a people consists of the continuous adjustment between them and their environment. The dry facts about education and dates cannot reveal the real significance of such adjustment.

CATHOLIC
IMMIGRANT ADJUSTMENT

CHAPTER ONE

The American Heritage of Europe's Culture

To assess and interpret the cultural forces of contemporary America, one turns to the grand epic of European immigrants sweeping across the continent overcoming the handicaps of wilderness and hostility of Indians, and embellishing history's record of free institutions built to protect natural rights. We can hardly overemphasize the fact that our ancestors were European—not Indian, that our country was a frontier of Europe, that our culture, our language and our religion burgeoned from European roots, and that even our ideals of liberty and constitutional government are part of a similar heritage. However social or geographic conditions may have modified the Western culture our immigrant parents brought with them, the regional communities of nations on both sides of the Atlantic are bound culturally. The continuity of that heritage outweighed, in a short time, anything new we got from the wilderness or the Indians. Such spiritual ancestry and nationality can be inherited but never acquired. Catholic education keeps both fresh in the minds of the inheritors.

Out of our European background centering around the Mediterranean (and for Catholics synthesized in the Eternal City—a fact particularly apparent in a Holy Year, such as 1950) has risen what Walter Lippmann designated the "Atlantic Community," the protector of Western civilization.

Lippmann regretted that our American public education, however, has created no common culture, no common faith, no common body of principles, no common moral code and intellectual discipline. It has failed because although individual subjects of the public school curriculum may be worthwhile in themselves, too much of the European world —and too many of its emigrants and their descendants—lost sight of the common purpose which integrated Catholic education through the ages.

Any history of American education should be sufficiently rich to encompass a survey of American and European culture and their relationship; but the integrating factor was rejected at the time of the so-called Reformation, and public education in American will never be normal until it returns to the path synthesized by St. Thomas and followed today only by Catholic schools and colleges. With economic prosperity, a forward-looking political and social philosophy, and an immense number of our adolescents in high school, the United States has a unique opportunity to contribute substantially to the civilization and culture of the world. Those adolescents (the next generation of adults) can be trained in disinterested devotion to the great cause of building the Kingdom of God on earth as it is in heaven.

The Burma Road was built from earth carried in baskets. World forces are the outcome of innumerable individual acts everyone does everyday. The bringing of Christian principles into domination of every individual's daily acts and then the subordination of all the ramifications of life to those same principles will solve world problems. All reform should begin with personal sanctification, and even waiting until adolescence to begin such training can be too late.

Airplanes, as well as vessels, have combated intellectual, political, and economic isolationism to such an extent that our American frontier, once thought of as west of the Alleghenies, now extends to lands in or bordering the

Pacific. The Declaration of Independence freed us politically, but an original American literature freeing us from the intellectual domination of European writers was slow in arriving. Evidently economic isolation is impossible; and some Americans' raucous shouts of superiority, jingoism, or exaggerated patriotism may be attributed to a suspicion of inferiority. Certainly Decatur's dictum, "My country right or wrong, my country" is unacceptable. If our country's leaders are wrong, they must be corrected. A Christian democracy tones down chauvinism or a lusty nationalism encouraged for utilitarian purposes or under romantic influence—its intensity directly proportioned to its artificiality. Consciousness that all are children of a Common Father counteracts the growth of isolationism and antagonism to fatherlands simply because their particular religions, nationalities, and languages differ. From the American melting pot has come a new and unique nationality, but it has ancestry.

The United States is, moreover, enmeshed in the entangling alliances against which Washington warned us. It is to be regretted that our armed forces have been embroiled in European and Asiatic conflicts. The lies of those politicians responsible for intervention are not to be excused; but in a large view, if Western civilization is to survive the Atlantic Community must co-operate. The United States intervened in World War I to preserve the Community but short-sightedly permitted politicians to keep us out of the League of Nations, which might, with our participation, have strengthened and guaranteed world peace. A survey of World War II will make that fact clear. Unfortunately Congressional appointments of delegates from the United States to the United Nations and the Commission on Human Rights have showed little discernment. The Soviet scrutinizes every member of its UN delegation for rigid adherence to Kremlin policies. Before Congress delegates the extraordinary power which the United States should have in this world body, it should demand of each candidate unqualified loyalty to American principles and to our form of Constitutional government. Even good intentions are insufficient without the intelligence, information, and other qualifications imperative for adequate representation of the American people.

Our religious heritage from Europe has been minimized too frequently. Our ancestors made vows most seriously and were thoroughly convinced of the sacrilege committed if one were broken as Hugh Osborn Taylor, a non-Catholic historian, shows in *The Medieval Mind.* When they vowed to spread Christianity or to perform a certain penance in reparation (even to leading a Crusade), they could find no excuse for dodging their responsibility. Bernal Diaz, companion to Cortez, wrote about him: He was a good cavalier, most true in his devotion to the Holy Apostle, St. Peter, and all other saints. "May God pardon his sins and mine, too, and give me a pious end, which is of more concern than the conquests and victories we had over the Indians."

At the first Mass in the Philippines (among barbarians who worshiped idols and demons) Magellan said to the leaders:

You must not accept our Faith from any fear of us in order to please us. If you wish to become Christians you must do so willingly. No harm will be done you if you do not embrace our religion; but those who do will be more loved and better treated than the others. Moreover, if you become Christians, I will leave you arms, as my King has commanded, and then you can defend yourselves against enemies.

The edifying stories of the fearless Franciscans who Christianized the Southwest are legion—Fathers Junipero Serra and Antonio Peyri, for example, and the Jesuit, Esebius (Kuhn) Kino. In *Death Comes for the Archbishop* Willa Cather has immortalized Archbishop John Lamy (who in 1854 reported to the United States government from his see at Santa Fe).

Father Rale, S.J., heroic on his Indian missions in Maine, murdered by the English, is never heard of by the Catholic child attending public school. He hears of Eliot, but the historian Bancroft says Eliot never approached the Indian tribe living within six miles of Boston Harbor until five years after the French had borne the cross, with religious zeal, from Lake Superior down the Mississippi Valley. In 1722, New England decreed imprisonment for life for Catholic priests and a reward was offered for the head of Father Rale. Harvard now has his Abnaki dictionary and the Massachusetts Historical Society has the strong box which held his papers. (On the lid are pictures of the scourging of Christ and the crowning with thorns—images rich in meaning for the meditation of one enduring Father Rale's sufferings.)

Canadian missionaries began to publish *Jesuit Relations* in 1732 and to include in them pleas for vocations, for example: "Alas! is there no charitable and virtuous lady who will come to this country to gather up the blood of Christ by teaching His word to little Indian girls?" Mme. de la Peltrie did. Mother St. Joseph, a timid, modest, sweet, delicate girl did. In 1639 with them and three hospital nuns came Margaret Bourgeois (who founded the first religious order in America—the Sisters of Notre Dame, one of whose schools is on Staten Island). The non-Catholic historian Parkman pays them high tribute for their courageous accomplishments in the midst of poverty almost incredible.

Mother Mary of the Incarnation (b. 1599) was the first Ursuline to come to America. She records:

The good education I had received from my parents, who were most pious Christians, laid an excellent foundation in my soul; and I cannot but bless the God of goodness for His gracious kindness to me in this connection. It is a great step in the way of virtue and a precious preparation for a high degree of piety to fall into hands which carefully mold the first years of our existence.

I now see that all the states of life, trials, and labor through

which I have passed, have had but one object—for forming me
for the work to be done in Canada.

Ideas of this sort the nuns passed on to their pupils.
Mother Mary's motto: "I should regard as lost a day passed
without suffering" was not sadistic or a love of suffering for
the sufferings' sake. She really united tribulations with the
sufferings of Christ in His passion and death—an excellent
check on hedonism or Manicheism (into which Augustine
of Hippo lapsed when his baptism was too long deferred).
The Ursulines opened the first school in the United
States at New Orleans and their pupils still learn the *Salve
Regina* (Hail, Holy Queen), the *Ave Maris Stella* (Hail,
Star of the Sea) and the *Te Deum* with which virgin forests
rang and their echoes adding to the beauty of lake waters.
The American Ursulines have special devotion to Our
Lady of Prompt Succor (the Blessed Mother holding the
Divine Infant who supports a globe) because in 1785 through
her intercession, Pope Pius VII (then Napoleon's prisoner)
permitted them to go to New Orleans. In 1814, by the same
intercessor they were saved from the plundering and torches
of the English under General Packenham, whose slogan
"Beauty and Booty" got them only defeat when Andrew
Jackson rescued New Orleans.
Our heritage as a frontier of Europe includes the Peace
of 1763, whereunder the French surrendered Canada, and
"Evangeline" became as much a part of our inheritance as
"Hiawatha." With the Colonists' aid the English winning
of the Battle of Quebec was a deadening blow to the mis-
sions because, even though the winners guaranteed to
Canada absolute religious freedom, they took unobtrusive
steps to get rid of the Jesuit Fathers. In 1775 deputations
from Maine and Nova Scotia attended the Massachusetts
Council, made known their intention of joining with the
Colonies, but begged that they be given a French priest.

Of the Council's regret that none were available, John Gilmary Shea remarks how strange that the very legislative body which less than a century previous had made it a felony for a Catholic priest to visit the Abnaki missions in Maine were now regretting they could not furnish these allies a missionary of the same faith and nationality as they had excluded.

After the Revolution, when Maryland's few Catholics selected Father John Carroll, S.J., as bishop, the Abnakis sent him the crucifix of Father Rale, whom the English had murdered, and asked for a priest. They got one for a decade; and when Father (later Cardinal) Cheverus visited the Penobscot tribe (after having studied the Abnaki dialect), he was inspired to discover they could still chant the music of the Mass and vespers.

Father Romagne succeeded Father Cheverus, evangelizing for the Penobscots and Passamaquoddies for a score of years. In July, 1827, Bishop Fenwick (once a Jesuit) visited Maine (then a part of the Boston Diocese) and in 1891 sent those Indians a resident missionary. A beautiful church was erected as a memorial to Father Rale, a prayerbook was printed in Abnaki; and since 1848 the Jesuits have been in charge. In a disgraceful Know-nothing riot (1844) Father John Bapst was almost murdered; but since then, the few remaining Penobscots still cling to the Faith first brought them at St. Saveur in 1613 by Fathers Biard and DuThet.

Because of Longfellow's poem the Acadians dwell in American memories. The descendants of Benedict Bellefontaine inhabit southwestern Louisiana and at St. Martinsville we can still see the live oak under which Evangeline rested. In one community over five hundred of the citizens (practically all) were descendants of Benedict—all "cousins." The poem is one of the finest pictures of home and domestic affection in any language and a choral reading group might recall:

When in the tranquil evenings of summer . . .
Solemnly down the village street came the priest, and the children
Paused in their play . . . Acadian farmers
Dwelt in the love of God and of man.

Parkman records that in a semipiratical descent on Port
Royal, an obscure stroke of lawless violence, began the
strife of England and France (of Protestantism and Rome)
which for a century and a half shook the struggling communities of the New World even after the crisis on the
Plains of Abraham. The aftermath of penal laws and hatred
by the government in the British provinces for "popish
priests" scarred America indelibly.

Paralleling the deportation of the Acadians was the
United States' scattering of the Wyandots (Hurons), whom
they deported to Indian Territory. Although they became
the smallest and wealthiest of the dispossessed, there may
be among them still legends of the French missioners
Brébeuf and LeCaron, who brought their ancestors the
Faith.

Over a thousand churches have been named in honor of
the Blessed Mother—rivers, lakes, bays, and mountain peaks,
too. The non-Catholic author of the famous *Education of
Henry Adams* showed in his *Saint Michel and Chartres* that
of soldiers dedicated to Our Lady the officers must be
skillful, diligent, prudent, unselfish, and prompt; troops must
be obedient, loyal, steadfast, and constant. Thomas D'Arcy
M'Gee eulogized the Catholic character of the great French
explorer LaSalle in his every act. Before each undertaking
he prayed for guidance. The first fruits of each completed
task were offered for the honor and glory of God. If he
stopped at a new place for but an hour, he planted the
cross. Hymns of adoration and thanksgiving accompanied
him on his travels. Whether he was exploring the Great
Lakes—and he was the first foreigner to navigate the Great
Lakes except Superior—crossing on foot the portage from
Lake Ontario across what is now Ohio to the Ohio River,

or planting the Cross on Starved Rock above the Illinois, he was ever the perfect knight, without fear and without reproach. Only his faith could console him, shot down at his zenith, unaware of his success.

In the current miasma of disbelief, malfeasance in high office, spoliation of political position, and cynicism as regards the survival of Western civilization—not to mention Christianity and the Church, we might look back to Civil War times and General Sherman's public acknowledgment that he would have sunk back many times were it not for the encouragement of his wife, a noble Catholic. Sheridan lost no opportunity to express his gratitude to his devout Catholic mother, typical of the group who in every time of national crisis have contributed the largest percentage of men to the Armed Forces. Recall also Thomas F. Meagher, Generals Rosencrans and Shields, and Colonel Mulligan, and the Sisters whose services are recorded in Ellen Ryan Joly's *Nuns of the Battlefield.*

Few contributions to one's country can compare with that of a person who believes in a personal God to whom he is strictly accountable. Brethren in Christ, children of the Common Father, the relationship of each one to his Creator is different in every case. With personal awareness of God, comprehension comes easy when as Christ said to St. John, "Son, behold thy mother"—all things through Mary. Don John of Austria and the sailors of the Holy Alliance believed firmly that the victory at Lepanto was due to Our Lady of Victory. Notre Dame de Bon Secours (Our Lady of Help in Need) relieved the French from the pestilence of epidemic.

The study of Mariology, of the troubadours' dedication to Notre Dame, Orbey Shipley's *Carmina Mariana,* the *Mariale,* Frank Sheed's *The Mary Book,* Henri Gheon's *The Madonna in Art,* St. Grignon de Montfort's *True Devotion to the Blessed Virgin,* F. Gabrini's *Mary the Model and Mother of Christians,* Daniel Lord's *Our Lady in the Modern*

World, and similar publications, all with the same goal, are evidence of continued devotion to the Seat of Wisdom, the Mother of Good Counsel. One needs but visit one of our towns where the Spanish or French influence lingers to see people stop on the street and men bare their heads for a few moments' communion with God during the Angelus. "Papists" have been accused to showing too much honor to Christ's Mother—even of idolatry; but the accusers are unaware that an indulgence is granted to Catholics who, upon entering a chapel where the Blessed Sacrament is reserved, turn attention first to Christ in the tabernacle. Missionaries, explorers, and pioneers who honored the Blessed Mother by naming places after her were pleasing her Son in reverencing her.

The Catholic immigrant was made aware of the strong feeling against devotion to Our Lady expressed by the powerful influence and consciences unhampered by a subordination of economics to ethics. Fortunate the youth protected in temptation by devotion to the ideal woman and innervated in their devotion by an atmosphere free from slight, misrepresentation, and deliberate lies as we have presented it through their voluntary class papers in *Faith and Youth, Stenciled of God, Spiritual Conferences for College Men,* and *Following the Liturgical Year.* No need to deny a delicate sentiment lest it be sneered at when in a Catholic college you can head your papers with O.L.P.H. (Our Lady of Perpetual Help), under whose aegis a girl with a severe physical handicap places her effort. In a materialistic atmosphere the youth who places a *T* as standard at the top of his class exercises might be asked what the "fetish" meant (one was); he hesitated to explain that, like St. Bernardine who had his trysts with the Queen of Heaven, he sought beauty in life and creed and was sure he got practical aid from the intercession of St. Thérèse (the Little Flower). A saint as ideal is psychologically much more effective than one's peer or an older adult whose clay feet become apparent when he is put on a pedestal. *Action Now* is a monthly magazine for Sodalists—very modern in its presentations—which encourages in youth more careful diligence for the soul than for the body, for eternity than for time; and the Queen of All Saints is its inspiration.

In keeping with the ideals of Catholic missionaries and explorers of primeval America, today no country has more reverent love and heartfelt devotion to the Blessed Virgin than America. Evidence of its deep roots and the ardor with which it is cherished appears in the author's *The Church of the Sacred Heart at Notre Dame.* Beyond the imagination of the exoteric is this unobtrusive but real influence which guides men's hearts and burns pure and glowing in the souls of Catholics, particularly in an unsympathetic atmosphere where the thoughtless are engrossed in daily affairs. In earliest childhood the young wear the symbolic medal or scapular, join a sodality or rosary society, and later enter the Armed Services fortified with a rosary which they may recite privately or unobtrusively on street or station or subway or in concert on an auto trip.

In the home parents have trained girls and boys thus, in school Sisters and lay teachers on all levels; Brothers and priests have directed boys and young men.

Currently, because of her appearances at Fatima in Portugal, devotion to the Queen of Peace is rising to amazing heights, for hundreds of millions of Catholics believe that only she can convert Russia, can bring peace to the world.

To think concretely about the United States as a European frontier, one might recall his ancestors as immigrants, why they came and where they settled. We might also approach the study of Dante humanly through realizing that today people bearing his name are Durantes and that he lived and had his being among fellow Italians, like any Durante living in the Bowery.

Many emigrants, especially the Irish, escaped to the New World "like birds in the night"—with few or no worldly possessions; but even if illiterate, Catholic immigrants could understand their relationship to God well enough to distinguish right from wrong and to train their children to choose the right unerringly. With no leaders in America (Emerson, Lowell, and similar writers had nothing to offer them) many got their greatest help from the Boston *Pilot,* just as today many non-literary Catholics are taught (as Christ taught— through parables) by such a magazine as the *Messenger of the Sacred Heart* (whose stories are parables) and by their diocesan newspapers.

In 1946 upon returning from a trip to the United States, a news reporter from the U.S.S.R. publicized his idea of a racial hierarchy established here—with the English, Scotch, and Irish at the top; the Scandinavians and the Germans below; then the French and the Slavs. Much lower were the Italians and still lower the Jews and Chinese. Puerto Ricans were next to the bottom, where the Negroes are found. Despite the meanness of this stratification, an Italian child, for instance, could be inspirited and the effect of that news report counteracted by revealing to him our debt to Dante, the greatest of Catholic poets. In fact, St. Bernard's prayer to the Blessed Virgin (*Paradiso,* Canto XXXIII) even non-Catholics concede the greatest poetry ever written, with the intellectual concept of God presented in the thinnest vowels and hardest consonants in contrast with the broad vowels and softest consonants of the Italian word for God—a full expression of the concept.

A study of the unique characteristics of the thinking of various nationalities would be most helpful in allaying misunderstanding, particularly for delegates to the World Peace Conference, the United Nations Assembly, and similar gatherings, and would lead into a liaison field—foundations of national leadership including comparative education, comparative government, contemporary civilization, comparative literature, and international relations.

A former member of the U.S. Government's educational missions to Japan and Germany, and for eighteen months Director of Education for the Allied Control Committee in Italy, reported that we may expect most of our way of life from the Japanese, although he knows nothing of their motives. General MacArthur found they are "sincere and on the square"—docile and imitative. The Germans (according to the same Director) insist on standing pat on German "principles," admit no compromise, and, as ever, are "efficient, but romantic, self-pitying and fanatical, crucifying reasonableness in the name of reason." He expected more from them than from the Italians because the latter refuse to prevent births (Catholicism forbids it) and overpopulation is the chief obstacle to re-education out of Fascism. The stupidity of sending non-Catholics to supervise the education system in Catholic countries of Europe and South America is patent.

Leaders in the social sciences feel that the comparative method in studying history diminishes, better than any other means, racial, political, religious, and national prejudices. By avoiding the narrowness of national history, through a wide acquaintance with other and comparable examples of the phenomena he meets therein, by emphasizing the continuity of history and stressing its cultural and social equally with its political and economic aspects, the growing mind tends to lose its provincialism.

The Catholic student, particularly, needs careful direction in comprehending the Communist regime in Russia since one cannot be Christian (for God, spiritual-minded, and a disciple of Christ) and also Communist (against God, materialistic-minded, and a disciple of Marx). From the standpoint of charity, Communists are men, our brothers. We must love them (which does not involve affection) in the manner of Christ, with all our hearts and, if need be, even to the giving of our lives. For clarity: we must realize that Communist doctrine and Christian teaching are incompatible. Accord is impossible even on the plane of practical action when the expression or affirmation of doctrine is involved. Communists have no conception of three things their opponents hold of greatest value—the human soul, human life, and human rights. The Communists and their fellow-travelers in America (who insist on living thousands of miles from Russia) try to destroy the very freedoms our immigrant ancestors came here to enjoy—freedom of political belief, of religion, and of opportunity, and freedom from prejudicial discrimination and oppression, poverty, and shame. These anti-Christians would termite American economy and terminate our freedoms.

If politicians would implement the Atlantic Charter and guarantee its Four Freedoms, Americans could get rid of any craven fear of the Soviet, which cost the world so dearly between World Wars I and II and which still forms the greatest menace to future peace and security. Safe in our Atlantic citadel Americans could co-operate more loyally and effectively (because the less suspiciously) with all the United Nations and thereby insure (through the fullest joint action) the new world order. We could thus contribute to more permanent settlements with Russia and China. Our fear of the U.S.S.R. banished (although Americans must always be alert against treachery), we could work out the more readily means of getting along in the world with the Soviet peoples on their way to material recovery and progress and at the same time also help China toward the same goal. As a result the entire world would be relieved and encouraged to adopt and support a genuine democracy and liberty characteristic of our western civilization and especially of its American frontier.

Walter L. White's *Land of Milk and Honey* presented the first days in America of Vashti, a deserter from the Red Air Force who is young enough to have no memory of times before Lenin. The exposition gives a perspicacious insight into the workings of the young Russian mind and the feeling that if Communist youth got away from Stalin's dictatorship they would not only be amenable to the ways of democracy but eager and enthusiastic about American democracy once they could believe it really exists.

According to the American standard of living, Russia is now overpopulated in relation to its resources. John Fischer's *Why They Behave Like Russians* reveals the Communist totalitarian despotism, a bureaucracy headed principally by ignoramuses in the field of science and research who know only terror and politics as whips to keep the people in line. Once the intelligent younger generation discovers there is a different sort of existence, particularly a republican form of government in which both capital and labor believe in a capitalistic philosophy, understanding between the United States and Russia will grow.

Hans J. Morgenthau's *In Defense of the National Interest* contends that in the present bi-polar world the presence of the United States army in Europe will warn Russia and prevent internal subversion of the countries behind the Iron Curtain. The Russians have two hundred divisions of soldiers; the Europeans, ten. The Swiss have the strongest army in Europe; so it is unintelligent to speak of the Elbe or the Rhine as the last line of defense. Weapons alone will restrain the Communists, but they will soon equal our stockpile of atomic weapons. The United States is once again—in another sense—the frontier of Europe.

Fortunately, an organized apostolate (the Pro-Russia Movement) hopes to assure the Christian Russians that they have the prayers and sacrifices of American brethren to help them in their great trials. In addition to the prayer campaign (the Mass and the rosary as requested by Our Lady of Fatima) the organization spreads information about the real Christian Russia—its language and history, and helps all refugees from Communistic tyranny.

CHAPTER TWO

History of Catholic Education in the United States

Historical and geographical research can aid tellingly our discovery of what the level of education in various periods was and why that culture and civilization passed away. In that process we have avoided both lists of names and dates and digests of educational reformers' theories. To avoid a post-mortem approach to history we have sought to discover in the daily life of a people how they strove continuously to adjust themselves to their surroundings. The dry facts about educators and dates cannot do that.

We have not feared being deemed "unscientific" because we followed this original pattern of interpreting what is of intrinsic interest to us as Catholics in the United States in the light of our purpose; it is a selective treatment in one sense, but our aim justifies the selection. In a descriptive bibliography we warn against several historians of education who ignore things Catholic or misinterpret because of bigotry, bias, prejudice, or ignorance. For that reason we are not concerned that our principle of selection will be considered invalid or unimportant.

For example, we note that Knight's title is misleading when he announces *Education in the United States* and treats only public schools—as if there never were any Catholic schools. We shall not try to give the impression that no one except Catholics helped build America; but as our title announces, we are discussing Catholic education in the United States and that limitation precludes the inclusion of anything not of intrinsic value to the topic. By both custom and precedent the Church has always gladly approved and helped forward whatever is honorable and praiseworthy wherever it is found. All truth is hers to defend foursquarely and there is no other institution with a like history. Special and greatest honors she reserves for those virtues most signally proclaiming a high morality because they are directly associated with the saving of souls, but she also honored natural virtues of all men in civil society. Morality, decency, justice, goodness, excellence of mind and spirit, all come from man's Creator.

As one continues the study of the history of education, he becomes more aware that the chief problem connected with the field is cultural—that is, people tend to lag (usually a generation) in adjusting to their environment. Scientific adaptations tend to speed up so that inventions and discoveries are always, as it were, ahead of time. No one doubts that education can increase or decrease cultural lag; but, as with the weather, little is done about the fact that usually what is discovered in the field of training the young is not adopted for a score of years or more.

In our selection from a survey of what has been handed on to us in the history of education, interest (which is the source of attention, which is in turn the mother of memory) centers in that material which has intrinsic value for us as Catholics in the United States. All material in the entire field of the history of education which does not contribute directly to our heritage is extrinsic and therefore not pertinent. Such a point of view is not necessarily biased or propagandistic; nor does the fact that it is not eclectic signify that the writer is partisan and wrong.

Because, as we shall show when discussing method, that of Catholic schools is eclectic—adapting in the light of Catholic philosophy and adopting any truth discovered through experimental research, our interest here lies in the philosophy of education rather than in the nature of schools and methods. We are not presenting the daily teaching in classrooms because ours is a larger view, including all educational agencies—church, home, physical environment, newspapers, motion pictures, radio, television, and so on. Individual teachers are fully presented in autobiographies and biographies in reading lists; there one will find background, details, the personalizing of human beings connected with educational movements. In such books appear pictures, examples, quotations, and anecdotes. Throughout this book there will be numerous opportunities to begin self-education—a lifetime of reading according to interest, purpose, or desire.

The advances and retrogressions of a people appear in their system of education; their educational history records their civilization and culture because their aims and methods reveal what they strove to achieve, what they tried to be. In this sense, education is the transmission of what has been thought and said and done from one generation to another. The record is enriched when descendants know not only what has been done but why.

Five principles underlie the Catholic teaching heritage; on them have rested the procedures by which each generation prepared those who followed for the task of living in all its ramifications. The religious principle must be known to understand the practice; and since the secularization of American education, Catholics have borne the burden of double taxes in order to have their system of schools where training in things of the spirit would supplement the education in the home. Parental obligation could permit no other course.

Those adults who in public schools had never read, for example, that Columbus sought above all other goals to discover new lands that might be Christianized, could think we distorted when repeating his words to King Ferdinand and Queen Isabella:

> Your glory will grow to immortality if you resolve to carry the name and doctrines of Jesus Christ into regions so distant. With His divine aid and grace may your majesties continue stead-fast in the desire to fill these new missionary shores with the truths of the Gospel. . . . I seek nothing from this enterprise except the increase and glory of the Christian religion.

A thoroughly unhistorical spirit (and, in consequence, a bad guide) pervades any treatment of the Catholic con-tribution to American history which derides or attacks the spirit of faith which is the foundation of that contribution. Such prejudice (judging beforehand) so hampers the intel-lectual processes of a writer that he presents a warped pic-ture entirely out of focus. That kind of unscholarly approach not only piles up gross errors in creating atmosphere but can be utterly wrong in the interpretation of specific detail. (The explanation of the fact that a man staggers may reveal the truth that he is approaching diabetic coma on the street or that he is drunk.) Bias leads to neglect of evidence, the ignoring of it, and even to deliberate mutilation. Instead of consulting primary sources the bigot repeats the precon-ceived opinion of a writer only a generation closer to the event—and a century was just as long three hundred years ago as it is today. Knowing nothing of the original evidence, his unreasonable predilection blinds him to his demonstrably false position and he repeats the garbled judgment without sufficient knowledge. (Heinrich Denifle's *Luther and Luther-dom* is a revelation of the contradiction of errors, suppres-sions, and misrepresentations which no German scholar could refute and thereby claim the Kaiser's reward of money. Hilaire Belloc's *Companion to Wells' Outline of History* in its first edition quit after listing a thousand errors of fact.) Catholics educated in public schools often fail to recog-

nize in what a welter of Protestantism they have been
nurtured and how, unconsciously, they have taken on its
coloration. (The author, because of circumstances, never
attended a Catholic school until after he had taught in a
Catholic university for a decade. His alma mater had exposed him to lectures by a history professor who, in his own
home, gave the youth his first meal after his return from
army service. Their friendship began when the youth ob-
jected to a lecture beginning: "The Catholic Church staggering under its weight of ignorance and superstition." The
professor had a doctorate in history from Yale and was teaching at Chicago; and yet he had never consulted *Catholic
Encylopedia,* Denifié, or any Catholic source before lecturing
on "indulgences.")

When Catholics look upon an anti-Christian (as some
English Catholics do on Gibbon) as a final authority and the
unmasking of his prepossession and ignorance as an outrage
against accepted historical science, it is exceedingly difficult
to get a hearing for the exposure of the lies and errors in
history. The Knights of Columbus established a chair of
American History at Catholic University to train scholars to
re-write our history truthfully. Certainly Reuben Parsons'
Some Lies and Errors of History, which has passed through
several editions, should make a thoughtful reader pause.
His exposure of Henry Charles Lea's bigotry and severe
handicaps as "historian" recall Belloc's exposure of the lies
connected with the so-called Reformation in England.

That any Catholic should accept the distortions and mis-
interpretations of violently anti-Catholic "historians" as the
normal thing ought to astound everyone. No child should be
exposed to enemy history irreligiously miswritten. We see
the process all about us today of Americans being soaked in
false history, with little assurance that the errors will be
corrected in our generation; and if they are not, we can fore-
see what little chance there is of later correction. Ignorance
and fear destroy truth in history. We can overcome the first

by going to primary sources, reading the originals in the light of present-day knowledge and discoveries through the centuries. The counter-attack must be launched with tremendous effort to get a foothold and a hearing.

Closely allied with the religious is the philosophical principle, for philosophy is to education what proportion and perspective is to drawing. To see life steadily and whole one must have unwavering criteria as standards of judgment—the same yesterday, today, and forever. On the Commandments, the Capital Sins, and the Laws of the Church, Catholics have built a philosophy co-ordinated and synthesized by St. Thomas Aquinas and adapted by theologian-philosophers to the needs of the centuries.

The ethical principle distinguishes right from wrong and is the basis for indoctrinating the immature with the ability to choose the right unerringly. The child is trained to put his proposed acts against the unwavering criteria underlying Catholic thinking so that he can tell when he is right or wrong without referring to what his neighbors are doing. To form a good character one must get at the inner life in order to have the dynamism of the most impelling motive— love of Christ. Unsupervised behavior is the test, and the Catholic child is trained to examine his conscience regularly and through a sacramental system to bring his thoughts, acts, and words in accord with the norm. The result is analogous to setting one's watch regularly by standard time or observing traffic signals.

Catholics cannot be indifferent in religious matters; but they welcome all contributions non-Catholics make to truth, which cannot contradict itself. If the pagans Epictetus or Marcus Aurelius, for example, discovered some truth as regards natural virtue or if Buddha or Confucius or Lao-tze pronounced a truth, Catholics make it their own; and priority of utterance means nothing. Although Martin J. Hillenbrand is not Catholic and Columbia University published his *Power and Morals*, Catholics welcome its ample confirma-

tion of their thinking when he shows the failure of modern
political theory resulting from evasions of natural law.

The relation to education of the political principle underlying a government is important. Not only is the form
of government basic to social customs; the correct interpretation of the word democracy is important. Not Jeffersonian
or Jacksonian or Wilsonian or Rooseveltian but true Christian democracy based on the fatherhood of God and the
brotherhood of man is acceptable to Catholics. Unfortunately, in the United States we have not had true Christian
democracy; and since the 1930's our republic (in which
the sovereign power should have resided in the electorate
who would delegate their power to representatives they
elect and whom they hold responsible) has deteriorated.
We now have an over-all social democracy in which a
bureaucratic, paternalistic government progressively relieves
the people of their powers and responsibilities.

In "The Novelty of Totalitarianism in the History of
Western Civilization" (*Proceedings of the American Philosophical Society*, Vol. 82, November 1, 1940), Carlton Hayes
made clear that today's dictatorial totalitarianism which
seeks to dominate the world is a revolt against all historic
Western Civilization—against the moderation and proportion of classical Greece, against the order and legality of
ancient Rome, against the righteousness and justice of the
Jewish prophets, against the charity, mercy, and peace of
Christ, against the vast cultural heritage of the Christian
Church in the Middle Ages and modern times, against the
enlightenment, reason, and humanitarianism of the eighteenth and against the liberal democracy of the nineteenth
centuries. It repudiates all these major constituents of our
historic civilization and fights to extermination any group
retaining affectionate memory of them. Against that sort
of encroachment Americans must stand foursquare.

The fifth, the psychological principle, related to the
soul and the mind, is confused in a viper's tangle of edu-

cational movements enmeshed in the intricate nexus of modern realism, whose form is at one time spoken of as psychological, at another philosophic or naturalistic or scientific. Our chief interest, as has been said, lies in the history of Catholic education in the United States; but because we do not live in isolation we must begin discussion of our heritage as a frontier of Europe with late sixteenth and early seventeenth century realism as it influenced European thinking.

We have included charts to give overviews, but such summaries are only for reference. From them one would learn little about the three overarching ideas of our approach —"Achieving Our Catholic Heritage," "Integrating Life Through the Liturgy," and "Inculcating a Catholic Sense," which replace the unscientific method of dividing history into ancient, medieval, and modern periods.

Graphically we might represent the Hebraic-Hellenic contribution to our heritage as a horizontal foundation. "Integration Through the Liturgy in the Ages of Faith" would be a similar horizontal base superimposed. The ramifications of "Inculcating a Catholic Sense" would be perpendicular uprights on these foundations, integrated by that title. The capstone would include Post-War problems and a survey of African, Chinese, Hindu, and Central and South American education as essential to missionary effort. An overview of the Catholic philosophy of education as contrasted with false philosophies would complete the background.

To achieve a Catholic sense, one must see eye to eye with the Church in all matters of Faith and morals—he does this most successfully when he has assimilated the Catholic heritage. It is because unmoored experimenters in modern times have not comprehended the Catholic heritage of the Christianized Hebraic and Hellenic culture on which Western civilization rests that in all fields—art, physical, natural, and social science, education, journalism, religion, ethics, and morality—their thinking and action has drifted to its present deplorable impasse. The liturgy represents an admirable expression of the Catholic *via media* or balance; in extremes lies danger.

Readers may accept the challenge in the following suggestions of items for a pageant surveying the history of Catholic education in the United States from 1650-1950. Listing choices chronologically will make discussion more pointed.

Twenty-five creative Americans who have made the most important contributions for the last three centuries might include: *Early nineteenth century:* Bishops John Carroll and John England, Father Gabriel Richard, and Madame Philippine Duchesne (whose cause is up for beatification). *Late nineteenth:* Cardinal Gibbons, Archbishop John Ireland, Bishop John L. Spalding, and Reverend J. A. Zahm, C.S.C. *Early twentieth:* Bishops Thomas Shahan and Philip McDevitt; Doctors Edward T. Shields, William J. Kerby, Peter Guilday, and George Johnson; Dom Virgil Michel, Fathers James A. Burns and Julius Nieuwland, C.S.C., Wm. J. McGucken, S.J., and Brother Elzear, F.S.C. *Current:* Bishops P. J. McCormick and John F. O'Hara; Msgr. Edward Jordan, Father Alphonse Schwitalla, and Sisters Joan and Nona, O.P.

Those authors most fitted to collaborate on scenes to dramatize the cavalcade of Catholic American education would include members of Catholic University's Department of Drama and of the Commission on American Citizenship and the Blackfriars drama group.

When citing in dramatic form American institutions which have contributed most importantly to the life cycle of the citizen, the following organizations might be cited together with their notable activity in relation to parts of the life cycle:

BIRTH: The school connected with Misericordia (Chicago) or any other maternity hospital.

CHILDHOOD: The laboratory school connected with Sisters College, Catholic University; the schools in the hospitals conducted by the Daughters of Wisdom (St. Charles, Brooklyn, for example).

ELEMENTARY: The activated curriculum of the school of St. Thomas the Apostle (Chicago), Corpus Christi (Manhattan), or any similar schools conducted by the Dominican Sisters of Sinsinawa, at Evanston and Winnetka, Illinois, and near Tuskegee Institute. Sister M. Joan Smith's *Guiding Growth in Christian Social Living* describes the procedures in three volumes (on primary, intermediate, and grammar grade levels).

SECONDARY: The procedures surveyed in Sister M. Janet's *Catholic Secondary Education* (N.C.W.C.)—specifically Sister M. Annetta's *Primer of Life Adjustment,* Brother Louis Faerber's *Provisions for Low Ability Pupils in Catholic High Schools* (C.U., 1948), Father Joseph Coyne's *Research Project on Vocational Education in Catholic Secondary Schools,* Sisters of St. Joseph (St. Paul, Minn.) *Christ-Centered World History,* and the work of the Confraternity of Christian Doctrine on both levels in various phases of catechetical and "released time" instruction.

MARRIAGE: Cana Conferences and courses given by the Ladies of the Grail (Loveland, Ohio) and their summer institutes in various dioceses of the United States.

PARENTHOOD: The work of the Catholic Conference on Family Life, Christopher Recordings (4) on sex education (2 double long-playing), National Council of Catholic Men —reprints of radio addresses (Father C. O. Rice's "The Catholic Church and the Family," May 19, 1946, for example).

CAREER: Numerous groups like the American Jocists (Columbus Club, 1 Prospect Park West, Brooklyn—the *Crusader,* their bulletin).

FAMILY LIFE: Cathedral High School of Duluth—course in family relationship, St. Mary's of Sandusky—a series of courses on home-making, and similar courses in the dioceses of Cincinnati and Covington.

RETIREMENT: Adult education and alumni activities in various Catholic universities and colleges; study clubs of the NCCM and National Council of Catholic Women, Catholic Daughters, and similar groups.

For a second section of this survey the heading suggested is "American Education Between the Wars (1918-1938)"—see the table with that head.

A third section would deal with American Education in World War II.

1. The characters in the educational scenes should be chosen from the American heroes of the period of World War II and the Peace, at home and abroad. As many as fifty might be listed.

The NCWC Department of Education, 1312 Massachusetts Ave., N.W., Washington, D.C., publishes a Directory of Diocesan Superintendents of Schools. Names from that list could furnish all the material wanted in regard to contributions of Catholic Schools on elementary and secondary levels. See Sister M. Leonita Delaney's *The Junior Victory Corps in St. Sylvester's Parochial School* (unpublished master's thesis, St. John's University, Brooklyn).

2. The outstanding contribution of American educational institutions to World War II and the Peace (military training, other training, development of understandings, and any other projects). List the school in each case which best represents each contribution: Courses in Teachers College, St. John's University, Brooklyn—Educating for Peace (a) on elementary level and (b) on secondary level; production of penicillin; St. John's Free School of Social Action; the work of Dr. Hugh Scott Taylor (Princeton) in connection with the atomic bomb; "Inter-American Institute," *Catholic Digest*, 8: 94 ff., September, 1944.

3. If you think a representative attitude of American education to World War II should be recognized state the attitude briefly.

You and I are responsible for the late war and for the atrocities that accompanied it. We are all guilty, for we are all one with all human beings the world over (the Mystical Body).

The last of these sections for a cavalcade would consider American education of the future.

1. Name the great problem and the potentiality of education in the United States from 1946 on.

A realization of the responsibility of each man for what men do. It is fundamental and universal that everyone accept the idea and persuade the world at large to believe and act upon it.

2. (a) Should organized education serve all "from the cradle to the grave" in the community? (No.) (b) What is the problem of community education?

To turn back to the home the numerous responsibilities that have been taken from it—as McConnell, Melby, and Arndt show in *New Schools for a New Culture*. See also Sister M. Janet's *Catholic Secondary Education* on life adjustment training.

3. Would you change the listing of the following instruments of education in the order of importance they should have for the future: faculties, curriculum, community experience, facilities, visual aids, finance, and others?

4. The authors best fitted to write scenes covering the various levels and activities in our Catholic education of the future: Sister M. Joan Smith, Father Wm. H. Russell, Sister Miriam (College Misericordia, Dallas, Pa.), Sister Monica, R.U. (Brown County, Ohio).

Originally, Protestant and Catholic school systems in the United States were public, that is, open to all. The story

AMERICAN EDUCATION BETWEEN THE WARS (1918-1938)

	Education characterized in terms of methods of effectiveness	Authors who could dramatize each level of the educative process	Notable experiments by teachers' colleges, administrators, P.T.A., public services, in quest of improvements in personnel methods, facilities, patrons' support, etc.	Educational heroes to be included in dramatic presentation because of their contribution to the improvement of schools
Kindergarten	Socialize the learner; rewards for serving among the society highest values and satisfactions any individual may attain. Education demands problem-solving. Teach responsibility.	Sister Supervisors in any Dioceses (C.S.J., D.W., H.F.N., O.P., R.S.H., S.M., etc.)	Model school in connection with Sisters College, Catholic University	Reverend Edward T. Shields (deceased), Catholic University

Elementary Schools	Applying the activated curriculum, grades 1-8.	Sisters Joan and Nona, O.P. (Sinsinawa, Wisconsin); S.S.N.D. (See *Catholic School Journal*, 33:127 ff., Jan, 1933.)	The activated curriculum in Corpus Christi School described in *Guiding Growth in Christian Social Living* (3 vols.)	*Mother Seton* by Sister M. Regis Hoare, doctoral dissertation, Boston College, 1933
Secondary Level	Democratic living is an ideal to be striven for — beyond the grasp. Christianity is the root whence came the substance which promoted democratic growth. Student councils.	Brother and Sister Supervisors of religious communities in any local area.	Father Wm. J. McGucken's *The Jesuits and Education* (Bruce) surveys competently. Presentation Academy, San Francisco, offers a four-year course in family living.	Bishop Philip McDevitt's Boys Catholic High School (Philadelphia)
College and University	Effective methods of teacher training through practice teaching at the Model School, Teachers College, Catholic University, Washington, D.C.	Bishop P. J. McCormick, Dr. Edward B. Jordan	Diocesan Teachers College, Cleveland (Doctoral dissertation of Bishop John R. Hogan, Catholic University, 1932)	Reverend Dr. George Johnson (Catholic University)

of American education is not, then, a record of the secular state or public schools of today. It is, instead, a history of the growth of two parochial school systems—the Protestant (supported by public tax funds) and the Catholic, maintained by an additional support from Catholic parishes.

While the Report of the March, 1955, national meeting of School Administrators of the National Education Association did not mention God, speakers recognized the moral and spiritual needs of children. General Eisenhower, President Conant, and Superintendent Jansen condemned opposition to religious training, emphasized the fact that no society can survive without moral order and the need for character education, and made clear that spiritual values arise from many sources and should be appreciated.

The Report recalled Dr. Arthur B. Moehlman's article in *School and Society,* 63:75 ff.; for we had been adapting his suggestions to the history of Catholic education in our country. He was in the Armed Forces when he wrote it, and within a few years we find the educational field again disrupted by students going into the Armed Forces. Once again Americans are urged to rebuild a faith in the United States such as the pioneers knew, to stress belief in God, and to emphasize the fact that Washington, Lincoln, and other outstanding Americans acknowledged a Creator. The confusion in young minds must be cleared so that no youngster will be stupid enough to be unaware of the contradiction in the remark, "Honest to God! I'm an atheist."

The daily life of a people consists of the continuous adjustment between them and their environment. Historical and geographical research can aid tellingly our discovery of what the level of education in various periods of human existence was and why that culture and civilization passed away. The dry facts about education and dates cannot reveal the real significance of education as an adjustment between a people and their surroundings.

In the only published history of Catholic education in the United States we met several omissions which have been supplied by diocesan superintendents of schools from primary source materials as follows:

Your brief note with its apparently simple request for information regarding the first Catholic school in Vermont has resulted in the beginning of a minor research project. As a matter of fact, there has been almost nothing worthwhile done for the history of the Catholic Church and Catholic education in Vermont.

At St. Michael's College Library I consulted with the Reverend Vincent B. Maloney, S.S.E., the College Librarian, who has taken a particular interest in the history of Catholicism in Vermont and who has recently begun a collection of source material. Father Maloney has among other things a typewritten copy of the diary of the first Bishop of Vermont, the Most Reverend Louis DeGoesbriand. The original manuscript of this diary is still preserved in the archives of the Diocese.

I found there this entry under the date of October 10, 1853:

Sisters of Providence have consented to take charge of the Pearl Street house where it is intended they will teach school, harbour orphans and perhaps sick persons.

Sisters Caron and Theresa came Saturday to see the house and make arrangements. Was agreed that three will come about the first of May to occupy the house and take care of the garden, and prepare children for first Communion. The others will come at the beginning of July.

Sit nomen Domini benedictum!

There is some obscurity as to the year under which this entry was made and, as you see, there is nothing in this statement of the beginning of the school but there is the promise of one.

The Diocese of Burlington was established in 1853 and I suspect that the correct date for the entry in the diary is October 10, 1853, not long after the arrival of the newly consecrated first

Bishop. However, this bit of information furnished me with a lead and I made inquiries of the Superior of the Sisters of Providence at St. Joseph's Orphanage.

There I found a very valuable primary source in the manuscript "Chronicles" of the Community. Under date of September 3, 1854, there is recorded that the Sisters opened a school on Pearl Street in Burlington with a beginning enrollment of 148 pupils. I am very sure that this is the first Catholic School in Vermont of any kind and most certain that it is the first Catholic school in Vermont conducted by Religious.

These Sisters of Providence, so-called, or Sisters of Providence of Montreal as they are usually designated, were founded in Montreal in 1943 by Mother Gamelin. The proper title is, in French, *Filles de Charite Servantes des Pauvres,* and sometimes, but rarely, is given in English as Daughters of Charity, Servants of the Poor.

The school which they opened on September 3, 1854, was known as St. Joseph's Providence School. These Sisters of Providence gave up teaching in this school upon the arrival of the Sisters of Mercy from Manchester, New Hampshire, who came here and opened a Diocesan Mother House in 1873. The Sisters of Mercy replaced the Sisters of Providence as teachers and these latter (from that date on) directed all of their efforts to the care of orphans. The modern St. Joseph's Orphanage on North Avenue in Burlington conducted by twenty-six Sisters of the same Community is caring for 200 children.

The successor to the school begun by the Sisters of Providence is the present Cathedral Grammar School in charge of the Sisters of Mercy with an enrollment last year of 749. I feel quite sure no Catholic school in Vermont conducted by religious or by laymen antedates this 1854 foundation. The next in matter of time is some nine years later, St. Joseph's School opened here in Burlington by the Community known here as the Ladies of Nazareth and known in some other places as the Nardine Sisters, who first took up residence in Burlington on October 28, 1863.

I did not go to the Orphanage to copy exactly the entry in the "Chronicles." It was read to me over the telephone by the Sister Superior, but if you have need of an exact copy of the words of the "Chronicles," I will be glad to procure it and to mail it to you.

From the Diocesan Archives, Nashville:

The first Catholic school in Tennessee was St. Joseph's Seminary, started in late 1839—probably November—located in Nashville, on Cedar Knob (now Capitol Hill), next to the Holy Rosary Cathedral. It was conducted by the diocesan clergy, who, at that time, one year after the establishment of the Diocese, consisted of Bishop Richard P. Miles, O.P., and Father Joseph Schat, the only clergymen in the young diocese. In 1839, the Seminary had two students.

The name of the seminary was later changed to St. Athanasius (*see Catholic Directory*—1842 and following). In 1843 the *Catholic Directory* says that there was an academy for boys attached to the seminary taught by diocesan priests.

About 1846 Bishop Miles established the Brothers of St. Patrick, who taught the boys' school but this order went out of existence about six years later.

The first female religious to come to Tennessee were the Sisters of Charity of Nazareth, Kentucky, who came in 1842 and began a school for girls on Capitol Hill, Nashville.

The source for this information is *The Father of the Church in Tennessee* (Life of Bishop Miles), by Rev. V. F. O'Daniel, O.P., 1926—Pustet & Co.—about the only printed source of the history of the Church in Tennessee.

The first Catholic school in the State of West Virginia was founded at Martinsburg on January 1, 1838. The school was named St. Vincent's Female Benevolent School. The school house was the parish priest's residence, which the future Bishop Whelan, then pastor of Martinsburg, gave to the Sisters of Charity from Emmitsburg, Maryland, for their use as convent and school. When the Diocese of Wheeling was established in 1850, the eastern panhandle of the State of West Virginia was not included. (The State of West Virginia was established in 1863.) Hence, the school at Martinsburg was the first established in what is now the State of West Virginia, then Virginia, but it was outside the present territory of the Diocese of Wheeling.

The first school in what is now the Diocese of Wheeling was established in the city of Wheeling in 1846. It was known as the German School and all of the teachers were laymen. The first principal was Anton Becker.

The Diocesan Superintendent supplied the information that the first Catholic school in Georgia, June 23, 1845 (incorporated by the State Legislature in 1849) was opened at Savannah as a boarding school, orphanage, and a private school for day pupils by the Sisters of Our Lady of Mercy, founded by Bishop England.

Sister M. Helen M'Carthy's *History of the Sisters of Mercy of Belmont, N. C.,* 1869-1933, records that the Sisters of Mercy from Charleston, S. C., opened the first Catholic school in North Carolina at Wilmington, October 11, 1869, with Mother Augustine as Superior. This "Academy of the Incarnation" was attended by both boarders and day students.

According to Arthur J. Heffernan's *History of Education in Connecticut* (1937), page 11, the first Catholic school was begun July 11, 1829, at Hartford. On July 25 lay men and women conducted the first Sunday school.

The Reverend Joseph Magri's *Catholic Church in the City and Diocese of Richmond* (pages 54 f.) lists the first Catholic school in Virginia as St. Joseph Academy and Orphanage, opened November 25, 1834. (Curiously, Bishop Patrick Kelly supported himself by teaching in Norfolk, 1821-22).

Catholics in Mississippi by the Most Rev. R. O. Gerow (1939) is authority (page 329) for the information that Bishop Chance's nieces began a Catholic school in Natchez, 1841.

Derwent Whittlesey's *The Earth and the State* is a political geography. Rudolph Geiger's *Climate Near the Ground* and V. Conrad and I. W. Pollak's *Methods in Climatology* are authoritative. See also *Climate and Man* (U.S. Dept. of Agriculture), Ellsworth Huntington's *Civilization and Climate* and *Principles of Human Geography,* S. F. Markham's *Climate and the Energy of Nations,* Clarence A. Mills' *Climate Makes the Man,* C. E. P. Brooks' *Climate in Everyday Life.*

P. M. Spurlin's translation of *Montesquieu in America* reveals the observant Frenchman's thoughts on the climate and geography of the United States as shoring up of his own philosophical ideas. De Tocqueville's *Democracy in America* helped many Americans to know themselves. Ellsworth Huntington's *Mainsprings of Civilization* analyzes the role of the biologic inheritance and physical environment in influencing the course of history. His life as a scholar he devoted to compounding generalizations about why our intellects work best in changeable, stimulating climates (moving toward colder regions).

Studies of pollution of the air in smog sections (Donora, Pennsylvania) by United States Public Health Service are comprehensive.

See Carl O. Sauer's *Morphology of Landscape* and recall Cardinal Newman's description of Athens as the site of a university in "The Site of a University" (*Idea of a University*). Carl W. Dreppard's *Pioneer America: Its First Three Centuries* contains 2,300 illustrations. Edgar B. Wesley's *Teaching the Social Studies* (pp. 604 ff.) amplifies methods in geography with regional studies, field surveys, and topical investigations. Houghton Mifflin publishes *Look at America* Series. See the volume on New York City, for example.

The Rivers of America Series (Rinehart) is growing—*Cumulative Book Index* will list new additions. The publications of the WPA (Writers' Project) and the volumes on local history the Writers' Program has produced appear in the same source. P. Lorentz' *River* (1938) attracted much favorable attention and was put in motion pictures. The

Mississippi was treated also in J. Delanglez's *El Rio de Espiritu Santo* (U.S. Catholic Historical Society, 1945). Many states publish beautiful brochures; see, for example, *Arizona Highways Series*. Arthur H. Carhart's *Water or Your Life* stresses need for conservation.

Diego Alvarez Chanca, a physician who accompanied Columbus on his second voyage (1493), wrote the first description of the flora and fauna of the New World. In *Myself When Young,* Henry Handel Richardson tells the effect that bodies of water in the immediate environment had on her family. She mentions the snow-fed, galloping Isar at Munich (in contrast to the fetid Pleisse and the muddy Cam at Cambridge, England). When describing her father's burial place in Australia, she notes that his natural surroundings (the open sea, the dunes) last longer than man.

Ellen Church Semple's *American History and Its Geographic Conditions* and Albert Brigham's *Geographic Inflences on American History* are fascinating reading. As regards the locations of cities, Bardstown, Kentucky, selected by Catholic pioneers as an important site did not turn out to be. The see of Boston was moved to Maine and to Ogdensburg, New York, because it seemed that Boston was unpromising as a Catholic center.

The 29th Yearbook of the American Association of School Administrators (*Conservation Education in American Schools*) emphasizes the official use of natural resources in a democracy.

Ladislaus Reymont's *The Peasants* presented that picture so tellingly he got the Nobel Prize. Louis Hemon's *Maria Chapdelaine* delighted readers with its impressive picture of simple French-Canadian family life as its members struggled with the land, the seasons, and the elements. Many such families crossed the border into the United States.

For a stimulating lecture on this relationship, see Richard Green Moulton's *World Literature*—"The Faust Story" (the plot germ of which is "What does it profit a man to gain the whole world and suffer the loss of his soul?") Book I of Goethe's *Faust* views man in microcosm; Book II treats him in macrocosm.

Wright Morris's *The Inhabitants* photographs America minus people in a Spoon River Anthology of pictures. See (a) Howard Mumford Jone's *Fifty Guides to American Civilization* and (b) *Pacific Spectator*, a journal of interpretation (Stanford University Press). Jay Monaghan's *This Is Illinois* records a State history by camera and sketchbook—in its political, cultural, and industrial growth. Theodore C. Pease, in his *Story of Illinois*, begins in Europe with the groping of navigators for a route to Asia and comes to focus on the explorations of Marquette and Joliet and the imperialistic adventures of La Salle and Tonty.

Nelson B. Keyes and Edward F. Gallagher published *Hope of the Nations.* Vol. I considers: What am I doing to build a better world? Vol. II: What am I doing to secure America's future? The latter reveals Christianity in action in the U.S. While the work is not fundamentally Catholic, it shows what our nation achieved through religion.

DESCRIPTIVE BIBLIOGRAPHY FOR HISTORY OF
EDUCATION IN THE UNITED STATES

Brown, Elmer Ellsworth, *The Making of Our Middle Schools* (New York, 1903). Valuable for the development of the Latin school, the academy, etc.

Burns, James A., and Kohlbrenner, Bernard, *A History of Catholic Education in the United States* (New York, 1937). A revision of the pioneer tent in this field.

Butts, E. Freeman, *American Tradition in Religion and Education* (and studies in cultural education). Biased writing, as shown in *School and Society* (72:436 ff., December, 1950) and *America* (83:579 ff., September 9, 1950). The pretense of fairness and scholarship is revealed in *America* by the citation of errors of omission and unsup-

ported claims. The author's announced purpose was to
present historical evidence but his specific purpose seems to
be argument that government policy in the United States
has always opposed religious training in public schools and
has always denied aid to religious education. That thesis
cannot be supported satisfactorily if one clings to historical
fact; so Butts' argument is confused.

Catholic texts often mention as Catholics: Jeremiah
O'Brien (who lost the Faith in pioneer Maine), Steuben of
Revolutionary fame (who had no right to the title Baron
and was never a Catholic; he was a Freemason of high
degree), James Hoban (architect of the White House, a
fallen-away who became Grand Master of the Federal
Lodge of Freemasons, Washington, D.C.), and Marquis
Lafayette (who renounced Catholicism to improve chances
of becoming an American officer of high rank).

Cubberley, Elwood P., *Public Education in the United
States* (Boston, 1934). The standard non-Catholic textbook
containing the most comprehensive treatment of the history
of American public schools. In the complementary *Readings
in Public Education in the United States* a lack of proportion
or false emphasis appears in the fact that Rugg is quoted
as often as Dewey (six times) but Kilpatrick and Bode are
excluded. There is neither an author nor subject index.

Curti, Merle, *The Social Ideas of American Educators,*
Report of the Commission on the Social Studies, Part X
(New York, 1935). An interpretation containing a large
amount of historical material. Its chief fault is that all of
the parts of the complete report of the Commission on Social
Studies of the American Historical Association (of which
this is an uncritical acceptance of a far-reaching economic
and social theory and an interpretation of the facts in the
light of that theory). Curti believes in a classless society
and consistently condemns the profit-motive and individual-
istic tendencies of every kind. On page 373 he condemns
Bishop Spalding for countenancing social and economic

Catholic Education in the United States 51

destruction, although social justice is one thing, communism is another. It is unfortunate that when this Commission was looking for a remedy for the gross injustices that certainly do exist so much encouragement should be given to the socialistic philosophy.

Ellis, John T., *Guide to American Catholic History,* a select bibliography with introductory notes concerning the nature and limitations of the items listed.

Kefauver, Grayson N., *Education During the War and After* (New York, 1943).

Knight, Edgar W., *Education in the United States,* new edition (Boston, 1934). Although this book is a standard text less comprehensive but more critical than Cubberley's *Public Education in the United States,* when its treatment of colonial education is compared with the latter, it appears a critical attack on New England tradition. Certainly the title is misleading because the book treats only public education—as if there never were any Catholic schools.

Knight, Edgar W., *Public Education in the South* (Boston, 1922). By far the most comprehensive and scholarly work on education in the South.

McCluskey, Niel J., *Catholic Education in America—* documents illustrating the development of Roman Catholic education for almost two centuries, together with an interpretative essay.

McCormick, P. J. (redacted by F. P. Cassidy), *History of Education* (Washington). Accurate, trustworthy. Includes references to research at Catholic University in the philosophies of current non-Catholic educators.

Monroe, Paul (ed.), *Cyclopedia of Education,* 3 or 5 vols. (New York, 1911-13). Full treatment of American education. Many articles on teaching Orders and Catholic educators written by Catholics.

Noble, Stuart G., *A History of American Education* (New York, 1938). Included because it gives emphasis to environmental influences, changing social and economic conditions, and so on. Page 403 reveals hasty and superficial thinking, for the author contends there are at present only two philosophies of education in the United States today—a philosophy of material success and the progressive idealism of Dewey and his adherents. Bode, Morrison, and Judd condemn material success as the ultimate goal and look upon organized and hard work as the best means of arriving at a development which will make any kind of a success possible. Catholic educators are neither materialistic nor progressive in the sense of accepting Dewey's philosophy in its entirety.

Thwing, Charles Franklin, *A History of Higher Education in America* (New York, 1906). Detailed histories of the founding of early colleges and state universities.

Vollmer, Edward R., *Catholic Church in America,* a historical bibliography.

When reading for background in education in the Old World, be on guard against A. F. Leach (an English educational historian). While he claims that the Reformation was absolutely destructive of education and admires episcopal (bishops') schools, he is always prejudiced against monks and derogatory of monastic schools.

Compayré (French) is a decided enemy of the Catholic Church as regards to the history of education. He contributed many articles to Buisson's *Dictionnaire.* Biased from the medieval period, inaccurate, untrustworthy, bitterly anti-Catholic, gave only 29 out of 400 pages to ten centuries of the Middle Ages, gave 10 pages to a French educator now unknown. By his claims that modern education began with the Reformation and that public education began in French after the Revolution, he forced Catholics to write histories of the various French dioceses before the Revolution.

Seeley, an American, is bigoted. In his *History of Education* Messenger reveals deplorable ignorance of the meaning of "indulgence" when discussing the Reformation. In the chapter which follows that, his idea of the *Ratio Studiorum* is entirely wrong. On page 136 he contradicts the three points he makes on the preceding page. The contradictions (in the 1931 edition) are so patent and unscholarly that he has no claim to a scientific attitude.

Cubberley, Ellwood P., *The History of Education:* Educational Practice and Progress Considered as a Phase of the Development and Spread of Western Civilization (Boston, 1920). This standard one volume textbook is still outstanding in the history of the development and spread of public school education. Unfortunately, it includes (page 261) a selection from Green's *Short History of England* which plays up the "benefits" of the mis-named Reformation in English education. Most non-Catholic historians grant what records show—that under Elizabeth and Edward VI education reached its nadir. (Neighbors hung their wash in Oxford classrooms). Green says the Puritans popularized the laity's reading of the Bible. Anyone who has read English literature recalls the familiarity with the Bible of authors as early as Cardman to Chaucer. Both the Old and the New Testaments had been translated into English at Douay before the King James Version appeared.

Eby, Frederick, and Arrowwood, Charles F., *The History and Philosophy of Education Ancient and Medieval* (New York, 1940). Two-thirds of the book is devoted to pre-medieval period and is always exceptionally well recommended for history of the first fifteen Christian centuries. Supplements Cubberley's book, which touches only lightly periods preceding the Middle Ages. Unfortunately, Eby and Arrowwood rely on Harnack who was decidedly anti-Catholic and whose interpretation of facts is for that reason always to be suspected. On page 621, discussing Christianity after the Apostolic Age and during the early Christian centuries, these authors maintain the primitive idealism and formalism were buried under credal formalism and hierarchical regimentation, that the Church quite lost its first simplicity and democracy by investing the clergy with powers distinct from those of the laity (page 656), and that in general the message of Christ has become quite distorted. These charges can be shown to be untrue, although the authors do not seem to be ignorant bigots.

Kandel, L. L., *History of Secondary Education:* A Study in the Development of Liberal Education (Boston, 1930). Deals with the pressing educational problems of this century in the light of their historical development.

Kane, Wm. T., *An Essay Toward a History of Education* (Chicago, 1935). An antidote for all ignorance of the non-Catholic histories—one of the very few histories of education that goes to primary sources instead of repeating others' misstatements. Read this volume and watch its stimulating footnotes.

Knight, Edgar W., *Twenty Centuries of Education* (Boston, 1940). Considers some of the economic, political, social and religious facts of history and their effect upon education. Prejudiced in an offensive way. His first eleven chapters discuss early Christian education as the foundation upon which today's schools have been built. His prejudice is revealed by a too critical attitude toward formal discipline as a means of education, his bias in favor of rich and varied curricula, and his reference to "the cruel doctrine of original sin." He does not know what the doctrine really is. He is sure that liberation of education from religious control is an altogether desirable development and that education conducted by the state is the only kind worth serious consideration.

Laurie, S. E., *Historical Survey of Pre-Christian Education* (London, 1900). Remains the best account of education among the Hamitic, Semitic, and Turanian races; less valuable for Greek and Roman. A little too sure at times of the schools and teachers of Babylon of which we know little. Be on guard against Laurie as regards Hebrews. He disregards revelation; to him the Hebrews are just another Semitic people. Too naturalistic—at times he rates the Hebrews but little less worthy than the Arabs. Refused to revise his work on medieval universities after the appearance of Denifle's work.

McCormick, P. J. and Cassidy, F. P., *History of Education*—should be listed here, too. The discussions and bibliographies are admirable.

Marique, Pierre J., *History of Christian Education* (New York, 1924). Good treatment of the Catholic point of view in the history of education. No contribution but, in contrast to many non-Catholic historians of education, does not make their mistakes about the medieval period.

Monroe, Paul, *A Textbook in the History of Education* (New York, 1920). A scholarly treatment; old yet still valuable for interpretation of the larger movements of the history of education. Fails to carry out what he announces as theory (individualism) in Introduction.

Moore, Ernest C., *The Story of Instruction,* 2 vols. (New York, 1936). Presents the story of education from the days of Sparta through the Protestant Revolt. Primary sources consulted and new light thrown on familiar movements.

Parker, Samuel Chester, *The History of Modern Elementary Education:* With Emphasis on School Practice in Relation to Social Conditions (Boston, 1912). Treats excellently the development of the theory of the elementary school.

Rashdall, Hastings, *The Universities of Europe in the Middle Ages,* 3 vols., edited by F. M. Powicke and A. B. Emden (Oxford, 1936). This new edition of an old study still is the best treatment by far of the development of medieval higher education. Especially good on English universities (Oxford and Cambridge). Only book in English on the subject which can be recommended. The earlier edition was in galley proof when he read the works of Denifle, the German Dominican whose *Luther and Lutherdom* gave the first real insight to that problem and for the contradiction of which the Kaiser offered a large money reward which could never be claimed. Rashdall made changes in his book in keeping with Deniflé's discoveries.

Wilds, Elmer Harrison, *The Foundations of Modern Education* (New York, 1942). Presents the history of educational theory up to the present world crisis. By using the Morrison Unit Plan, Wilds presents seventeen units on great movements in education—utilitarianism, humanism, nationalism, formal discipline, social education, and so on, and avoids confusing a conglomeration of facts which often are devoid of interest and lacking any apparent significance. For each unit there is an assimilation chart synthesizing aims, types, content, agencies, organization, and methods of each movement. The flaw in the text is a too-ready acceptance of certain supposedly scientific findings, for example, that the earliest religion was animism (page 19), man has existed on earth for hundreds of thousands of years (page 115), and G. Stanley Hall intended to apply his catharsis theory to all instincts and tendencies (page 489).

Willmann, Otto, *The Science of Education* (translated, with additional bibliography by Kirsch), 2 vols., Philosophy and history of education (Latrobe, 1930). Willmann wrote many articles for *Catholic Encyclopedia;* that on the seven liberal arts is authoritative.

For an admirable survey of the literature on history of education coming from non-Catholic sources, see *School and Society,* 72:436-44, December, 1950. That article looks back to 1946. Possibly similar surveys will follow.

Catholic Encylopedia is an excellent source. (See *Catholic Encyclopedia and its Makers* for photographs of Catholic scholars). *The New Catholic Dictionary* is an abridgement of the *Encyclopedia.* Under "United States," for example, treatments of these subjects are referred to a partial list: abbots (mitred), Apostleship of Prayer, art (Lafarge),

Augustinians, Baltimore Councils, mission of Cardinal Bedini, Benedictines, Bible (translations), Brothers of the Christian Schools, Bureau of Education on co-education, Bureau of Statistics on Irish in America, Sisters of the Blessed Sacrament, Canon Law, Capuchins, Carmelites (and tertiaries), Archbishop Carroll, catechisms, census, Central Verein, chancery officials, chaplains (military), charities (statistics), Sisters of Charity, S.C. of Our Lady, Children of Mary, Christian Brothers of Ireland, Church in U.S., patron saints of churches, Cistercians, converts (baptism of), Coptic Rite, Corcoran, Jas. A., councils (plenary), Creighton U., Croatians, Dominican regular tertiaries, education (subheads— associations, co-cd. in U.S., college graduates, colleges, high schools, universities, arts faculty of a u., M.A. degree), Emigrant Aid Society, Bp. Flaget, Foresters, Franciscans, Friars Minor, geography (various dioceses), Sisters of Good Shepherd, Grey Nuns, Historical Society and Thebaud (first president of St. John's—later Fordham), patronage of Our Lady of the Immaculate Conception, Indian missions, Irish in U.S., Religious of Jesus and Mary, language question— liturgy in national tongues?

Lazarists (Vincentians, C.M.'s), literature for blind, Sisters of the Little Company of Mary, Maronite Rite, marriage, Missionary Union, early missions, number of missions, National Catholic Educational Association Bulletin, Northwestern U.S., ordination, provision for orphans, parishes formed, Passionists, patron, periodicals, Plenary Councils, care of the poor, Poor Clares, Congregation of the Precious Blood, of the Presentation of the Blessed Virgin Mary, Presentation Sisters, U.S. and Propaganda, property, protectorates, Provincial Council, retreat houses, Sisters of St. Joseph, Salesians, schools, seminaries, John Gilonary Shea, Bible Society, Catholic Truth Society, Society for the Propagation of the Faith, Society of Jesus (Jesuits), Society of the Blessed Sacrament, St. Vincent de Paul Society, statistics,

Sulpicians, Syro-Catholic Rite, Syro-Jacobite Rite, U.S. Catholic Historical Magazine, U.S. Catholic Magazine, U.S. Miscellany, Ursulines, Viatorians, Visitation Nuns, Xaverian Brothers, James Ward (a founder of the present system in the U.S. Naval Academy).

Willging's "Index to Pamphlets" lists helpful material. Consult mimeoed additions to Willging and recent titles published by America Press, Paulist Press, International Catholic Truth Society, Queen's Work, and other Catholic presses. National Catholic Welfare Conference, and *Our Sunday Visitor* pamphlets are instructive.

Watch the Catholic magazines your school or home subscribes for (such as *America, Catholic World, Thought, Sign*), especially those reviewing books on items pertinent to history of Catholic education in the U.S. as we treat it.

Keep in touch with Abstracts of Theses, particularly those from Catholic graduate schools. Examine *Bibliographies of Research Studies in Education* from the Office of Education.

Catholic Periodical Index directs to Catholic magazines (and includes references to *Catholic Mind*).

Compare John H. Meier's *Catholic Press Directory* as a source with Ayer's *Guide* and Ulrich's Periodical Directory. Read your diocesan paper weekly, for example, such stimulating items as (December 18, 1948) the Vermont Mission of the Redemptorists, begun at Bradford, 1944. Catholic Mission Crusade publications, Catholic Youth Society pamphlets, and *Catholic University Bulletin* yield occasional items relevant to our study.

American Catholic Philosophical Association Proceedings will help on the history of Catholic education and adjustments of Catholics (individuals and groups) according to our subheads under "People," "Adaptation," "Surroundings." Helpful, too, are *American Catholic Quarterly Review, Ecclesiastical Review* (Index to Vols. 1-50 printed in 1914; for

Vols. 51-81 in 1944), *Historical Bulletin* (St. Louis U.), *U.S. Historical Society Records and Studies*, and *Cumulative Book Index* under "Catholic," "Roman Catholic Church," "R. C. Liturgy," and so on.

The Committee micro-filming American periodicals, 18th century, included not one Catholic magazine. To see what might have been drawn on, consult Paul J. Foik, C.S.C., *Pioneer Catholic Journalism*.

CHAPTER THREE

America as a Frontier

Not counting names of rivers, valleys, and lesser geographical formations, there are over two thousand Spanish place names in the United States. Counting such variants as "Austin" or "Austen" for Augustine, that figure would mount in any atlas.

Not only does one become aware of how much our country owes Catholic culture and how basic that Catholic culture is in America; study of geographical influence on history is fascinating.

St. Augustine was the first center from which Catholic influence radiated, but the Spanish missionaries and explorers left an equally deep impression on the Southwest. Citizens of San Francisco resent the shortening of the name because they recall the work of the Franciscan Friars, the beautiful legends (that of the annual return of the swallows to San Capistrano, for instance), and the inspiring names with which followers of St. Francis adorned the landscape.

"Sacramento" recalls the apotheosis of the Catholic sacramental system. San Joaquin Valley was named in honor of the father of the Blessed Virgin.

Anyone unfamiliar with St. Joachim—or any other name mentioned here—has some stimulating reading ahead of him.

Information about the complete name of Los Angeles

(Our Lady, Queen of the Angels of the Portiuncula) con-
trasts the Catholic influence in the United States with that
of the Puritans (who felt that it was not in keeping with
Christian humility to name a man Gabriel or Raphael or
Michael or to use the names of angels for human beings).

Reading about Santa Barbara will reveal why she is
the patron protector against lightning—why her father was
destroyed by thunderbolts, why she is patron of gunners.
Point Reyes gets its name from the Three Kings who visited
the Christ Child on the first Christmas. Santa Fe (Holy
Faith), Santa Croix (Holy Cross)—and there is a Holy
Cross, Indiana, seat of a famous women's college, St. Mary's
—Conception (The Immaculate Conception), Las Cruces
(the Crosses), and Florida (flowers) merely suggest the
wealth of Spanish place names. The last meant Easter
(*pascua florida*).

With the name Louisiana (recall St. Louis, who was King
Louis IX) one associates the Mississippi Valley and the
French missionaries (Marquette, Hennepin), explorers (La
Salle, Joliet), and martyrs.

Their association with the Chicago and the Wisconsin
portages and the Great Lakes leads back to the Quebec
area. Quebec exemplifies the effect of the missionary work
of the Church when unhampered. The influence of the
Church in the social development of Quebec's citizens always
has been deep and lasting, since its foundation in 1608.
As in Quebec, so in the mission lands the Church endeavors
to enrich every phase of life by sanctifying it.

Jacques Cartier's dedication of a river and a gulf to
St. Lawrence recalls the fact that he had mapped Plymouth
Harbor at the turn of the sixteenth century, before the
Pilgrims ever thought of coming to Massachusetts. Some
of the original French names (Sault Sainte Marie, for
example) still persist, although many have disappeared in
garbling or translation. "Des Moines" means "of the monks."

Try the gazeteer section of a dictionary or explore the

Great Lakes Region on a map to list French Catholic names.

Bishop Carroll was the first priest born in the United States to be consecrated bishop. He was consecrated August 15, 1790, and had all the thirteen original states for his diocese. Now, there are almost 200 bishops in the United States, but less than 80 native bishops in the mission countries. Bishop Carroll dedicated the United States to Our Lady of the Immaculate Conception. In 1846, the Hierarchy repeated the dedication in a pastoral letter:

We take this occasion, brethren, to communicate to you the determination, unanimously adopted by us (the 6th Provincial Council of Baltimore) to place ourselves and all entrusted to our charge throughout the United States under the special patronage of the Holy Mother of God, whose Immaculate Conception is venerated by the piety of the faithful throughout the Catholic Church. By the aid of her prayers, we entertain the confident hope that we will be strengthened to perform the arduous duties of our ministry, and that you will be enabled to practice sublime virtues, of which her life represents her most perfect example.

In 1847 Rome confirmed the dedication.

Spanish, French, and English Catholics used the various forms of Our Lady's name: Our Lady of Portiuncula was patron of western missions, with numerous pioneering expeditions at Carmel and Guadalupe. Eighteenth century maps of Texas list Nuestra Senora de la Concepcion, de Rosario, and Loreta (Loreto); the Rio Grande was Our Lady's River. One of the early conquistadors (Mendoza) called his campsite Our Lady of the Pillar of Saragossa. On the eighteenth day, his camping ground became Our Lady of the Immaculate Conception; on the nineteenth it was Our Lady of Solitude; on the twentieth, Our Lady of Happy Voyage; on the twenty-first, Our Lady of Good Success; on the twenty-second, Our Lady of the Rosary; on the twenty-third, Our Lady of Good Order; on the twenty-fourth, Our Lady of Bethlehem; on the twenty-fifth (the Nativity) Our Lady of the People; on the twenty-sixth, Our Lady of Atocha; on the twenty-seventh, Our Lady of Guadalupe; on the twenty-eighth, Senora de los Remedios.

First Pro-Cathedral in the United States—When Baltimore was made the first diocese in the United States under Bishop Carroll, there was no church in the diocese considered fine enough for a cathedral. The church that was temporarily designated as the cathedral was simple and noble, as are many of the cathedrals in the nearly 200 dioceses of the foreign mission countries.

At least 350 American cities and villages, ranging from such metropolises as St. Louis, San Francisco, San Antonio, and St. Paul down to the by-road hamlets and communities named for neighboring monasteries, have taken the names of the Saints of the Church. Catholic influence on place names in Connecticut is limited to one—Mount Carmel. Delaware has no Catholic place names. Georgia has St. Charles, St. Clair, St. George, St. Mary's, and St. Simon's Island. In George R. Stewart's *Names on the Land,* the first item in the Index is "Abbeville."

A check of the list of postal addresses in the United States and its possessions shows 22 places named in one way or another after St. John, 15 after St. Joseph, 14 apiece after St. Mary and St. Charles, and 12 after St. Paul. Other popular saints' names in the directory of cities are Saints Francis, George, Louis, Clair, Anthony, Michael and James.

Catholic Encyclopedia and its Index and supplements are a basic reference for the field of action of these saints in the Western Hemisphere: Mother Cabrini (died 1917, the first citizen of the United States to be canonized—St. Francis Xavier Cabrini), Blessed Mother Duchesne, St. Louis Bertrand, Sebastian of the Apparitions, St. Philip of Jesus (patron saint of Mexico City), St. Peter Claver ("Apostle of the Negroes"), Mary Anne Paredes of Jesus, St. Rose of Lima (first American-born saint) and her assistant, Bl. Martin Porres, St. Turibius Alphonsus de Magrovejo, Blessed Mariana of Quito, St. Francis Solanus ("wonder

worker of the New World"), John de Massias, Ignatius of
Azevedo, Bl. John de Britto, and the Martyrs of Uruguay
(Bl. Roch Gonzales, Bl. John del Castillo, Bl. Alphonsus
Rodriguez). St. John Berchmans might be added because
one of his major miracles was performed at Grand Coteau,
Louisiana, where the Religious of the Sacred Heart opened
the oldest college for women in the United States.

  Heroes of the Cross by Marion F. Habig, O.F.M., is a
complete martyrology of those who consecrated American
soil with their life blood. The cause of canonization of the
early missionary martyrs of the United States as a group
has been introduced in Rome. Father Habig's book will
verify many dim traditional stories of the members of his
own Order which give an excellent idea of the sanctity and
apostolic zeal of these missioners. A non-Catholic historian's
tributes appear in Herbert E. Bolton's *Historical Memoir
of Pimeria Alta, The Rim of Christendom,* and *Spanish
Borderlands* (Florida and the Southwest). Later we shall
mention fiction; here Willa Cather's *Death Comes for the
Archbishop* is appropriate.

  As a cumulative project which will continue throughout
a study of the history of Catholic education in the United
States, (a) one might collect "firsts"—First in discovery,
first in the establishment of Christianity, first in the organization of civil government, first in proclaiming religious
toleration, first and unanimous in the support of Washington,
the First Mass in the Western World.

  When Christopher Columbus landed on the island of
San Salvador, named after the Holy Savior, his first important act was to have Mass celebrated by a diocesan priest
named Father Pedro de Arena. Today in the United States
alone, more than 42,000 Masses are celebrated daily.

  In the mission lands, half that number are celebrated in
a territory seven times as large as the United States. The

point to keeping alert about missionary endeavors lies in the fact that the culmination of a study of Catholic education appears in sharing the Faith with those peoples who do not have it. The chief purpose of Columbus' first voyage was to Christianize the Indies.

(b) To enrich this project, a subsidiary might be started —that of listing Catholic place names, with a "first" as point of departure.

First church in the United States, the Cathedral of the diocese of St. Augustine, was built shortly after the Spaniards took possession of Florida, in 1565. The church has a full set of records dating from 1594. The United States alone has more than 20,000 churches and chapels. In the mission lands, there are only some 10,000 churches in an area seven times as large.

Ottmar Mergenthaler (American Catholic) invented the linotype, 1885. Dr. J. Takemine (Catholic of New York) discovered the drug adrenalin. Father Julius Nieuwland, C.S.C., discovered neoprene (synthetic rubber), 1931. The first Catholic university in the United States—the present Georgetown University began with the barest essentials in 1789. The United States now boasts 228 Catholic universities and colleges, with an enrollment of over 240,000 students. In all the mission countries, there is not one great university as Georgetown, but there are ambitious beginnings in more than 700 institutions.

First seminary in the United States, 1791. The beginnings of St. Mary's Seminary, in Baltimore, were primitive indeed. The One Mile Tavern was taken over by the Sulpician Fathers under most discouraging conditions in 1791. The present seminary building at Roland Park is a monument to their zeal and courage. There are now 401 seminaries, major and minor, in the United States with more than 22,000 students. The missions have over 400 seminaries, but many are no finer than the One Mile Tavern.

First priest trained in the United States, Prince Dimitri

Gallitzin, a Russian, was trained in St. Mary's Seminary and was ordained for the diocese of Philadelphia in 1795. His chapel is preserved as a monument in the diocese of Altoona, at Loretto. The United States now has more than 42,000 priests. All the mission countries together have less than 7,000 native priests.

Before Columbus, St. Brendan, a Catholic Irishman, has been traditionally spoken of as the first to reach America (on his voyages to the Happy Isles). Some historians favor Lief Erickson, a Catholic Norseman, as the discoverer of our mainland.

The first book printed in America was the work of Catholics. In 1536, Bishop Zumarraga printed his *Spiritual Ladder* in Mexico City. (Dr. James J. Walsh's *Education: How Old the New* introduces one to the Catholic firsts in universities—a century before Harvard—in Mexico City and Lima. The first university of the United States was that of St. Thomas (Manila, P. I.), which today has 15 faculties and a large student body. Mother Mary of the Incarnation was the first Ursuline to come to America. Father Juan Padilla, O.S.F., was the first American martyr (in the Southwest, 1544).

St. Margaret Bourgeois founded the first religious order in America. Lydia Longley, a Puritan brought to Canada for ransom, joined the Congregation of Notre Dame two years after conversion, and 1694 saw the first woman of the United States (by birth and residence) enter the religious life. (Fannie, daughter of Ethan Allen, entered 114 years later. Even Marie Jurpin, often listed as first, entered the Ursulines at New Orleans in 1747.)

Father Jogues first planted the cross on the soil of Michigan; he was the first priest to set foot on Manhattan Island.

Fathers Chaumonot and Dablon built the first Catholic chapel in what is now the State of New York.

The second wife of President Tyler (Julia Gardiner of East Hampton, L. I.) was the first Catholic First Lady of the White House. Charles O'Conor (N.Y.) was the first Catholic to run for the Presidency (1872). Mrs. Mary Hayes (Mollie Pitcher of Revolutionary fame) was the pioneer WAC and a Catholic.

Since the founding of our country the first Catholic priest elected as Chaplain of Congress Rev. Dr. Charles Constantine Pise, 1801-1866, eminent scholar, author and preacher, was attached to St. Patrick's Church, Washington, D.C., at the time of his appointment.

The Jesuits were the first Europeans to attempt the extremely difficult task of grasping the Indian language (unwritten) and putting it into writing. (Father Parega's catechism was printed in 1593).

Fathers Biard and Du Thet first brought Christianity to the Penobscot Indians at St. Sauveur, 1613.

Oliver Pollock (Catholic) gave such outstanding assistance to American troops that he is known as "Financier of the Revolution." He assisted General George Rogers Clarke similarly in his conquest of the Northwest.

Father Peter Martinez was the first Jesuit American martyr.

Father Louis Tolbiniere, appointed by General B. Arnold as chaplain for Col. Jos. Livingston's "First Congressional Regiment" (1776), was the first officially commissioned U.S. military chaplain.

Father De Smet helped build St. Louis University (1828), the first west of the Mississippi.

In 1872, Father Moore (Boston) was given charge of a culprit by a criminal court judge and thus became the first probation officer.

The Catholic colony of Maryland, under Lord Baltimore and his Calvert brothers, was the first to grant religious freedom; Alaska now has a glacier bearing his name. On

the Delaware coast we have a "Dragon Creek" into which
the "St. George" flows. (English settlers were familiar with
St. George and the Dragon in their homeland.)

Myles Standish, closely related to Bp. Henry Standish
(confessor of Henry VIII's wife, Katherine of Aragon),
traveled great distances to Canada to make his Easter Duty.

Du Luth was an admirable French officer, noted for his
devotion to the Indian maiden who has been made St. Kateri
Tekakwitha in our century. He acknowledged publicly answer to his prayers through her intercession.

Cardinal Gibbons and the American hierarchy, in 1886,
got the ban of excommunication lifted from the Knights of
Labor (forerunner of the AFL), an alleged secret society.
(Pope Leo then issued the *Rerum Novarum* in 1891.)

St. Paul (Minnesota) and St. Peter were so named
because of their juxtaposition. A look at the gazeteer section of a dictionary will amplify our list. To open up the
spate of Catholic names of schools in the New York area
we might mention the First Cardinal in the United States.
John Cardinal McCloskey was named to the College of
Cardinals by Pope Pius IX on March 15, 1875, and was given
the Red Hat by Pope Leo XIII on March 28, 1878. He was
the first native of New York State to become a diocesan
priest.

The first white child born in what is now the U.S. was
Snorre Karlsefne (near Buzzard's Bay, 1008)—580 years
before Virginia Dare. When the boy's father died, his mother
joined a Religious Order.

To emphasize the closeness of Catholic education and
missionary effort we list Thomas Cardinal Tien is the first
cardinal of the mission lands. He received his entire training
in China and was named Cardinal in 1946. (Catholic Students' Press, Jefferies and Manz, 521 Vine St., Philadelphia,
publishes *Catholics Do "Do Things"* listing over 130 additional "firsts.")

A cumulative project: Throughout your study of history

of Catholic education in the United States, list in the form of question (with answer) items such as follow. The results from the lists made by your group may be pooled from time to time and used as a quiz.

The nieces of Bishop Chance opened the first Catholic school in Mississippi at Natchez, 1841. The diocesan clergy of Nashville, Tennessee, started a seminary, 1839; three years later, a school for boys began next door. St. Vincent's Female Benevolent School was founded in Martinsburg, what is now West Virginia, January 1, 1838. (The State of West Virginia was not established until 1863. When the Diocese of Wheeling was established in 1850, the eastern panhandle of the State of West Virginia was not included. The first Catholic school in what is now the Diocese of Wheeling opened in Wheeling, 1846. Known as the German School, all of its teachers were laymen—the first principal Anton Becker)

The Academy of the Incarnation of the Sisters of Mercy began in Wilmington, N.C., October 11, 1869. The first Catholic school in Georgia opened at Savannah, June 23, 1845—a boarding school, orphanage, and private school for day pupils conducted by the Sisters of Our Lady of Mercy (whom Bishop England had founded) and incorporated by the State Legislature, 1848. The Sisters of Providence of Montreal opened the first Catholic school in Vermont at Burlington, September 3, 1854.

The first Catholic school for women in the United States opened in New Orleans, 1734. This Ursuline Convent is the oldest standing building in the Mississippi Valley. The Church in America has made tremendous sacrifices for the education of girls and women, knowing their important role in the training of the young. It may truly be said that the educational system of the Church in the United States rests on the shoulders of women, devoted to God as Sisters. The same is true in the mission fields, where there are 33,000 foreign and 22,000 native Sisters.

Under the direction of the French Catholic, Count Rochambeau, Newport, R. I., was the first community to honor publicly Washington's Birthday (1781).

The first alien to become legally naturalized was a Catholic importer of New York—Antonio Trappini.

Father Joseph d'Aillon, O.S.F., made the pioneer discovery of oil in the United States, at Cuba, N. Y., 1627; Father Louis Hennipen sighted coal at La Salle, Ill., 1673; Father LeMoyne, S.J., discovered salt near Syracuse (seat of LeMoyne University).

The Englishman Bessemer was refused a U.S. patent on his steel process because a Catholic (Wm. Kelly, Pittsburg) had patented a process of decarbonizing iron by a current of air.

CHAPTER FOUR

Pioneering in America

Dixon Ryan Fox's "Civilization in Transit," *Ideas in Motion*, New York, 1933. Herbert Bolton on the transit of culture from Europe or from already Europeanized areas to the frontier as well as with reverse culture (All his books on the southwest). *Wider Horizons of American History* (in the Appleton Historical Series with D. R. Fox's *Sources of Culture in the Middle West* and Wm. E. Lingebach's *Approaches to American Social History*). Arthur M. Schlesinger's *New Viewpoints in American History*, 1922. Katherine B. Shippen's *The Great Heritage*. In fiction form, Carl Sandburg's *Remembrance Rock* (a wordy attempt to show the spiritual, intellectual, and physical inheritance of an American, a tolerant training of ideologies, and a dark picture of faulty thinking, prejudice, ignorance and immorality).

In 1949 Heath began publication of a series dealing with clash in issues in American History, including *The Turner Thesis Concerning the Role of the Frontier in American History* (whether the forest divested Americans of European influence [except through institutions]—as Professor Turner held.)

Carlton Hayes, "The American Frontier," *American Historical Review*, 51:199-216, January, 1946, and R. V. Coleman's *First Frontier* (east of Alleghenies).

Sister Monica, *A Cross in the Wilderness*. See also J.

Herman Schauinger's *Cathedrals in the Wilderness* (the American complement to the European Liberalism movement.

See Ross Hoffman's "Europe and the Community," *Thought*, 20-25 ff., March, 1945. For further evidence that every state on the North and South American continents stems from Western European Christendom, see also his *Great Republic, Christendom and Durable Peace.*

Burton Confrey's Catholic Action tetralogy amplifies this idea. *Social Studies, Catholic Action, Original Readings in Catholic Action,* and *Reading for Catholic Action* base Catholic Action on the liturgy, motivate it with love of God, put it under the direction of the Hierarchy, and show that the first requisite for the individual who would co-operate is living in a state of grace. Training for peace on the elementary level represents the type of course the author has offered teachers in preparation for such an apostolate.

Charles Beard's *Study of Appearances and Realities* is but one of several studies of the great moral bankruptcy of this mid-century, the duplicity dominating our day, the abandonment of American principles. Any periodical index will give reference to abundant material on the Secretary of State, the Secretary of Defense, and their fiasco as regards China for example; Communist infiltration of our government, and so on. The names involved fade from current interest, but their infamy lingers.

The Carl Schurz Memorial Foundation, 225 S. 15 St., Philadelphia, published *The German Contribution to American Culture.* See also Colman J. Barry's *Catholic Church and the German American* and (in fiction) Richard Sullivan's 311 *Congress Street.* Alma Routsong's *A Gradual Joy* pictures a young couple's married life.

An Italian by birth, Pope Pius XII, with sources of knowledge unknown to many other leaders, did more for world peace and for the betterment of human life than any other person.

Dr. George Speri Sperti, Director of the Scientific Research *Institutum Divi Thomae*, Cincinnati, received the Christian Culture Medal as an outstanding exponent of Christian ideals.

See "The Irish Emigrant and American Nativism," *Dublin Review*, 219:174 ff., Oct., 1946 (a wealth of references in the footnotes). James H. Moynihan's *Life of Archbishop John Ireland* quotes that leader: "Not to know one's rights is low-minded; not to defend them is cowardice. . . . The rights of Catholics are the rights of the personal conscience of the Catholic citizen. . . . Catholics demand no special power—merely equal rights for all.

In the *American Journal of Physical Anthropology*, Dr. Alice M. Brues reported five American types distinguished by head measurements in the Army. Those of Irish extraction could not, however, be classified. Equally common everywhere, they hit the dead center of the American average in their measurements.

Michael Laverty's *The Three Brothers* depicts what happens to the average Irish citizen (as it does to everyone else) when the desire for material success overcomes the more spiritual longings of the heart. Arthur R. McGratty, S.J., presents a typical American boy against the background of a large Catholic family in *I'd Gladly Go Back*.

To balance the decline in family size Americans rushed into fraternal organizations of all sorts. Currently there is too little family life; but Roger B. Dooley's *Days Beyond Recall* pictures that of Irish-Americans so convincingly as to give to these staunch Americans the old-settler status too often denied them by the descendants of Anglo-Saxon and German immigrants. Here we have an honest picture of the transition period in which immigrants and their descendants became Americans, recorded with extreme patience and insistence. The supposed realism picturing sordid, superstitious peasants transplanted has been blasted. Mr. Dooley can present a dispassionate and candid story of the Irish-

American losing the hyphen—in his occasional backsliding and his durable virtues. See also his *House of Shanahan* and *Less Than the Angels.*

The name of the Notre Dame Football Team "Fighting Irish" is a memorial to the long uphill fight for equal rights in a free land. See "The Irish in the United States," *Catholic Digest,* January, 1948. Dr. Richard Purcell, historian, declared that half the Catholic population in the United States are of Irish origin. See also "The Irish in America in the Eighteenth Century," *Catholic World,* 164:58 ff., October, 1946. Wm. G. Schofield's *The Deer Cry* is a colorful, heroic picture of St. Patrick, one of the greatest figures in Christian history.

See Michael Demiashkevich's *The National Mind* (British, French and German), 1938, and *Shackled Diplomacy: the Permanent Factors of the Foreign Policy of Nations,* 1934; D. W. Brogan's *French Personalities and Problems;* Wm. McDougall's *The Group Mind* (Chinese, Hindu, etc.), 1920; Anna W. M. Wolf's *Our Children Face War* (1942)—a blueprint of education for life, with a bibliography on foreign nations; Thos. J. C. McCormick edited *The Peoples of Germany;* Elizabeth Boettinger's *Your Child Meets the World Outside*—a guide to children's attitudes in democratic living; Denis W. Brogan's *The English People* examines their understanding of other people. Gerald W. Johnson's *Our English Heritage* (one of Lippincott's Peoples of America Series) disregards other inhabitants of the British Isles, makes no mention of the English economic revolution in the industrialization of the U.S. or of the influence of English philanthropists on American reformers of the nineteenth century. Denis W. Brogan's *American Character* (title in England, *American Problem*) reveals that neither we nor the British have changed much since Mrs. Trollope and then Charles Dickens visited us. Professor Brogan (political science, Cambridge) notes that normally English self-esteem (or indifference to outside criticism) is a striking and often a most valuable national quality.

George S. Counts' and Nacia P. Lodge's *The Country of the Blind* discusses the Soviet system of mind control. Their horrible use of scientific tools to reduce a human spirit to a state of complete disintegration has been recorded in Stephen K. Swift the *Cardinal's Story*. Ida A. R. Wylie's *My Life with George* exposes the German mind (and the Nazi: "I'm free from freedom") and the English mind in contrast to the American. Jeffrey E. Jeffrey's translation of *Plutarch Lied* (from the French) analyzes the military mind. Sinclair Lewis's *Babbitt* shows the American mind a collection of conventions, an approach underscored by current squabbles among chiefs of the Armed Forces—all our wars have been conducted under the domination of conventionalities (of traditional methods of procedure).

In a *Thought* review (Dec., 1942) of Elizabeth Aldrich's *As William James Said,* his opinion of European national traits is quoted:

The English insist on keeping the amateurish attitude without suffering from any lack of the deepest insights. The Slavs seem to be the great radical livers-out of their theories, while the Germans, for all their brilliant gifts, are most easily submerged in "a broth of sentiment."

Currently there seems to be special meaning in his saying that there is a plane where men occasionally meet each other moving, and recognize each other as brothers inhabiting the *same depths.*

Frank Monaghan's *Heritage of Freedom* is a permanent record of the 127 documents on the Freedom Train, revealing phases of thinking in a republic. Haile Selassie, Emperor of Ethiopia, studies each issue of the *Reader's Digest* to get at a cross-section of the thoughts, the moods, the ways of life of citizens in the United States.

Saturday Review of Literature devoted an entire issue

(Jan. 13, 1951) to "America and the Mind of Europe." See also Halvdan Koht's *The American Spirit in Europe*. In it Norway's leading authority on American history stresses the impact of the U.S. on Scandinavia, on the United Kingdom, France and Germany—particularly in the fields of political philosophy, economic activities, scientific knowledge, and cultural achievements. He discusses American idealism and materialism, reforms and literature.

"Town Meetings on the Rhine," *Reader's Digest*, January, 1949, reveals the German mind as it was encouraged to express itself in open meetings.

See the chart on Communism in B. Confrey's *Catholic Action*, p. 271.

Catholic Periodical Index will keep a reader in touch with the spate of materials about Russia. We are warned of Red tricks, of Red Fascism in America today (by the FBI) and of Communist-dominated organizations seeking to ensnare the unwary into joining.

See Leland Stowe's *They Shall Not Sleep* (1944) on the training of China in totalitarianism.

When asked to collaborate in a permanent entente with Communists (because, they claimed, they, like Christians, were opposed to Fascism and social regression), a French Bishop said, "The Communist doctrine must be rejected as incompatible with Christian doctrine; but Communists as men must be treated by Christians as brothers." Since Communism is built on Marxianism and materialism in the field of social action we cannot collaborate with the Soviet; divergent ideas cannot lead to convergent actions. We do not ask for a profession of Catholic faith, but we must demand observance of the principles of the natural law. However, their doctrine as regards man, society, and the world ignores Revelation. By their rejection of God, Communists require of their followers acts that break the Commandments. With Christian charity we must love the Communists, secure in the hope that eventually Russia will again be Catholic and become a strong protagonist for good in reparation for the evil emanating from the country under its present criminal governors. Our Lady of Fatima has promised help (*Catholic Periodical Index* will guide to numerous expository articles) and gradually parishes throughout the world are being consecrated to the Immaculate Heart of Mary for aid against the encroachments of totalitarian states on the freedom of the Church and the rise of crass secularism.

Dostoevski has recorded what the Russian people themselves are like (*Journal of an Author*):

I assert that our people became enlightened long ago, by taking into its essential soul Christ and His teaching . . . I may be told that it has no knowledge of Christ's teachings, for no sermons are preached to it. But this is an empty objection. It knows indeed everything that it needs to know, though it cannot pass on every question in the catechism. It came to know this in the churches where for centuries it had heard prayers and hymns which are much better than sermons. The people repeated and sang those prayers while they were still in the forest, in hiding from their enemies. They sang, "Lord of Powers, be with us." . . . The greatest school of Christianity through which they have passed are the centuries of innumerable and endless sufferings which they have endured through their history. . . . The Christianity of our people is and must forever remain the chiefest and most vital basis of its enlightenment. . . . I have seen the people and know them. I have lived with them years enough. I have eaten and slept with them and I myself have been reckoned with the transgressors; with them I worked real work and hard. I do know them. From them I received Christ into my soul once more, whom I knew in the home of my childhood, and whom I all but lost when in my turn, I changed into a "European Liberal." In the West, wherever you will, in whatever nation you choose, is there less drunkenness and robbery, is there not the same bestiality and into the bargain an obduracy which is not to be found in our people, and a true

and veritable ignorance, a real unenlightenment, because it is
often connected with a lawlessness which is there no longer
considered as sin but which has begun to be held for truth?

Sin is a stench, and the stench will pass away when the sun
shines fully. Sin is passing; Christ is eternal. The people sin and
defiles itself daily, but in its best moments it will never mistake
the truth. The ideal of the people is Christ.

Diocesan newspapers (March 17, 1951) reprinted from
Counter-attack "What You Can Do to Fight the Communists."

In *Education for Peace* Catholics amplify this material
on Russia when discussing one of Pope Pius XII's five principles for peace—triumph over mistrust. Stalin and his fellow
dictators did not want peace because a dictatorship must
have opposition in order to thrive, to lie to their subjects
about planned attacks from without. The Communists want
to destroy the property-owning class and hope to do it by
bleeding the United States of resources when rearming, rebuilding, feeding, clothing, and medicating the world. If,
however, Russia refuses to join a world federation, the
world must federate without them.

Horrifying revelations about the Communists appear in
these non-Catholic sources: Wm. H. Chamberlain's *We
Cover the World* (ten million starved), Victor Kravchenko's
I Chose Freedom, Jan Crechanowski's *Defeat in Victory*
(massacres of millions in Poland), and Benjamin Gitlow's
The Whole of Their Lives. Felix Morley's *Human Events,*
Isaac Don Levine's *Plain Talk* and *Counterattack* have done
highly commendable anti-Communist work as periodicals.
In *My Russian Yesterdays,* Catherine de Hueck presents
attractively Russian family life before the Communists
took over.

The Board of Regents of the State of New York investi-
gated the slighting of American history for one-world-ism.
They found too much of that and a light treatment of the

ideals of the Founding Fathers, which fellow travelers of the Communists wanted played down.

Enough has been said to open up the possibilities of reading widely of the growth of the Church and education (simultaneous because teaching the school always accompanied building of a church) in central, southern, and western United States. Choose an archdiocese—Detroit, Milwaukee, St. Paul, St. Louis, Omaha, New Orleans, San Antonio, San Francisco—, or a diocese—Leavenworth, Dubuque, Nashville, Denver, Seattle—and let one milestone lead the reader to another. Or choose names: Bishop James O'Gorman (a Trappist who came to America to found a New Melleray and became Bishop of Nebraska, Dakotas, Wyoming, and Montana, 1851), Bishop Baraga of northern Michigan, Bishop Loras of Dubuque, Bishop Cretin, first of St. Paul, or Archbishop John Ireland (St. Paul, 1888). One simply must know Archbishop Ireland's zeal, energy, activity, versatility—his building up the State by immigration, his fight for temperance, his Faribault Plan for solving the school question, his presidency of the State Historical Society of Minnesota, first president of the Catholic Historical Society of the United States, the districts in Minnesota permanently Catholic because he settled them with Catholic immigrants, his national appeal (not to mention President Theodore Roosevelt's blunder in asking that he be made Cardinal). *The Official Catholic Directory* lists all the religious foundations in a diocese. Check on the Religious Orders—the Benedictines, for example, their Abbey and College at Atchison in the Diocese of Leavenworth and the first Bishop one of their men. From earlier volumes trace the growth of these institutions.

Martin Dempsey, *St. LaSalle and His Institute* (founder of Christian Brothers). John Talbot Smith, *Brother Azarius.*

Katherine Burton's *Celestial Homespun* (Father Hecker).
Walter Elliott, *Father Hecker* (Founder of the Paulists).
Wm. J. Fitzpatrick's *Life of Very Rev. Thos. N. Burke, O.P.*
(No author) *Very Rev. A. L. Magnien* (Sulpician, St. Mary's
Seminary, Baltimore). Brother Joachim (Trappist), *The
Man Who Got Even With God.* Brother Julian, C.F.X., *Men
and Deeds.* S. C. Lemoyne's *Ven. Don Bosco* (Salesian).
Thomas Merton, *Seven Storey Mountain* and *Waters of Siloe*
(Trappist). W. N. Bischoff, S.J., *The Jesuits in Old Oregon*
(bibliography on missions in Washington, Oregon, Montana,
Idaho, and Wyoming). Katherine Hughes *Father Lacombe,
The Blackrobe* (Jesuit). Martin Scott, S.J., *Isaac Jogues.*
F. X. Talbot, S.J., *Saint Among Savages,* and *Saint Among
the Hurons* (Jean de Brébeuf—Martyr). Wm. E. Shiels,
Gonzalo de Tapia (1561-94), founder of first permanent
Jesuit Mission in North America. Agnes Repplier, *Père
Marquette.* Reuben Thwaites, *Père Marquette.* Chas. Dan-
iel's *Alexis Clerc* (sailor and one of the Jesuit Martyrs).
Frederick Easterly, C.M., *Bishop Rosati, C.M.* (first Bishop
of St. Louis). L. V. Jacks, *Claude Dubuis, Bishop of Galveston.* (The author comments on early relations between
the clergy in the U.S. and their fellow-priests in Mexico.)
Mary Ellen Evans, *The Seed and the Glory* (Father Mazzuchelli, O.P.).

Anyone attending schools taught by these Orders can
get biographies through the members or can refer to *Catholic Encyclopedia.* Mother Mary Frances Clarke (Presentation
of B.V.M.)—Clarke College, Dubuque. Mother Katherine
Drexel, founder of the Sisters of the Blessed Sacrament for
Indian and Colored People (Xavier U., New Orleans). Very
Rev. C. Fournier (Viatorian)—Bourbonnais, Illinois. Mother
Theodore Guerin (Sisters of Providence of Charity)—St.
Mary of the Woods, Terre Haute. Father Moreau (Brothers
of Holy Cross)—Ave Maria Press, Notre Dame, Indiana,
publishes brochures on several Brothers. Mother Warde,
who brought the Sisters of Mercy to Pittsburgh (Mount

Mercy), was educated according to Fénelon's ideas. Where is a Sisters of Mercy College in your area? Sisters of the Immaculate Heart of Mary (Marygrove, Detroit) and Marywood (Scranton, Pennsylvania).

Charles G. Herbermann, *Province of St. Joseph of the Capuchin Order in the U.S.* V. F. O'Daniel, *Dominicans in Early Florida* (U.S. Catholic Hist. Soc. Monograph.). Sister Maria Alma, *Sisters Servants of I.H.M. Mother Caroline and the School Sisters of Notre Dame in North Carolina* (2 vols.). Sister Maria Kostka, *Sisters of St. Joseph of Philadelphia,* 1847-1947. Scranton Community, *Sisters of Immaculate Heart of Mary.* Mary A. Sharkey, *New Jersey Sisters of Charity* (3 vols.). Helen M. Sweeney, *Golden Milestones,* 1846-96 (Sisters of Mercy, N.Y.C.). John Cavanaugh, *Priests of Holy Cross* (C.S.C.). Leo P. Johnson, *Daughters of Charity in Milwaukee,* 1946-96. James M. Gillis, *The Paulists.* James A. Garvin, *Three Centuries of Vincentian Missionary Labor* (the centenary of the C.M.'s in the U.S., 1917). Camillus P. Maes, *Life of Father Chas. Nerinckx* (early Catholic missions in Kentucky; progress of Catholicism in U.S.A., 1800-25. Founded Sister of Loretto, Ky., Mo., and N. Mex.). *Catholic Periodical Index* will refer to such articles as *Cahokia's 250th Birthday, America,* 81: 257 f., May 21, 1949. Sara M. Brownson, *Life of Prince Gallitzen* (first priest trained in America). Harold J. McAuliffe, *Father Tim Dempsey* (poor man's friend, St. Louis). William J. Fitzpatrick, *Life of Rt. Rev. Dr. Doyle* (vindicated). A Nursing Sister of the Sick Poor, *Monsignor White* (Brooklyn). Gordon Blair, *Father Tabb.* Francis E. Litz, *Study of Life and Works of Father Tabb.* J. M. Tabb, *Father Tabb.* Peter P. McLoughlin, *Father Tom McLoughlin* (priest of N. Y. Archdiocese). Rev. Wm. A. McGuire (Navy), *Rig for Church* and its sequel *Captain Wears a Cross.*

Richard Clarke's *Lives of the Deceased Bishops of the Catholic Church in U.S.* Jos. B. Code's *Dictionary of the American Hierarchy* and *Great American Foundresses.*

Bishop Francis Kelley, *The Bishop Jots It Down* (Church Extension Society). Hugh J. Nolan, *Most Rev. Francis P. Kenrick, Third Bishop of Philadelphia,* 1830-1851). John G. Shea, *The Two Kenricks* (Archbishop of Baltimore and Archbishop of St. Louis). Theo. Maynard, *The Reed and The Rock* (Bishop Simon Bruté). Jos. Gurn's *Charles Carroll.* Ellen H. Smith's *Charles Carroll.* Dorothy Fremont Grant's *Margaret Brent* used colonial Maryland as background; her *John England: American* is a biography of Bishop England; her *Night of Decision* uses New York (1683-1690), when Colonel Dongan (a Catholic) was governor and anti-Catholic bias prevailed. Sister Blandina Segal, *At the End of the Santa Fe Trail*—the part the Catholic Church has played in genuine Americana. Catholic University has microfilmed theses that were out of print. (*M* will designate that fact.) J. Hugh O'Donnell's *Catholic Hierarchy in the U.S.,* 1790-1922 and Thos. P. O'Rourke, *Franciscan Missions in Texas,* 1690-1793.

Allen F. Will's *Life of Cardinal Gibbons* and the Cardinal's *Retrospect of Fifty Years* introduce the reader to a quietly militant Catholic leader whose influence was felt everywhere and who delighted Americans of all creeds. He began humbly, with missions to non-Catholics (out of which the best-seller *Faith of Our Fathers* grew) in North Carolina, where the Church had made the least impression. He made clear to those who feared Rome's influence in America that all just governments are alike to the Church. Particularly interesting in his story are his connection with Mt. St. Mary's (the Sulpician Seminary for priests at Baltimore), with the founding of Catholic University (1889), with demonstrating that the Church in the United States knows neither fear, nor fatigue, nor discouragement, and that Catholics here dare not be false to the principle of religious liberty which for them is sacred and inviolable.

Archbishop Carroll was as beloved by Catholics in America as Washington was by the whole country. Archbishops

Kenrick, Spalding, and Bayley (Mother Seton's nephew) were equally religious of highest caliber.

Bishop John England (Charleston, 1830) at one time had but two churches in his enormous diocese; in fact, before 1800 Father P. J. O'Gallagher of the area had supported himself by teaching in the Protestant Charleston College. Bishop England's contribution to education included incessant preaching and teaching, establishing of a Book Society (1812) and the *U.S. Miscellany,* the first Catholic weekly in the country (1822). (*Catholic Mind,* vol. 16, no. 23, December 8, 1918, printed from the *Miscellany* of August 12, 1826, Washington's stepson's address on Irish freedom.) Bishop England's writings have been collected in five volumes, but one must read history to realize his impact on the sparsely settled country. He was the first Catholic clergyman to preach in the House of Representatives; he supplied for a Protestant minister in his pulpit at the latter's request. He was stopped on the road with a request, "Give us a sermon, Mr. Bishop" and complied; his kindness and instruction to Negroes led Protestant plantation owners to welcome him. When hoodlums threatened to burn a Charleston convent, he examined the flints of his defenders' rifles to be sure they would not miss fire—and the bigots slunk away.

Bishop Loughlin, first in Brooklyn (1853), made that city "the city of churches" and deepened the hold of Long Island on its title "Island of Apostles."

In the Ohio Valley, Father Badin was the first priest ordained in the United States. The story of Bishop Flaget of Bardstown, who had taught at the historic Mt. St. Mary's Seminary at Emmitsburg, Maryland, recalls that while the city (like the original Catholic settlement near Pittsburgh) did not flourish and another city (Louisville) became the Bishop's see, Father Nerinckx's founding of the Sisters of Loretto and Mother Catherine Spalding the Sisters of Charity of Nazareth, together with the Xaverian Brothers, made a dynamic Catholic cradle. Bishop Martin Spalding (later

Archbishop of Baltimore) brought the Xaverians and the Brothers of the Christian Schools (de la Salle) to Kentucky. Bishop Fenwick started the *Catholic Telegraph* in Cincinnati (1831). Bishop Gilmore founded the equally well-known Cleveland *Universe* and published an excellent series of texts for Catholic schools. Bishop Purcell and Archbishop Elder are connected intimately with the Cincinnati St. Mary's of the West (seminary for training priests). The name of Bishop Bruté (Sulpician) is associated irrevocably with historic Vincennes.

Sister of Mercy, *Catholic History of Alabama and the Floridas* (reviewed, *Catholic World,* 88:394 f., Dec., 1908). *History of the Catholic Church in the Diocese of Brooklyn* (by a Sister of St. Dominic). Roger Baudier, *Catholic Church in Louisiana* (1939). John O'Kane Murray, *Catholic Pioneers in America; Lives of Catholic Heroes and Heroines of America; Popular History of the Catholic Church in the United States.* W. H. Bennett, *Catholic Footsteps in Old New York.* Charles G. Hebermann, *Sulpicians in the United States in 1883; Three Quarters of a Century* (1807-85); *Diary of Lord Russell's Visit to the United States in 1883.* J. L. J. Kirlin, *Catholic Church in Philadelphia from Earliest Missionaries to Present Time.* Wm. A. Leahy, *History of the Catholic Church in New England; Catholic Churches of Boston and Vicinity.* E. Leveille, *Peter De Smet, S.J.* Chas. H. McCarthy, *Columbus and His Predecessors.* Article on "U.S." in *Catholic Encyclopedia.* C. E. McGinn, *Catholic Builders of the Nation.* (As a class project consider bringing this material to date.) John Gilmary Shea, *Hierarchy of the Catholic Church in the United States; History of the Catholic Church in the United States; History of Catholic Missions Among Indians; Isaac Jogues.* Don Shearer, *Pontifica Americana: A Documentary History of the Catholic Church in the United States,* 1784-1884. Augustus T. Thebaud, *Forty Years in the United States.* Helen Margaret, *Father De Smet.* Justine Ward, *William Pardow, S.J.* Father Wynne, S.J., *Golden*

Jubilee. The *Grail,* September, 1946, carried an article ("Teachers of Life") on the Benedictines; the work of various religious communities in the U.S. has been so recorded; locate material on any community that interests you especially.

These Master's theses (available through interlibrary loan) were chosen from those at St. John's University, Brooklyn, to represent the work by Religious of different Orders. (They are catalogued according to year submitted and the first three letters of the author's family name.)

(50 Mul)   Contribution of Peter Guilday to American Catholic Historiography
(50 Fli)   The Humanitarianism of John Boyle O'Reilly
(46 Gly)   Mother Catherine McAuley, Foundress of the Sisters of Mercy
(43 And)   Brief History of the Sisters of St. Joseph in Brooklyn 1856-1903

Brother Angelus Cabriel, *The Christian Brothers in the U.S.,* 1848-1948. Daniel Sargent, *All the Day Long* (Bishop Walsh, founder of Maryknoll). Joseph E. Walsh, *Father McShane of Maryknoll;* G. A. Donovan's *When the Sorghum Was High* (Maryknoller from Pittsburgh slain by Manchukuoan bandits). Rev. James A. Keller, *Men of Maryknoll.* Rev. Wm. A. Hayward, *Rt. Rev. Wm. McGarvey, Founder of the Congregation of the Companions of the Holy Saviour* (helps Episcopalian ministers to live more perfect lives). Sister Columba Fox, *Life of Bishop David of Bardstown;* Huen-Dubourg's *Bishop Cheverus of Boston;* Joseph L. O'Brien, *Bishop England, Apostle of Democracy;* John R. G. Hassard, *Life of Archbishop Hughes;* John M. Farley, *Life of Cardinal McCloskey;* James Jamison's *By Cross and Anchor* is a biography of Bishop Baraga (pioneer in northern Michigan); Frederick J. Zwierlein, *Life and Letters of Bishop McQuaid* (3 vols.)—unique in information about the Church at the turn of the century.

Brother Francis Xavier assisted Father Edward Sorin (of the Congregation of the Holy Cross) in founding Notre Dame (1841). The museum and the archives at the University are repositories of invaluable materials to the history of the Church in Indiana. The Sisters of Providence opened what has become an excellent college (St. Mary's of the Woods) in 1840. St. Mary's College at Holy Cross (near Notre Dame) is a leading Catholic college for women under Sisters of the Holy Cross.

The growth of Catholicity in Chicago has become phenomenal. From the time Father Marquette had Christianized the Indians (of whom Chicago was chief) to the arrival of Father St. Cyr (sent by Bishop Rosati of St. Louis) a century and a half later, Chicago was indeed an outpost, subject to the Bishop of Bardstown. Father G. J. Garraghan's *Catholic Church in Chicago* (1673-1871) surveys from the coming of the first resident Bishop Quarter to Archbishop Feehan's start. *Mid-America* (organ of the Illinois Catholic Historical Society) continues the story of the magnificent accomplishments of Archbishop Quigley and Cardinals Mundelein and Stritch. At Bishop Foley's request (1877), the Diocese of Peoria was formed from part of that of Chicago. Bishop John Lancaster Spalding, nephew of the Archbishop of Baltimore, was chosen first Bishop. His biography begun in *Mid-America* was not continued, but his numerous volumes reveal him an outstanding thinker and educator of first rank.

E. T. Dehey's *Religious Orders of Women in U.S.* will introduce readers to the magnificent work of teaching groups, builders of hospitals, and varied charities which began when the Carmelites driven by the horrors of the French Revolution to Maryland (1792). The Poor Clares, and the Visitation nuns founded by Alice Lalor (1797) closed the eighteenth century in the United States; (no author) *Venerable Margaret Bourgeoys* (Congregation of

Notre Dame) now canonized. Marjorie Ersine's *Philappine Duchesne* presents the pioneering of a Religious of the Sacred Heart in the Mississippi Valley near St. Louis (Duchesne College in Omaha).

Code, Joseph B., *Letters of Mother Seton* (convert). Agnes Sadlier, *Mother Seton.* Charles White, *Mother Seton* (history of Sisters of Charity to 1879). Joseph J. Dougherty, *Mother Elizabeth Boyle* (one of Mother Seton's first companions). (Anonymous) *Soeur Eugenie* (Sister of Charity). (No author) *Life of Rev. Mother Julia* (history of the Sisters of Notre Dame de Namur in the U.S.). Sister M. Pauline Fitts, G.N.S.H., *Hands to the Needy* (Mother Marguerite d'Youville, foundress of the first religious order of women in North America—the Grey Nuns). Mother Francis d'Assisi's *St. Angela of the Ursulines.* S. M. Johnston, *A Light Shining* (Mother M. Joseph, R.U.). K. Burton, *Sorrow Built a Bridge* (Rose Hawthorne Lathrop), Nathaniel Hawthorne's daughter—Mother Alphonsus. James J. Walsh, *Mother Alphonsus, O.S.D.* (founder of Society for Treatment of Incurable Cancer). Blanche M'Eniry, *Woman of Decision* (Sisters of Charity of Convent Station). Mother M. Williams, *Second Sowing* (Mother M. Aloysia Hardey—Religious of the Sacred Heart). Mother M. Eleanor, *The Triumph of Truth* (Mother Connelly, foundress of the Society of the Holy Child Jesus).

Katherine Burton's *Mother Butler of Marymount.* Theodore Maynard's *Too Small a World* (Mother Cabrini). In 1945 (her centenary) appeared Ignatius Jeiler's biography of Frances Schervier, whose cause for beatification has been introduced at Rome; she founded the Sisters of the Poor of St. Francis. In 1951 Theodore Maynard's biography of her was published. In the same year we have Sister M. Hester, S.S.N.D., *Canticle for the Harvest* (centenary volume). John L. Bonn, *So Falls the Elm Tree* (Mother Valencia, Franciscan Hospital, Hartford). Jos. Rosata's *Life of Felix de Andrew* (first Superior of the Vincentian priests in the U.S.

and Vicar General of New Orleans). W. H. Judge, *Father Judge, American Missionary* (to Negro). Joachim V. Benson, *The Judgments of Father Judge, C.M.* (who founded the Missionary Servants of the Most Holy Trinity—Trinitarians). P. Classen's *Life of Father Bernard Murray, Redemptorist.* John A. Berger, *Rt. Rev. John M. Neumann* (Redemptorist Bishop of Philadelphia).

The cause of Fra Junipero Serra has been introduced at Rome. "San Juan Capistrano Swallows Punctual" (National Catholic Welfare Conference News Service annually)—The swallows of the old Franciscan Mission here celebrated the nameday of the Franciscan friar whose prayers and miracles turned back the Turks from Hungary in the fifteenth century in their traditional way, flying out to sea at dawn. Agnes Repplier, *Junipero Serra, Pioneer Colonist of California.*

This type of material appears at the foot of pages in B. Confrey's *Following the Liturgical Year:*

1. What Catholic was called "The Father of the American Navy"? (Captain John Barry)
2. How many Catholics signed the Constitution of the U.S. (Two)
3. Who was the first priest ordained in the New World? (Father Las Casas)
4. Who among Colonial laymen was the greatest Catholic patriot? (Charles Carroll)
5. Of what nationality and religion was Columbus? (An Italian Catholic)
6. Which was the last of the States to grant equal rights to Catholics? (New Hampshire)
7. Which American convert contributed most to the Church in the U.S.? (Mother Elizabeth Seton)
8. What great American city is called after an English Catholic nobleman? (New York)

9. How many Catholics have served in the U.S. Supreme Court? (Six)

10. Where in what is now U.S. territory was the first Catholic Church founded? (St. Augustine, Florida)

11. Which is the oldest Catholic university in the U.S.? (Georgetown)

12. Why does the future of the U.S. as a democracy depend upon the Catholic Church? (Because the Catholic Church believes in freedom of the individual under the laws of God and the just laws of man.)

13. In which nation has the Church in all her history grown most rapidly? (U.S.)

14. What priest was largely responsible for the accession of the States in the original Northwest Territory? (Father Gibault)

15. In how many states do Catholics outnumber members of any other religious organization? (Thirty-three)

16. What Bishop was the first to be made a Cardinal in the U.S.? (Bishop McCloskey)

17. Why is a good Catholic a good American? (Because the Catholic Church teaches the social principles upon which the U.S. is founded.)

18. Who was the only priest to serve in the House of Representatives? (Father Gabriel Richard)

19. Where in all colonial days did Catholics receive the best treatment? (Penn.)

20. Why have all anti-Catholic organizations in the U.S. ultimately failed? (Because they were un-American as well as anti-Catholic)

21. Why should a good American be a Catholic? (As a Catholic he would be a better American citizen)

22. According to Catholic teaching, what is principally needed for the furtherance of social justice in the U.S.? (The payment of an annual living wage)

23. How does the Constitution safeguard the natural

rights of all Americans? (By establishing a check
and balance among the three branches of
government)

24. What is the Church's greatest contribution to democracy? (The insistent teaching of the supremacy
of the individual)

25. Which amendment of the Constitution is of most
importance to Catholics? (The first)

26. Why is Communism bound to fail? (Because it ignores man's nature)

27. Who gives our President the right to govern? (God)

28. What is the principal cause of prejudice against the
Church? (Ignorance of her teaching)

29. What is the greatest danger facing the Church
today? (Indifference toward religion)

30. Who is regarded as the outstanding convert of the
last century? (Cardinal Newman)

To lengthen this test include items from the preceding
section on "firsts."

Bernard J. Kohlbrenner's redaction of James A. Burns'
History of Catholic Education in the United States (1937)
furnishes a chronological account of the development of
schools, information about religious orders, historical names.
To their lists might be added the following information
about first Catholic schools in several dioceses. In Connecticut, at Hartford, July 11, 1829, the first Catholic school; a
Sunday school conducted by men and women opened July
25. In Virginia, St. Joseph's Academy and Orphanage was
first, November 25, 1834. (Bishop Patrick Kelly supported
himself by teaching in Norfolk, 1821-27.)

Projects based on Burns—Kohlbrenner's *History of Catholic Education in the United States* might include: (1) On
an outline map of the states in our country, locate, with date,

the site of the first school in each state. (The activity may be enriched by listing names of the founders and an authority for the facts. For the information we added in the preceding paragraphs, consult: Arthur J. Heffernan, *History of Education in Connecticut* (1937); Joseph Magri, *Catholic Church in the City and Diocese of Richmond*, pp. 54 ff.; R. D. Gerow, *Catholics in Mississippi* (1939), p. 329; V. F. O'Daniel, O.P., *Fathers of the Church in Tennessee* (1926).

Choose from the Index names you would like to know about (Badin, Baraga, Bardstown, Bruté, Dubois, Dubourg, Fenwick, Flaget, Gallitzin, Gibault, Mazzuchelli, Nerinck, Neumann, Rosati, Seton, Shields, Spalding).

On a sketch map of the states of our country show "The Original Catholic Settlement of the U.S.," revealing the sign of Christ's Cross over it all ("A soil fertilized by the blood and sweat of Catholic explorers, founders, and missionaries"). One might show, for instance, Spanish settlements in Washington, Oregon, California, Montana, Idaho, Colorado, Arizona, New Mexico, Texas, Alabama, and Florida. (A cross could designate Catholic settlement.) The French settled Dakota, Minnesota, Nebraska, Kansas, Indian Territory, Louisiana, Mississippi, Arkansas, Missouri, Iowa, Illinois, Wisconsin, Michigan, Indiana, Ohio, Vermont, and Maine. English and Irish Catholics settled Maryland.

CHAPTER FIVE

Geographical Surroundings of the Frontier

When seeking the vivifying element in a civilization we must study its relationship to its physical surroundings—both in particular regions and in the world. The climate [1],* the land [2], the water [3], the plants and animals [4] influence strongly a people's adjustment, their means of livelihood, the choice of sites for cities [5] and their courage and fighting spirit. Distinctly to the American pioneer's advantage, to be sure, was the fact that axe, plow, fire, and grazing domestic animals had not destroyed trees, grasses, and other plants. So long as the mulch of vegetation accumulated on the sod was not washed away, the uncontrolled flow of water did not affect fertility. When settlers first came to what is now our country about half the area was forest-covered—and the forests protected watersheds. Fish and game were plentiful. But in a century and a half we lost one-third of our topsoil, an unknown proportion of reserve water, more than half of our high grade lumber, and much of our wild life. Rex Beach's *The Spoilers* fictionalizes dramatically the devastation of our forests by greedy lumber companies. (For years the Diocese of Grand Rapids was known as the "pine stump diocese.") Pioneers need not worry about an expanding economy becoming a contracting one, because our pri-

* See notes to this Chapter in the Appendix.

meval forests were so thick a squirrel could travel from the Atlantic to the Mississippi without ever touching the ground.

Since missionaries first discovered our nation's wealth, despite the "rugged individualism" which Protestants brought into our civilization, Catholicism underlies much of America's material progress and prosperity. Recall the days of pioneering and discovery to realize how Catholicity opened up the economic possibilities of the fertile acres and the grazing plains. When missionaries realized the boundless productivity of the alluvial plains of the Mississippi Valley— and they were first to comprehend that wheat grown in Illinois (and corn in Iowa) could make us the breadbasket of the world, under their direction the Middle West bloomed like a garden. Not only did they record our amazing timber resources; they emphasized the necessity for reforestation.

Consideration of what the production of citrus fruits has meant to our South and Southwest, recalling that Catholic missionaries first introduced cultivation of the orange and the lemon, suggests our debt to them for these sources of wealth and prosperity. Nor can we estimate the aesthetic value of the sight of orange groves in what had been wasteland, the perfume of their blossoms, or the shimmering gold of their harvest. Grapes they introduced—take time out to think of their significance in all ramifications. They introduced sugar cane—realize how independent that has made us of other sugar-producing areas; or, since we use such incredible amounts of sugar, think how handicapped our economy would have been had we never had sugar plantations. Our missionaries introduced apples in the western hemisphere. New York State's salt wells they discovered. Not only were they first to unearth copper deposits in the Lake Superior region; they developed them. They first detected the oil fields in Pennsylvania—the source of gigantic fortunes. And their most impelling motive was *Ad majorem Dei gloriam*—the love of God.

"Our poisoned waters" [6] reveals the fact that streams and

rivers from which Americans get drinking water contain organic pollution equivalent to eight million dead and disintegrating mules dumped into waterways every year. Harbor and bathing beach pollution, too, is a terrifying problem for a metropolis like New York or Chicago; yet the fact that such fertilizer is wasted and allowed to endanger health is surely a sign of educational lag—but no problem to our pioneers.

The early pioneering days in America had a much more social and economic inequality than the present; and yet at that time when men had to fight the severe handicaps of physical environment the temper of America was not, as it is today, one of pessimism and foreboding but of courage and hope.

"What's Right With America?" [7] presented the hospitality of the new, uncrowded land as a frontier of Europe, its climate, geographical position, fertility, and economic conditions. Frederick J. Turner's frontier hypothesis was upheld by F. L. Paxon as the most attractive single explanation of the distinctive trends of American history; but L. M. Hacker contends that Professor Turner's thesis of the role of the frontier as the true point of view in our history has blighted man's proper understanding for half a century. Hacker feels that it is only by a study of the origins and growth of American capitalism and imperialism that we can realize the nature and complexity of the problems the United States faces today.

American-born Poles remark their parents' love of the earth and their ambition before World War II, when they had accumulated sufficient money to go back to Poland to be land-owners [8].

Many young fathers have struggled to get out of a metropolis to the less complicated living, closer to nature. Therein lies the history of real estate developments, of shifts in population, in dwindling parishes and the necessity for building new ones in suburban areas. David Grayson's delightful *Adventures in Contentment, The Friendly Road, Adventures in Friendship,* and others, corral the enchantment of daily living far from the madding crowd [9].

Various authors have glorified waterside environment where one actually learns to feel part of the sea and the sky. Since man likes a certain amount of beating, sailing is an experience wherein one's opponents are not human.

Clarence A. Mills' *Living with the Weather, Medical Climatology,* and *Climate Makes the Man* uphold the thesis that, no matter what one's family or racial heritage, the climatic background of his life will always affect his aggressive attack or his complacent sluggishness. Human geography is a study of the distribution and activities of man and his constant dependence on interrelationship with his physical environment. Geography is a more powerful memorial than history, and in geo-history we have the greatest source of information about man's past adjustment.

Our geography of the future will be in the heavens—in air routes. Everyone who looks up should realize that the sky is a revelation of God's handiwork. Materialists, with eyes on the ground, have denied the Creator; but Catholics coming to America to escape persecution looked up—and in astronomy found a guidebook to God's kingdom. Viewing the vast expense of the heavens, particularly at night, the pioneer learned to think of self in macrocosm [10], and realized his relative insignificance among the wonders of the universe. Contemplating all the glories of the heavens helps man realize the shortsightedness of living in microcosm. When he thinks of self as the center of things, he should be overwhelmed by the secularization of his life and of that of the world around him.

No one questions the educational influence of the Christian mother in the Christian home. Certainly to the pioneer mother can be attributed 75 per cent of the educational influence of the succeeding generation. But today with one out of three marriages in the United States ending in divorce

—and that proportion rapidly approaching one out of two, Capital and Labor strife, high public officials betraying their trust with contempt for law and for man, the low morality of the motion picture, stage, and commercialized amusements, the febrile and highly successful campaigns to drive recognition of God not only from public education but from the world, the moral law subordinated to the power of knowledge, a sense of accountability for one's acts shrugged off [13], all bespeak man's selfishness.

The chief factor in the daily life of pioneers is their adaptation to environment; so the history of Catholic education in the United States consists, in the main, not of facts about educators and dates but of the reaction of Catholics to frontiers—whether they be the agricultural borderland or the industrial wastelands [13] with which the bourgeoisie and proletariat in an American metropolis confront churches, or the missionary fields which the Pacific world thrust suddenly into new prominence since World War II. Several authors have traced our growth from agrarian innocence through the Civil War and into the era of the Robber Barons and ruthless industrial expansion. In *Catholic Action* [14], we included a chart on training for life adjustment which surveyed the changes in education because of our shift from an agrarian to an industrial civilization and the effects on administration, control, employment, interdependence, place of women and children in the working world, and rate and standard of living under three phases of our development— pioneer agrarianism, what the United States has passed through (first Industrial Revolution), what we are experiencing (Industrial Revolution II), and the pedagogical implications in such changes. An honors course might well be devoted to training superior students to make the most of their national and Catholic heritage [15].

Before leaving this considereration of geographical surroundings and frontiers we might recall the historian Bancroft's tribute to the zeal of missionaries in sixteenth and

seventeenth-century America and the innervating challenge
of sparsely inhabited places. The simplicity and freedom of
life in the wilderness was not without charm. Men's hearts
could tumesce with delight when, under serene sky in mild
temperature and pure air, they crossed waters as transparent
as the most limpid fountain. When the missioner halted, his
companions could hunt wild fowl and animals undisturbed.
Masters of all they saw, they were unencumbered by ownership or the cares of possession. Though, like Jacob, their
pillows were stones, like him, feeling the presence of God,
they could dream of a ladder leading "Nearer, my God, to
Thee." Eating in the open, like Abraham under a tree breaking bread with angels, they could look forward to receiving
the bread of life before they broke their fast next morn.
Daily they changed their dwelling site; in a short while they
could erect anew a shelter of branches over a floor of grass
enlivened with blooms. All around them their eyes met beauties unspoiled by art and by it inimitable.

A project continuing your interest in philately would be
that of watching for Catholics honored by having their faces
on our postage stamps and adding to the list which follows.
While several of our Postmasters General have been Catholics (they were unusually effective managers of Presidential
campaigns), they have no choice of the subjects used. Catholics represent one fifth of our population (which does not
mean that four-fifths are Protestants).

Of more than 150 historical characters and events so
honored, however, very few are Catholics. (Hoover is the
only President not on a stamp.) Since July 1, 1847 (when
the first U.S. postage stamp was sold in New York City), 13
honored foreigners (10 of whom were Catholics—a historical necessity?). Only two Catholics born in America have
been included (General Sheridan and Governor Alfred E.
Smith). Captain John Barry, father of our Navy (born in

Ireland) became an American citizen; and General Kosciusko was naturalized.

The recognition of those few Catholics came very late. On October 13, 1933, the Kosciusko stamp commemorated the 150th anniversary of his naturalization. Captain Barry appeared with John Paul Jones on a stamp, December 18, 1936 (over a century and a half after the War of Independence). General Sheridan appeared with Grant on February 18, 1937 (seventy years late). Is it curious that he and Barry had to share a stamp with others?

Other foreign Catholics commemorated: Columbus, Queen Isabella with him, Balboa (upon the opening of the Panama Canal 400 years after Balboa discovered the Pacific), Pulaski (150 years after his death), Count Rochambeau and Admiral de Grasse shown with Washington for the 150th anniversary of the surrender at Yorktown, Father Marquette (1898), Jean Nicolet (for the Wisconsin Tercentenary—he was the first white man to reach what is now Wisconsin, at Green Bay), and in 1940 Coronado (fourth centenary of his exploration of the Southwest, long before the Pilgrims landed).

An ignorant slight to Catholics came in 1940 when President F. D. Roosevelt (whose stamp collection sold for over $134,550) selected a famous American series. The thirty-five included seven groups of five each—authors, poets, educators, scientists, composers, artists, and inventors. All Catholics were omitted; commemorative postage stamps missed, then, their unprejudiced function of recalling important people or historical events in our national life.

In 1943, Congress proclaimed November 11 Pulaski Day to honor the Father of American Cavalry. Other Catholic leaders in the Revolution included Stephen Moylan, Rochambeau, Kosciusko, Coudray, Neuville, and Duportail.

There were 45 Union Generals in the Civil War who were Catholics or became converts. The list includes Sheridan, Sherman, Ewing, J. A. Hardie, H. J. Hunt, T. F.

Meagher, and D. H. Rucker. Eighteen Confederate Generals
belong in this category: Beauregard, W. J. Hardee, Theodore
Hardeman, Longstreet, and R. H. Anderson.

Edison is the only electrical genius with more patents
than Thos. E. Murray, a Catholic who had more than eleven
hundred.

The *Catholic Mind* is an admirable source of material
not readily available any place else. For the periodical
America Press collects sermons, addresses, and reprints, including these titles:

The North American Indian and the Catholic Church
(1903); Isaac Jogues, Missionary and Martyr, and the Jesuit
Martyrs of North America (1925); Cardinal Gibbons' Ju-
bilee; and Scotland in Penal Days (1911); Catholicism and
Americanism by Archbishop Ireland (1913); Magna Charta's
Centenary by Peter Guilday; The Church's Mission in
America Today, The Catholic School the Country's Bulwark,
and The Laymen We Need (1919); Preserve all Catholic
Records (1920); The French Clergy's Gift to America, 1780,
and Education in the Middle Ages (1920); the American
Catholic Historical Association, Freedom of Thought, History the Witness of Truth, and Luther at Worms (1920);
Catholic Toleration in Maryland; and the Graduates' Responsibility (1926); The First American Sister of Charity
(Elizabeth Bayley Seton). These titles are listed from a
stack at hand; but if they are not available, treatment of
the subjects can be located elsewhere.

America Press publishes also books pertinent to this
unit. Arrange individual reports on: T. J. Campbell's *Pioneer
Priests of North America*—Among the Iroquois (vol. 1),
Among the Hurons (vol. 2), Among the Algonquins (vol. 3);
his *Pioneer Laymen of North America* (2 vols.)—Cartier,
Menendez, Champlain, De La Tour Maisonneuve, Le Moyne
Radisson, Le Moyne d'Iberville, Frontenac, La Salle, Le
Moyne de Bienville, De La Vérendrye, and Dr. John
M'Loughlin; T. J. Campbell's *Isaac Jogues, Discoverer of*

Lake George; Life of Venerable Philippine Duchesne; Life and Letters of Henry Van Rensselaer; Anna C. Minogue's *Loretto* (accomplishments of pioneer Catholic women of Kentucky).

Special interest might be found in (a) Columbus's preserving his chains as memorials of the rewards of his service, (b) Among Ponce de Leon's most successful warriors was a dog named Berezillo, renowned for its courage, strength, and sagacity—it could distinguish those Indians allies of Spain from enemies. To the names already listed might be added: (c) Verazzano and (d) the Cabots. In piety, virtue, and integrity they equal any cross section of a corresponding number of the world's great men. Human frailty was theirs, but their virtues outnumbered their faults. Their daring adventures they undertook from Catholic motives and succeeded through Catholic co-operation. Those who were not great missioners were daring explorers—their virtues have been engraved on the tablets of our memories.

Try for special investigation these ideas: (a) Columbus's Catholicity: religion his guide, piety his companion. Denied by Genoa and Portugal, in Spain at La Rabida he got his first inspiration from a Franciscan friar—Father Parez (former confessor of Queen Isabella) was a scholar who loved mathematics and cosmology. Before sailing Columbus safeguarded his soul with the Sacraments, implored the Queen of Heaven to direct his course and assist his voyage, would have no sail hoisted until he had invoked the help of the Holy Trinity. This reliance on God gave him a tranquil constancy of mind which protected all when the sailors later threatened mutiny. On the voyage Columbus and sailors sang "Star of the Sea" (the Blessed Mother); he named his place of landing San Salvador (Holy Savior), and all chanted the "Te Deum" (We Praise Thee, O God). (b) The devotion of Father Marquette, S.J., to the Blessed Mother led him to name the Mississippi (Immaculate) Conception; but like its earlier Spanish name (River of the Holy

Ghost—*Rio del Spiritu Santo*), it has yielded before the Indian name. On December 8 (the Blessed Mother's Feast Day) he got permission to visit the Indian nations on the Mississippi. With him were Louis Jolliet, five Frenchmen, and two Algonquin guides. Report on the fascination of reading about Marquette.

The author's home is in La Salle, Illinois, which is the Diocese of Peoria (Pewaria)—the heart of the Marquette country. The names of streets of the city include: La Salle, Crèvecoeur, Chartres, Marquette, Joliet, Hennepin, Tonti, Crosat, La Harpe. One hotel in the city is the Kaskaskia. Starved Rock (La Salle's Fort St. Louis) is nearby. Near it the first Mass was celebrated west of the Alleghenies. A similar report on some settlement with a historical background might attract attention.

Share with your group your enthusiasm for Thomas A. Shaw's *Story of the La Salle Missions*. Why does it (not?) give you the impression that the accomplishment of the Sisters outdistanced that of anyone else? (The objection has been made.) *The Story* (2 vols.) relates the work of the Vincentian Fathers, whose missionary headquarters were at La Salle as late as the twentieth century.

Explain Marquette's point of view as recorded in his narrative of the voyage down the Mississippi:

Had all this voyage brought but the salvation of a single soul, I should deem all my fatigue well repaid. And it was, I have reason to think; for, when I was returning, I passed by the Indians at Peoria. I was three days announcing the Faith in all their cabins, after which, as we were embarking, they brought me to the water's edge a dying child, which I baptized a little before it expired, by an admirable Providence, for the salvation of that immortal soul.

Read about him in John Gilmary Shea or a biography. He promised to return to Kaskaskia (on the upper Illinois River). His health broke when he reached the Chicago

River, but he returned to the Kaskaskias and on Maundy
Thursday (April 8), 1675, and offered Mass on the River
bottomlands between Utica and Starved Rock.

The Protestant historian Bancroft said about him, "The
West will build his monument." Honors paid him were un-
sought and uncontemplated. He sought no place among
contemporaries, and he died without thought of posterity
or fame.

The Ottawas lived in the upper part of the lower penin-
sula of Michigan (between Lakes Huron and Michigan).
Father Menard's death closed the first mission to the Ottawas—who were almost as close to Santa Fe as they were
to Montreal. (Check those distances on a map.) See what
Bancroft says of Menard: It may be asked if those massacres
quenched enthusiasm. I answer the Jesuits never receded
one foot; but, as in a brave army, new troops pressed forward to fill the places of the fallen. There was never wanting
heroism and enterprise in behalf of the cross under French
domination. Consider the idea that the most impelling motive is love of God.

Investigate Parkman on La Salle, a Catholic French
nobleman and magnificent seventeenth-century explorer,
who secured Fort Frontenac as basis of his operations. (b)
What of the two Franciscan friars, his companions—Luke
Buisset and Louis Hennepin and the Italian officer Henry
de Tonti he brought with him from France? (c) Why did
he name his fort at Peoria on the Illinois Crèvecoeur (broken
heart)? (d) What effect on American history did his naming
the land drained by the Mississippi and its tributaries "Louisiana" have on our history? (e) Why did he build Fort
St. Louis on Starved Rock (1687)? (f) How did the Rock
get its name?

(a) Map his voyage up the Great Lakes, through the
strait of Detroit and the Sault Ste. Marie. (b) Trace his
voyage from the Falls of St. Anthony (Minneapolis) to the
Gulf.

On an outline map locate the Illini on both sides of the Mississippi, pressed from the west by the Sioux and Dakotas and from the east by the fierce Iroquois. Locate such places as Cahokia and such Illini as the Tonicas.

Read about (a) Mme. Ako (Mary, daughter of the Chief of the Kaskaskias), who married the French Michael Ako to save Father Gravier and other missionaries from attack; (b) the Illini Christians who frequently sailed to New Orleans and edified all by their conduct under their chieftain, Chicago (who had been in France); (c) Father P. J. DeSmet's mission to Oregon and Washington.

Follow any leads which fascinate members of your group. For instance, in 1828 Father De Smet, S.J., actually helped put up the building for St. Louis University. In 1853 his travels equaled five times the distance around the world. Report on his letters, particularly the one describing his expedition against the Mormons (when as chaplain he accompanied the United States army sent against the Mormons and savages).

Consider (a) Father Simon LeMoyne's conversion of the Indian chief John Baptist, his Council's establishing Christianity at Onandaga, the capital of the Iroquois nation; (b) the founding of Le Moyne College at Syracuse (1946). (c) the Catholic Iroquois' refusal to fight the American Colonists; and (d) the harsh treatment missionaries, who took no part in the French and Indian Wars, received from Americans during the invasion of Canada. (e) St. Catherine Tekakwitha (died 1679) deserves an extended report. This "Lily of the Mohawks" was born in their chief town on the Mohawk River in 1656; her mother was a Christian Algonquin. Both her parents and her brothers and sisters died when she was four. (f) Father Claude Allouez, who went to the lower shore of Lake Superior in 1665 and labored among the Indians of Michigan, Wisconsin, and Illinois with unabated zeal for thirty years deserves the title "Apostle of the West." Report on the superstition and vice he battled to elevate these people morally and mentally. (g) The Marquettes deserve special consideration. Not only Father James, who followed Father Allouez in 1768 and whose name is linked forever with DeSoto and LaSalle and the Mississippi, but the three Marquettes sent from France to the American Revolution. The mother of Father James was a de la Salle, connected with the founder of the Brothers of the Christian Schools, who for over a century have been distinguished in American education, particularly for popularizing religious education. Their founder had opened the first Sunday School a century before Raikes, who is usually listed as its founder.

Initiate a project on the only true native Americans. (a) On a sketch map of aboriginal America, locate the nine great Indian families. (b) Special interest may add the five Iroquois Nations. Since the Indian tongues are not written, the inventing of a dictionary or the printing of a catechism was a tremendous task. (c) Arrange a symposium on these contributors: Father Garnier's Seneca and Cayugan catechisms and grammars; Father Le Boulanger's Illinois dictionary and catechism; Father Brébeuf's Huron catechism; Father Chaumonot's Huron dictionary; Father Bruyas' Onondaga and his Iroquois dictionary; Father White's dictionary for the Maryland Indians; and Father Rale's for the Abnekis of Maine. Father Alonzoa Barcena wrote grammars and catechisms (16 century) in most of the S.A. Indian languages he knew. (All these authors were Jesuits.) Bishop Baraga was the best Indian scholar of the nineteenth century; Father Sagard's Wyandot Dictionary appeared in 1632. Father Garcia printed a Texan manual. Father Francis Pareyna, O.S.F., wrote grammar, catechism and prayers in the Tirnaquan language of Florida (printed 1593 & 1606). Others include Rev. Dr. Vetromile, Father Joseph Marcoux, and Dr. John Gilmary Shea. Father John M. Cooper of the twentieth century deserves a special report not only for his work with Indian language but his leadership in the Catholic Anthropological Society.

In Pettit's famous study of American Indian education he praises the learning of the language of a people whose cultural changes one hopes to observe at first hand. Anthropologists realize that a people can be advanced by materials already existing bearing on the cultural areas in which the anticipated special work resides. The Church has always used whatever of natural virtue her missioners found among pagans and built on that apperceptive mass. Creating dictionaries in an unwritten language is not a superhuman task for those who labor for love of God.

ADDITIONAL ACTIVITIES ON AMERICA AS A FRONTIER

The Church not only discovered America but civilized its interesting people. (d) Report on the apostolic brief of Pope Paul III (1537) pronouncing that the native Indians were really and truly free men and must not be enslaved. (e) The work of Father Bartholomew Las Casas (Spanish dominican), "Protector of the Indians" (in Cuba) deserves Washington Irving's tribute. Report on his sixteen crossings of the Atlantic and his famous address before Emperor Charles V (in which he gained his point): "The Christian religion is equal in its operation, and is accommodated to every nation on the globe. It robs no one of his freedom, violates none of his inherent rights on the ground that he is a slave by nature, as pretended. . . ."

Show on a sketch map that the boundaries of the thirteen colonies after separation from England at the close of the War of Independence revealed the Catholic impress left on the area. The new nation rested in the embrace of the Holy Family, the boundaries being the River of the Holy Cross, the River of St. Mary, the River of St. Joseph, and the Rapids of Sault Sainte Marie. Further, each later additional proof of our debt to the Catholic Church—St. Augustine and St. John in the south, St. Lawrence in the north, St. Louis, Sante Fe, and San Antonio in the southwest, and San Francisco on the west coast, all indicate Catholic pioneering.

The following special investigations at Marquette University, Milwaukee, are available on inter-library loan. Which arrest your attention particularly?

Blied, B. J.: A Survey of Austrian contributions to the Catholic Church in the United States derived largely from the publications of the Leopoldine Society, 1830-1860. Ph.D. 1943.

Cudahy, Sister Eutropia: Religious Liberty in Maryland prior to the Act of 1649. M.A. 1948.

DeMarsh, E. M.: Some principles of religious and civil liberty developed by Maryland Catholics, 1632-1789. M.A. 1941.

Kerschen, Sister M. Donata: Father Mazzuchelli's influence on the frontier prior to his appointment as Provincial. M.A. 1946.

Lynch, Sister M. Claire: Jesuit missionary activities in North America from 1572-1773. M.A. 1934.

McGee, Sister M. Ignatius: Early explorations and rivalry between Spain and France of the Southwestern United States to 1763. M.A. 1938.

McSorley, Sister Ann Noreen: Cultural factors due to French Catholic influence in the region around Detroit, 1608-1812. M.A. 1945.

Mannix, M. W.: The contribution of Eusebia Francisco Kino, S.J., to the exploration and civilization of the American Southwest. M.A. 1941.

Martin, Sister Mary Stella: Some missionary activities of the Lake Superior region of the United States. M.A. 1940.

Patterson, Sister M. Hyacinth: The life of a Jesuit missioner in New France. M.A. 1934.

Raynor, Sister Miriam: The development of the Catholic Church in the Lake Erie region to 1850. M.A. 1941.

Sanford, G. F.: Paul de Chomeday, Sieur de Maisonneuve, and the founding of Montreal. M.A. 1933.

Zarse, F. M.: Life in the posts and towns during the French regime in Canada. M.A. 1933.

On an outline map of the United States show the 1822 division into nine dioceses. One could have each of the maps made throughout the course much enlarged and left to the history room as a permanent record.

In Bishop Gerald Shaughnessy's *Has the Immigrant Kept the Faith?*, Chapters 2 and 3 summarize well conditions of the Church in colonial days. Share them.

Arrange a panel on the Church and the immigrant. *Catholic Mind*, Vol. XIII, No. 17, September 8, 1915, included (a) an address by the President of the Catholic Church Extension Society on that subject, (b) "The Immigration Problem," and (c) "The Catholic Immigrant." (d) What Catholics in your area are doing to teach immigrants English and citizenship. (e) Essay contests like that of the Italian Historical Society of America on Italy's or Italo-American contributions to our civilization. (f) A current problem such as receiving displaced persons (DPs) and in real American style fighting the shutting out of Catholics (or any other minority group).

For a cumulative project lasting throughout the year select from the following booklists on the pioneering achievements of Catholics in America, their favorable or successful reaction to a frontier environment, whether it was wild prairies or the wasteland near industrial mammoths where mushroomed American cities.

A. The roll of Irish (debarred from fighting for the liberty of their own land) and French officers who came to America's aid from France during the War for Independence makes inspiring reading. Brice, Conway, Roger, Dugan, Arundel, and Stephen Moylan (brother of the Bishop of Cork)—this last, the Murat of the Revolutionary Army, had three brothers with him. Lt. Col. De Franchessen, Col. Dubois, De Kermorvan, De la Neuville, Malmady, De Saint Aulaire, St. Martin, Vermonet, Dorset, Du Portail, Du Coudray, Pelissier, Vibert, Fleury, Manduit, Gouvion, Rochefermoy, Armand, Dorat, Gimat, and Lafayette.

Aedanis Burke (who, like the Carrolls, had studied at St.
Omer) became Chief Justice of the South Carolina courts
after having represented her in the Continental Congress.
Chevalier de Ternay brought the French soldiers commanded by Count de Rochambeau. On the fleet with Count
de Grasse were an army of Catholics with Catholic chaplains. We got Spanish aid through Count Bernardo de Gal-
vez (Galveston), governor of Louisiana.

John Barry is looked upon as the father of the American
Navy. Catholic officers in the American Forces included:
Guillot, Louis, Loseau, Orono, Aller, Basadé, Landais,
Menard, and the Italian Col. Vigo, sturdy adherent of Father
Gibault. Those last two, with George Rogers Clark, got the
Northwest Territory for us; their co-operation recalls Clark's
words when Father Gibault asked if Catholics would be
allowed to practice their religion: "I have nothing to do
with churches except to defend them from insult. By the
laws of the State your religion has as great privileges as any
other." The journal of a Catholic soldier in the War of Independence (McCurtin) has been printed.

Msgr. Peter Guilday, "Catholic Church in United States,"
Thought, 1:3 ff., June 1926; *Catholic Church in Virginia,
1815-22; Catholic Philosophy of History; History of the
Councils of Baltimore; Introduction to the Literature of
Church History*—Note items (pp. 293-324) relating to education in the United States, our goal in using these biblio-
graphical items; *Life of Times of Bishop John Carroll; Life
of Times of John England; National Pastorals of the American Hierarchy*, 1792-1919. Jesse W. Lonsway, *Episcopal
Lineage of the Hierarchy in the United States*, 1790-1948.
Sister M. Angela, *Four Decades of Catholics in Texas* (1820-
60). George J. Waring, *United States Catholic Chaplains
in World War*. Benjamin A. Webb, *Century of Catholicity
in Kentucky*. Michael Williams, *American Catholics in the
War; The High Romance* (his conversion); *Catholic Church
in Action; Catholicism and the Modern Mind; Shadow of*

the Pope—anti-Catholic cartoons in the appendix. Msgr. Edward C. O'Reilley, *Looking Back Over Fifty Years* (Catholic Church in Wisconsin). Groups have found it time-saving to list (as a project) the call numbers of these books from their university library.

Special mention might be made of the several volumes of Centenary Chronicles of the Sisters of Holy Cross, of which Anna S. M'Allister's *Flame in the Wilderness* is volume VI. This biography (with letters) of Mother Angela Gillespie, American foundress of the Sisters (1824-1887), recalls their notable service as nurses in the Civil War. (So commonly known was their headdress on the battlefields and in hospitals that the exoteric thought it part of a nurse's garb.) One expects Mother Gillespie's life to have more trials than triumphs and admires her perspicacity as an educator. She regarded the mere imparting of information as valueless; students must be taught the distinction between information and culture and learn to evaluate facts as the raw material of culture. The spiritual life of students she considered of prime importance, and one of her main goals in education was to strengthen the natural endowment of each girl with a sound knowledge of Christian philosophy.

The Brooklyn *Tablet* reported (Jan. 10, 1953, p. 4) that the American Catholic Historical Association planned marking historic spots. Discover what has been done to date on the project.

B. As always, during the War for Independence Catholics in the United States were of different races and from many nations—blended by the same Faith. The colonists of Maryland were mostly English and Irish Catholics. One can understand their dislike of the Hanoverian dynasty that had usurped the English throne and together with Scotch Catholics in the Colonies loyal to the Stuarts ("Bonnie Prince Charlie") saw the fallacy of "divine right of kings." In Pennsylvania the Catholics (who had not come in groups) were scattered not only in space but in social position—

bondsmen, redemptioners, and people of wealth. German and French Catholics there were in the Colonies, too— not forgetting the Acadians banished from Canada and resettled from Detroit to the mouth of the Ohio, from Vincennes to Lake Superior and in southwestern Louisiana. England neglected the Colonists shamefully; and when she traded Havana for Florida, the Spanish Catholics in the latter area felt the difference.

Catholic Indians inhabited northern Maine. Ohio had Catholic Wyandots—among the tribes practically all Catholic. Maryland was the only Colony not stained with Indian blood. Protestant historians record that Catholic Maryland treated Indians better than Protestant New England and Virginia.

Constantin-Wiger's *Champlain*. Morris Bishop's *Champlain: the Life of Fortitude*. Richard W. Clarke's *Old and New Light on Columbus; Columbus' Voyages Told by Himself*. Samuel E. Morison's *Columbus*. Daniel Sargent's *Columbus*. W. H. Browne's *George Calvert and Cecilius*. Wm. Clarke's *Gallant John Barry*. Joseph Gurn's *Commodore Barry, Father of the American Navy*. H. Basso's *Beauregard of the Great Creole*. Peter Guilday, *John Gilmary Shea*. Henry E. Davies, *General Sheridan*. Katherine Burton, *Three Generations* (Ellen Ewing, Wife of Sheridan). Condé B. Pallen, *Andrew J. Shipman*. Wm. P. Trent, *Wm. Gilmore Simms*. Elting E. Morison, *Admiral Sims and the Modern American Navy*. Theodore Maynard, *De Soto and the Conquistadores*.

In the nineteenth century the Church's mission consisted of establishing itself—it grew so rapidly and spread over such an enormous area that the growth was necessarily not deep. In the present century that growth must be deepened and the American people evangelized. The latter can be accomplished through championing the inviolable rights of the individual. Should the State trespass on these natural rights of the humblest citizen, the conscience of us all has been violated.

Biographies will enrich background. See these: Jas. J. Roche's *John Boyle O'Reilly* (editor, Boston *Pilot*). Thos. F. Meehan's *Thos. M. Mulry* (St. Vincent de Paul Society). *Joel Chandler Harris* (by his wife). Alvin F. Harlow, *Joel Chandler Harris* (plantation story teller). Natalena Farrelly, *Thos. F. Meehan* (Catholic Historical Society). Carl B. Swisher, *Roger B. Taney* (Justice Supreme Court). Daniel Sargent, *Catherine Tekakwitha.* Kate H. Becker, *Christian Reid* (Mrs. Tiernan, one time popular Catholic novelist). Richard T. Montgomery, *White-headed Eagle* (John McLoughlin, M.D., northwest pioneer). H. L. Lear's *Chas. J. Bisson, Dominican Artist.* Jos. T. Durkin, *John Dooley* (Confederate soldier). Francis A. McNutt, *Papal Chamberlain.* Maurice F. Egan, *Recollections of a Happy Life.* J. F. Daly, *Augustine Daly.* Frank Graham, *Alfred E. Smith.* Jas. A. Farley, *Behind the Ballots.* (See *Jim Farley's Story.*) Wm. T. Kane, S.J., *Jean Garnier, Librarian.* David T. Dwane, *Early Life of Eamon de Valera.* Eddie Doherty's *Gall and Honey* (newspaperman who married Baroness de Hueck). Katherine Conway's *Chas. Francis Donnelly* (politician). Margaret Chanler, *Roman Spring* (Marion Crawford relatives in Rome) and *Autumn in the Valley.* Maude H. Elliott, *My Cousin F. Marion Crawford* (novelist whose Catholicity was never militant). Elizabeth Jordan, *Three Rousing Cheers* (Catholic freelance writer). Lowell M. Limpus, *Honest Cop* (Valentine).

Continue to add to your list new publications, for example, Theodore Roemer's *Catholic Church in the U.S.* (1950), George Paré's *Catholic Church in Detroit, 1701-1888* (1951), Sister Helen Angela Hurley's *On Good Ground* (Sisters of St. Joseph in St. Paul), Sister M. Hester, *Canticle for the Harvest* (centenary of the S.S.N.D.).

Particularly the Polish, but all interested in Our Lady should be acquainted with the history of the Madonna of Czestachowa and the sudden demise of the Swedish soldier who slashed her painting in the shrine when Gustavus Adolphus' men desecrated it. (The University of Notre

Dame has a copy of the painting on cedar.) Count Pulaski, our helper in the War of Independence, defended Czesta- chowa against Russian soldiers. St. John's U. library (Brook- lyn) has a thesis by a Sister of the Holy Family of Nazareth (48BIL)—*Influence of Czestachowa on Polish Nationalism.*

Catholic Mind, March 22, 1928, includes "The House of God," a sermon preached at the dedication of St. Mary's Church (Mobile, Alabama) located on the site of the church founded by the Rev. Abram Ryan, poet-priest of the Con- federacy. The sermon is a beautiful exposition of the signifi- cance to Catholics of their church.

In contrast to the environment of these missioners and explorers, despite modern conveniences, we must face the vices of civilization, the love of money, cheating in consumer transactions, the ensnaring of youth by appealing to their baser appetites (because therein lies easy money), moral dangers, poverty, and crime. The arching aisles of the forest have been replaced by the canyons between skyscrapers. The laughing water tumbling over the falls' edges, the wild and beautiful lakes and rivers (uncontaminated by cities' sewage) seem preferable to hot, narrow, treeless streets. For those who like the madding crowd, there need be no regret that we lack the challenge missioners and explorers faced. Today there are idols in the market place that must be shattered, human passions dominating hearts which, like temples, must be renovated. Catholic education must re- claim the drunkard, the criminal, the skulker, the apostate Catholic—and the geographical surroundings may not be so attractive as those of the pioneers; but the challenge is there. The physical handicaps may, at times, be less severe; the most impelling motive still remains the love of neighbor as oneself for the love of God.

CHAPTER SIX

Geography and History Influence
People's Plans

When considering people (the individual and the group), their physique and numbers, intelligence, psyche or mind set, and emotions we must take into account the fertility of valleys, the waste areas irrigated, and the natural resources of those regions selected for settlement. Arthur M. Schlesinger and Dixon Ryan Fox's *History of American Life* is our best survey of the social history of our country—of manners, dress, amusements, painting, architecture, journalism. business, and other infinitely varied phases of the more average human life in America. Otis W. Coan and Richard G. Lellard's *America in Fiction* annotates a list of novels interpreting aspects of life here, dealing with various geographical areas of the country, the Negro, the Indian, city life, business, modern war, the leisure class, and so on. John T. Flanagan's *America Is West: an Anthology of Middle Western Life and Literature* includes material little known—the writings of explorers, travelers, and obscure country people. No historical or geographical record of the past is too trivial to contribute to current operation and future planning of American education. Instead of being transmitted for its own sake, cultural heritage must be brought to influence current living; added to the contribution will be current materials which because of their general application lose their specificity with the passage of time. Hans Kohn's *The*

Twentieth Century: a Midway Account of the Western World surveys the main currents of political and social ideas in our milieu since the European revolutions of 1848. The crux of his discussion ("The Challenge of Old Myths and New Trends") surveys the beliefs and programs of imperialism, racialism, fascism, national socialism, and communism. In juxtaposition he places democratic ideals and the possibilities for a realistic American co-operation with western Europe and Latin America against totalitarianism.

The emigrants from Europe had to flee persecution, with few material possessions; but their mental backgrounds, their spiritual, cultural and intellectual heritages they brought with them. Nor were these immigrants merely the offscourings of metropolitan gutters. A few American settlements had a greater proportion of college graduates among their population than any American city today. P. S. Duponceau, who came as aide to Baron Steuben in the Revolution, founded the science of ethnology and linguistics in the United States. Nor were the Catholic missionaries priests who would discredit a parish. We read in *Jesuit Relations* the narrative of Father Andrew White's voyage as Chaplain with Lord Baltimore. A finished scholar who had filled the chairs of Scripture, Hebrew, and Theology in Spain and Belgium, with forty-six other priests he was banished perpetually from England—under the Penal Laws—with the same price on his head as for that of a wolf. Among the Sulpicians was the famous Fenelon, adviser of Mme. de Maintenon, who at his advice amazed the educational world by adding mathematics to her curriculum for girls (because unscrupulous lawyers and adventurers had taken advantage of many heiresses and widows who knew nothing about accounts). He is famous for his work *The Education of Girls*, written while connected with the convent of New Catholics—for the training of young women who were or planned to become Catholics. Here he acquired his deserved great reputation for teaching, defending the Faith, and preaching. During a sermon he was interrupted in the pulpit by a note saying that because of his health his superiors had decided against permitting him to go to America as missioner. He turned from the interruption to give a magnificent sermon on obedience.

In the period after the revocation of the Edict of Nantes when Louis XIV tried to stamp out heresy and restore religious unity, Fenelon's missionary zeal had full sway. Despite maligning of him during that period of religious strife, today Protestant historians of education believe his statement: When hearts are to be moved, force avails not.

More brilliant than his work among the Huguenots was his training of Louis XIV's grandson, the Duke of Burgundy —cruel, passionate, vindictive, and headstrong. To teach him Fenelon wrote *Dialogues of the Dead* (biographies of great men) and *Adventures of Telemachus* (the characteristic education of a young prince and future governor). The Dukes of Burgundy were notoriously vicious—even Shakespeare alludes to such characteristics in the Duke de Burgoyne; but Fenelon's pupil became civilized, conscientious, and kind.

Religious organizations of the seventeenth century which left deep impress on Catholic education in the United States because their members came here and have grown amazingly in numbers and influence include: the Brothers of the Christian Schools (founded by St. John Baptist de la Salle), who organized and improved free elementary instruction for training lay teachers; the Congregation of the Mission (followers of St. Vincent de Paul) who, like the Sulpicians, trained priests (but have for years conducted colleges for lay students); the Sisters of Notre Dame of Montreal (whom we have discussed in the Activities of Unit I); the Sisters of Charity (of St. Vincent de Paul), who not only teach but have hospitals (Hotels de Dieu), and several other orders of Sisters; the Brothers of Mary (founded by Chaminade, who successfully fought the false philosophies of

Voltaire and Rousseau and the aftermath of the French Revolution). Both Protestant and Catholic educators tried to counteract eighteenth century naturalism and nineteenth century secularization. which is rampant today.

Since the early schools here used as models the schools in the various countries from which immigrants came and the schools in all the colonies were related to the Church, naturally Catholics would imitate Christ in their teaching. To make learning easy and attractive, we have but to follow the natural steps in presenting new material to the mind; and we find their naturalness best revealed in His teaching.

1. What we know as the Pre-test or *Exploration* our Lord used with effective informality. His oral, personal instruction and indefinable personal characteristics won from his audience the desire to listen. He won their confidence and suited His teaching to their individual needs. He aroused wonderment and curiosity and caused them to ask questions about what they saw and heard and felt, rebuking them when they did not say what they were thinking. "Reading their thoughts, He said unto them . . ." His directness and simplicity made His thought clear: "I am the Way, the Truth, and the Life." "I am the Bread of Life." "I am the Good Shepherd." From the effectiveness of this approach, we infer that if when teaching we fail in our exploration of what the student already knows, if the students are not interested or eager to proceed, if our manner and material are not attractive, we must reorganize our exploratory material from the students' point of view; and in appealing to the mind through the senses lies the secret.

2. The greater the truth Christ was to present, the more detailed was His *preparation* of the minds of His hearers for it. To be sure, many things He left for the Holy Ghost to teach because even the Apostles were not ready for them. Recall how our Lord prepared for the doctrine of the Real Presence by His miraculous multiplying of the loaves and fishes. St. John tells us that the doctrine was not presented

until the patent objections to it had been made and answered; and despite Christ's careful preparation of their minds for what He was about to say, "many of His disciples found the saying hard and walked away." So clearly did He get their minds ready that His hearers had to understand what He said even though they did not understand Him.

If our presentation of material to students is unsuccessful, we must re-teach it. We can save ourselves that additional preparation in most instances, however, by imitating our Lord's method of stating our truths in language so simple that everyone in the class can understand. We can gain and hold interest as He did by using illustrations that our hearers can understand easily. Recall how often, in the Parables, Christ used similitudes of things familiar as points of contact for His lesson. ("And without similitudes He did not speak to them.") "Two men went up to the Temple to pray," for instance—the Jews hated both pharisees and publicans, but they understood our Lord's illustration perfectly.

3. By weaving the new ideas into the hearers' past experience closely, assimilation followed quickly. By *correlating* the new with the old (the only way we can integrate knowledge and use it), He bound His teachings up with their experience; and they remembered. The Jews disliked Samaritans and were splitting hairs over who was their neighbor. Knowing that they had a particular place in mind for Samaritans, Christ told the story of the Good Samaritan (from the Gospel for the Twelfth Sunday after Pentecost), thereby painting a picture which was hung before the world for two thousand years and has not faded.

4. The *organization* of the new ideas led to a *generalization*—"Follow Christ." Our knowledge advances only by generalizations, by drawing conclusions and seeing applications of the new. While Christ is the only teacher who can point to Himself as a model to be imitated in all things, we can strive to be worthy of imitation, for what our pupils

see and hear they tend to imitate. Recall St. Paul's drawing
the conclusion: "For me to live is Christ." "I live now not I,
but Christ liveth in me." "Be ye followers of me as I also
am of Christ."

5. The *application* of what we learn crowns the achievement. "Follow Me" invited the Apostles to imitate Christ
and to represent Him to others. We need to have the application borne in on us repeatedly; and there is no more successful way than that of discovering whether we learn
best through the eye, the ear, or the muscle pull (kines-
thetically, as, for instance, in letting our fingers spell a word
we are in doubt about) and strengthening our strongest
impression (visual, for instance) through approaches by
way of other senses. If one learns to spell most readily
through seeing a word, his mastery of it will be most complete when he has strengthened his picture of the word by
auditory impressions of how it sounds (pronouncing it—
even without moving his lips) and by kinesthetic impressions of how it feels to write correctly.

In St. Thomas Aquinas we find Christian teachings (as
well as Aristotle) synthesized; and while the former never
labeled his pedagogical theories as such, it is a mistaken
notion that the modern science of teaching is of recent
origin. Unfortunately many non-Catholic theorists seem to
know nothing of the noble tradition in the philosophy of
education prior to the Renaissance. We mention that Movement rather than the mis-called Reformation, for the Protestant Revolt added nothing to the theory or practice of
teaching which had not been carried over from the Renaissance. By turning attention to the child instead of to his
final destiny, modern non-Catholic educators have gone
astray and can never get back to the norm until they go
back to St. Thomas to pick up the lost trail. Without a
definite goal, they cannot determine their action clearly.
Rudderless striving gets them no place. Since they do not
recognize the real purpose of the child's existence, without

a definite sense of direction they turn to the child to observe him under the miscroscope, they appeal to his senses— they prod him to activity; but they are unable to interpret their immense mass of findings, to formulate basic principles of activity. If only they might achieve sound criteria of interpretation, they could enjoy with Catholic educators the benefit of new discoveries in the field and the co-ordination of the new, the results of more accurate methods, with the Catholic deposit through the centuries. Ecclesiastes (12, 13) speaks of the whole man; Dewey and Kilpatrick speak of integrating personality as the aim of modern education. For twenty centuries the Catholic Church has been basing the unity of pedagogy on the synthesis lent man's existence by viewing his training in the light of the purpose of his creation. While various laws direct the growth of different phases of human nature, the unity and totality of view which Catholic philosophy alone affords finds its synthesis not in the child but in his destiny. Such a viewpoint sees the child not as a mere aggregate but as an entity.

CHAPTER SEVEN

People as Individuals and Groups

PHYSIQUE AND GROWTH

The relation of a knowledge of geography and past history to a people's future planning and operation is so inclusive a topic that we have split it into two large co-ordinate subjects ("People as Individuals and as Groups"—Chapter VII—and "Missionary Efforts"—Chapter X). Subordinated to the subject of Chapter VII are three coordinate Units, which shall consider people under aspects of: Physique and Growth (with Chapter VII), Immigrants Meet American Education (Chapter VIII), Achieving the Catholic Heritage (Chapter IX).

Statistics on the growth of the number of Catholics in the United States and the expansion of their dioceses and school systems the *Catholic Encyclopedia* (7) will supply, and the *Official Catholic Directory* will keep up to date. Catholics do not maintain a "secondary system of schools" (as has been charged by those who do not know the history of education in the United States and consider public schools the first system), because religious schools were the first and only kind until the third decade of the nineteenth century and Catholics carry on the tradition. Immigrants, more than any other group, increased the number of Catholics from 195,000 (out of 9,638,000 inhabitants) in 1820 to twenty out of one hundred million a century later and about thirty out of one hundred thirty million at the beginning of World War II. As usual there was a greater percentage of Catholics in the Armed Forces than of any other religious group. The suitability of Catholicism to true Christian democracy is patent; in fact, there can be no real democracy without acknowledging a Common Father and the practice of the charity preached by His Son. The Church's spread has been astoundingly rapid and, as must be expected, in spots thin. When Bishop Edwin O'Hara entered his see at Great Falls, Montana, he was photographed with a group of Catholic men who had never seen a priest. Truly American as it is Catholic, the Church has attracted a number of distinguished converts—each outstanding, in his own way, as an individual. D. J. Scannel-O'Neill's volume brings the record to 1907. Claude Williamson's *Great Catholics,* John A. O'Brien's *Road to Damascus* and *Where I Found Christ,* and Maurice Leahy's *Conversions to the Catholic Church* amplify. Clare Booth Luce's conversion caused a stir.

Of autobiographies Thomas Merton's *Seven Storey Mountain* is unusual because moves from Columbia graduate to self-effacement as a Trappist monk—for the love of God. Sisters of the Visitation recorded Bishop Alfred A. Curtis's turning from Episcopalianism and Bishop Frederick J. Kinsman, Episcopal Bishop of Delaware, recorded the steps in his conversion in *Salve Mater* (1920); Dorothy Day's *From Union Square to Rome* (from Communism) and Louis Budenz' *This is My Story* (from Communism back to the Church); Sister M. Ignatia, O. M. presented the history of New Hampshire's First Catholics in the *Magnificat,* beginning January, 1946. (The Daniel Barber family converts were inspiring.) Ethan Allen's daughter (a convert) was the first nun taking vows in the United States. (See *Catholic*

Digest, December, 1948). Theodore H. Dorsey's *From a Far Country* (1939); Arnold Lunn's *Within a City* and *Come What May;* Louis Stancourt's *A Flower for Sign;* John Moody's *The Long Road Home* and *Fast by the Road;* Thomas Sims Lee (convert) was Governor of Maryland; Herbert E. Cory's *Emancipation of a Freethinker;* Dorothy Freeman Grant's *What Other Answer;* Rachel Maria's *The Divine Pursuit;* Michael Williams' *The High Romance* was a conversion. Selden P. Delany (Rector of the highest Anglican church in New York City) wrote *Married Saints* after his entrance into the church and his ordination. Katherine Burton devotes a chapter to him in the story of her conversion (*The Next Step*). John L. Stoddard's *Rebuilding a Lost Faith* and Orestes Brownson's *The Convert* are classics. Daniel Sargent's *Four Independents* treats Brownson. Theodore Maynard (whose author-wife was also a convert) did a biography of Brownson, as did Henry Brownson. Henry A. Staunton (Rector of an episcopal church in Rochester) and his family became Catholics in the 1920's; his brother (also a minister) was later ordained. Georgiana Pell Curtis's *Beyond the Road to Rome* appeared in 1914. Katherine Burton's *In No Strange Land* and "Great Converts and Their Testimony" (*Catholic Mind,* 22; 322 ff., November 22, 1924) presented several famous converts. See also Gladys Baker's *I Had To Know* and Paolo Manno's *Conversion of the Pagan World.* H. Stuhldreher presents a famous convert in *Knute Rockne, Manbuilder.* Elizabeth L. Adams' *Dark Symphony* tells beautifully the conversion of a Negro; John Wu (former Chinese Ambassador to the Vatican) records his story in *Beyond East and West.* Rose Marie Levy and David Goldstein (converts from Judaism) have presented their stories interestingly as has Karl Stein (Bavarian psychiatrist) in *Pillar of Fire.* Brother David's *American Catholic Convert Authors* is an impressive record. Lives of Fathers Isaac Hecker (Paulist) and the Passionist, James Kent Stone (Fidelis of the Cross) are inspiring. The conversion of Col-

onel William F. Cody (Buffalo Bill) celebrated pioneer
Indian scout and star of wild west shows, attracts young
readers. Burton Confrey's *Method in Literature* includes a
lengthy list of biographies and autobiographies of converts
not included here.

Stephen A. Douglas, who debated with Lincoln and lost
the Presidency because of a split in the Democratic Party,
became a Catholic before his death in 1861. *The Catholic
Encyclopedia* suggests that he came from Illinois Irish stock,
and the Irish who settled in southern Illinois were remarkable; but Douglas was born in Vermont and we have no
evidence either way as regards his connection with the
well-educated group in Illinois. Of that coterie John Doyle
became the first schoolmaster in the State and half of Illinois'
first Governors were of Irish descent.

Douglas' second wife was Adele Cutts, a Catholic grand-
niece of Dolly Madison and an acknowledged leader of
Washington society in 1857-58 while her husband opposed
President Buchanan's pro-slave policies. The ifs in history
give rise to thought of what might have happened had
Douglas defeated Lincoln or had his conversion come earlier
when he might have helped the Catholic cause at a time
when it needed badly gifted leaders of position.

Another "if" concerns Douglas's contemporary, Jefferson
Davis, who wanted to join the church while studying in St.
Thomas' College opened by the Dominicans in Kentucky.
Father O'Daniels' *Fathers of the Church in Tennessee* says
the Superior did not encourage Davis because of his youth.
After the Civil War, the destitute Mrs. Davis wrote: "No
institution of my own church offered to teach my poor children" but one day the Sisters of Charity called, bringing five
gold dollars—all the money they had. They almost forced
her to take the money. When she refused, they offered to
take the children to their school in the neighborhood of
Savannah, where they could be comfortably cared for during
the hot summer months.

Certainly the biological is a foundation of education; the child with a good physique has an advantage over one handicapped by an enfeebled body. Reference to big, handsome police officers chosen from a nationality noted for its brawn is frequent; but it may be more suitable to the development of the topic to defer discussion of health education until considering adaptations of Americans with health as a human need.

Educational and Vocational Supervision includes a Chart on Family Life (p. 71). In Column I the problem is cited. Column II carries the Catholic solution. Column III shows the place of the problem and solution in everyday life. For example:

I	II	III
Catholic home. Ideal christian family. (See *Catholic Action*, pp. 100 ff.)	Imitates the Holy Family at Nazareth	The family is the basis of christian civilization, etc. Citizenship

CHAPTER EIGHT

Immigrants Meet American Education

The mental ability of Catholic immigrants and their descendants may be inferred, in part, from the biographies in such reference works as *American Catholic Who's Who, Who's Who in Catholic Education, Catholic Literature from 1888-1948* (four volumes), *Catholic Authors* (four series), The Library of Living Catholic Authors, *Catholic Theatre Guild,* Blackfriars productions, David P. McAstocker's *Current Catholic Verse* and American contributions in Alfred Noyes' *Golden Book of Catholic Poetry,* the Legion of Decency, Catholic book clubs, National Organization for Decent Literature, and Pro Parvulis (books for children). Catholic scientists, doctors, lawyers, and members of other professions appear in *Who's Who in Science* and *Who's Who in America.* The variety of Catholic periodicals and newspapers is potent at the exhibits each February, Catholic Press month. Every Catholic is encouraged to read regularly his diocesan newspaper (which subscribes to the NCWC News Service) and Catholic papers of wider circulation for materials and reports unavailable anywhere else, particularly in regard to things Catholic. Their communications to lawmakers and radio and television and recording studios help tremendously in counteracting pagan or secularizing influences in American civilization. Broadcasters who are Catholic recall the number of Catholics connected with public communication.

A delightful broadcast of a St. Patrick's Day Parade resulted from an announcer's Catholic training. A bond salesman from Wall Street, he communicated his joy to listeners by singing the hymns children sang as they passed, reciting Mrs. Dorsey's "Lovely Lady, Dressed in Blue" when a sodality appeared, and included heart-warming remarks about group participants as seen through the eyes of a young Catholic father. The next day was Easter, and the pitiful broadcast about the exhibitionists in that Parade brought into bold relief the results of two types of education —no matter where they were received.

Our listing of names of famous Catholic scientists, discoverers, explorers, artists, musicians, and patriots throughout this book grows not out of the desire to boast or the belief that Catholics have a monopoly on intelligence. The purpose is, instead, to indicate that there is nothing in the Catholic faith that prevents intellectual development to the highest peaks of achievement in every department of human activity and that Catholics have contributed their full share to the march of humanity upward and onward.

Raphael, the world's greatest painter was a Catholic, as are all the others we list: John Cabot discovered the mainland of North America, June 24, 1497. Thomas Lloyd was the father of American shorthand. Magellan first sailed around the world. Count Kosciusko started West Point Military Academy. America was named after Amerigo Vespucci. Leonardo da Vinci was the greatest architect, engineer, and painter of his time.

The finest stained glass in the world is in the Cathedral at Chartres. Most of the world's greatest musicians have been Catholics—Verdi, for example. Marshal Foch, St. Camillus de Lellis, founder of the Red Cross idea, and Cardinal Mezzofanti, world's greatest linguist, were devout Catholics. Queen Katherine, wife of Henry VIII, the best educated woman of her time, was daughter of Queen Isabella, the Catholic Columbus' patron. Bishop Mullock of

New Foundland first proposed the laying of the Atlantic Cable. Peter Menendez founded our oldest city, St. Augustine, Florida. The world's largest building, St. Peter's Cathedral at Rome, Catholics designed and built. Bramanti is the world's greatest architect. Ponce de Leon discovered Florida. Cartier discovered Canada. Father Lawrence Hengler invented the horizontal pendulum used in seismographs. St. George Mivart, biologist, was one of the many who showed there was no conflict between religion and science.

When, in the middle of the nineteenth century, the Church defined the dogma of the Immaculate Conception, Dr. Edward Preuss, a German Lutheran theologian, attacked it. On the voyage to the United States he became aware of his error; his conscience bothered him because he had ascribed sin to the Blessed Virgin. A year after immigration he became a staunch Catholic and three of his sons became priests.

An arresting phenomenon in Catholic education is the thread of love for our Lady which gives richness of meaning to the tapestry of Catholic life. While it may be incomprehensible to those who know nothing of the experience and while history is not surmise, opinion, prejudice, lie or error, the fact of Catholic veneration for Christ's mother and its influence in Catholic training can be truly interpreted only by one who has experienced it. Here inexperience or detachment does not lend objectivity. One cannot hope to understand Catholic disciplining of mind and character through study and instruction if he does not comprehend or realize the inspiration of the "Cause of our joy." An Ordo or a Catholic calendar will reveal the numerous and varied titles under which the Queen of Heaven is venerated.

The beauties of charity, altruism, unselfishness, and gentleness which accompany that devotion the non-Catholic German from Bavaria or the Rhineland saw at wayside shrines where niches sheltered statues which are milestones or heard her name as a beloved household word. The school of modern art at the Abbey of Beuron is a successor to earlier groups who through the centuries reproduced her wondrous fair image in painting and sculpture.

French emigrés, too, knew wayside shrines, poets' praises chanted and simple, heartfelt hymns in her honor. The faith of the Irish immigrant in God and the Blessed Virgin Mary was deepened by centuries of such inhuman religious persecution, enslavement, conquest and starvation as blacken history's pages. Their descendants are taught that they gain a plenary indulgence once a month under the usual conditions if they recite daily the *Salve Regina* and another for daily recitation of the *Memorare* ("Remember, O Most Gracious Virgin Mary"). Their brawn cut roads through forests, dug canals, and built bridges and railroads binding our sprawling nation into physical unity. To each community came the priest to build a church and Religious to man the school; and even today in metropolitan hotels descendants of Catholic pioneers gather during their noon half-hour to recite the rosary in petition to Our Lady of Fatima to convert Russia and bring peace to the world.

Italians and other immigrants who can cultivate hillsides have brought with them from their fatherlands their trust and affection for the Queen of All Saints into their daily employment in minor industries and less desirable ways of earning a living. Their steadfast devotion, their innate love of simple beauty (typified by the man who would not move his wheelbarrow because a blooming morning glory entwined its wheel), encouraged in them deep love for a country whose patroness is Our Lady of the Immaculate Conception.

Study of and meditation upon the biographies of a newspaper man, a baseball exhibitionist, a gourmand, a "philosopher," a playwright, a woman radio programmist, a dramatist, a radio reporter, who were baptized Catholics but lost the gleam may properly be included in a history of Catholic education in the United States. Even if all did not attend

Catholic schools, like a novelist notorious for his poor style, they were born into Catholic families. This writer's father was a strict German Catholic, but his son's skepticism makes one wonder how long positive life-value can persist when faith is lost. Achieving a Catholic sense, which we shall discuss later in this unit, is imperative in any Catholic child's training. Parents and teachers can set the emotional tone, but God acts in the child's soul to inspire him to seek direction and helps to build the basic natural virtue which can prevent collapses in adult life.

Cardinal Newman's *Loss and Gain* is thought-provoking in this connection. In addition to statistics on leakage from the Catholic Church published by the Church itself, anyone can become aware of the losses in his own group of those who find Christ's sayings hard and no longer hear them—the fallen-away Catholic in a parish, the Irish names in the Protestant ministry or on the roster of an anti-Catholic lodge.

The young are warned that to have the Faith is not a pledge that one is going to keep it. Witness the old English poem "The Pearl," in which a man mourns his loss of the pearl of great price. Even the young can see that the problem is a relative one of loss and gain. Despite heavy losses, the Church moves forward rapidly—"the gates of hell shall not prevail against it." Conversions, new churches, schools and buildings, attention given papal encyclicals and the Vatican radio, the Pope as front page news always, all attest that the losses are more than repaired by gains. Century after century the increase in numbers of Catholics has always been greater than the increase in world population.

We recall that when the Arian heresy seemed devastating, Ireland outgrew the Druids; in place of various Greek defections Poland and Germany were Catholicized; and more American Indians were baptized than Europeans left the Church during the Protestant Revolt.

"I fear Jesus passing by" means not that one be afraid of our Lord but that he fear Christ will pass him by to go

to someone who will not toss his faith aside. When George
Moore boasted that he had left the Church, a Protestant
remarked, "No gain except for the Church." When some of
Christ's disciples "walked no more with Him," they were
let go. He did not change His doctrine or its interpretation
to bring them back. He asked faith and those who were not
with Him were against Him. Graces rejected go to others
more worthy—that is one explanation of fervent interest in
foreign missions. Inconsistent Catholics prevent non-Catholics from inquiring about the Faith. One needs disbelieve
but one teaching of the Church in regard to faith and he
is no longer a Catholic—and his loss is the Church's gain.

Generation after generation of descendants can be lost
to the Faith because a youth refuses to give up a girl who
is an occasion of sin, because someone will not restore ill-
gotten goods—whether it be cheating laborers of their hire
or swiping money to meet a gambling loss, because of
laxity blamed on a non-Catholic marriage partner who
neglected to get him or her up for Sunday Mass because he
gets his moral guidance from a charlatan preaching promis-
cuity under one guise or another, or because he reads
Spencer or Kant or other matter forbidden for the same kind
of reason (but a more important one) that guards people
under the Pure Food and Drug Laws.

Vernon B. Hampton's *Religious Background of the White
House* could be an interesting point of departure for discussion. Biographical sketches of Catholics currently in the
public eye of lawmakers or generals suggest a fruitful field
of reading. Actors in motion pictures appear with pro-Communist groups and professional men and women who are
Catholics address public gatherings, but no listener would
suspect their religion—it is not lack of militance that amazes;
it is lack of functional grasp of their Faith in fields where
Christian principles underlie the only answer.

Another field of stimulating readings deals with lapsed Catholics who return to the Fold. Each story of how these people who lost the pearl of great price temporarily varies, but the joyous end of the quest—the rescue of the one (while the ninety and nine remained in the Mystical Body intact) is always an inspiring story.

The Catholic Digest, June 1946, includes seven articles about persons in the news whose work or activities make the sketches a cross-section of Catholic life today. An editor of *Reader's Digest* and author and producer of an unusual current radio program of Bible stories is a convert. Katherine Brégy is a convert of long standing. Pascal P. Parente (nationally known theologian) has written the biography (*Susanna Mary Beardsworth*) of an American mystic and stigmatic who has the gift of prophecy. A Negro athlete entering the Church after the mid-century (his wife and daughter with him) said a year in a parochial school in Cincinnati convinced him that the Church is really interested in Negro youth. The Franciscan clerics of Holy Name College, Washington, campaign to make St. Benedict the Moor known throughout America and bring the Negro saint closer to members of his own race in this country.

Actors, producers, and playwrights including Dion Boucicault, Augustin Daly, John Drew, and James O'Neill were Catholics. St. Malachy's Church, Manhattan, is known as the actors' church. *Catholic Builders of the Nation* lists numerous artists, authors, scientists, sculptors, and architects. Such books as Genevieve Taggart's *Biographical Sketches* introduce John Carroll of Carroltown who included with his signature of the Declaration of Independence his place of residence so the King of England would have no difficulty in finding him, Chief Justice Roger B. Taney (of the Supreme Court), Commodore John Barry (father of the American Navy), and Generals Philip Sheridan and Rosencrans (Civil War).

The Columbian Jubilee or Four Centuries of Catholicity

in America reveals that many people whose theater of action was local or regional (and frequently neither military nor political) have had much greater influence on American development than those usually included in conventional American histories. Individuals influencing that development negatively are, moreover, not difficult to uncover.

Academic training will be treated later under "education" but surely it is unnecessary to amplify the contribution burgeoning from the ability of Catholic immigrants and their descendants to adjust to the American scene, to live successfully as a minority group, and always to contribute more than their share to the American way of life. Nor should we ever forget what the public schools would have been like (after they had become dominated by a Godless philosophy) were it not for the thousands of Catholic teachers who by their example counteracted the evil influence of secularism in public education. Numerous Catholic immigrants (driven from European homes by religious persecution) rose from the penniless state in which they arrived and advanced their families in the social scale by turning to teaching as a means of livelihood.

When considering the intelligence of Catholic immigrants to America and their descendants, we shall turn to current American education as a phase of background.

The educational philosopher most frequently referred to at the present time by non-Catholic theorists is John Dewey (1859-1952), the leader of the Experimentalist (or Instrumentalist) Movement. Most unfortunately, because of his lead, less able educators took on skepticism as the characteristic pose of the supposedly "educated" mind. In his *Moral Principles in Education,* Dewey says: "Apart from participation in social life, the school has no moral end or aim." Further, his scheme for social education includes no religious training. Since he himself lacks belief in the soul's immortality, his educational theory includes no preparation for a life after death. In fact, for Dewey the child has neither

Creator nor soul; but real educators know better because through experiment and observation of the whole child, of his integrated personality, they have seen that personality is not individuality; it is primarily spirituality. It is the mirroring of God.

The blind spot in Dewey's mental set prevented his seeing that should we throw the child into his life as member of the group with no direction except the promptings of instinct, he would be a destructive influence. If it is to contribute to the social group and to help in the child's normal development, the social, like other instincts, such as, for instance, the reproductive and self-preservative, must be controlled and directed. There could be no social training without the power objectives—based on discipline, mortification, and mastery of self.

John Locke warned against rewards lest they become the premium the child works for rather than the doing of the right act—the senses register to the child their immense appeal. Placing the child in disgrace or ostracizing him temporarily provokes self-condemnation and regret and encourages (as does esteem) an internal reaction which leads, Locke held, to self-correction. Punishment should always lead a child to new resolution.

A spoiled child brought to a Montessori school by an indulgent parent heard the latter tell how difficult the child was, how his parents could go for a drive only when he felt like it, and so on. Having given him a reputation to live up to, the mother withdrew. Immediately he refused to do anything suggested; so he was excluded from the class activities. When the children grouped for a game, he refused to take part. The director put him in a part of the room by himself. Later, when despite his being ignored he came over to join the group, he was firmly but gently led back to his isolation. After similar treatment continued, for the first time he realized that he must conform to the common order, and within a year he was most active and conformable.

Dewey, like all the naturalistic pedagogues, reveals his lack of comprehension of the integrated human being. Passions must be controlled; man must co-operate with grace in order that of his free will, having learned right from wrong, he may choose the right unerringly. This same fallacious ignoring of the existence of flesh and spirit in the child and of the struggle between good and evil in every personality, we find underlying Dewey's teachings in regard to interest and effort, his ignorance of the part will plays in effort.

The child must be taught to control his senses; but, in addition, in order to intensify the learning without lowering standards, educators can economize in teaching by stressing sensory aids—visual, audio, visual-audio, tactile, kinaesthetic, olfactory, and taste. With such equipment greater amounts can be learned within a similar length of time, with greater satisfaction to the learner, and a greater retention after a lapse of time. Fewer pupils have to repeat work, with a consequent saving in the length of the child's school life.

Further, sensory education increases the opportunity for actual experience; and the Church has always insisted on vitalization as opposed to passive learning (as, for example, in her continuous use of symbolism). Hence the appeal of the sensory education idea down the centuries. Since the advent of Realism, sensory education has been influenced by such educational theorists as Montaigne & Herbart, innovators such as Francis Bacon, and writers such as Rabelais, Ratke, Comenius, Pestalozzi, Froebel, Montessori, and Dewey.

Catholic education is activated, because it embraces the desirable features, utilitarian and cultural, of education. It is Christocentric for it is taught on the life and teachings of Christ. It teaches the necessity of the Christian virtues in man's every contact with his fellow men. Knowledge of ideals, training of will, formation of good habits, emotional stability, all must lead to moral integrity and tend to assimilate man more closely with God.

Hence the true Christian product of Christian education whether it follows the formal traditional or activated technique is the supernatural man who thinks, judges and acts consistently in accordance with right reason illumined by the supernatural light of the example and teaching of Christ.

The Catholic concept of education is as a training for eternity, as a preparation of the mind and will and soul for the matter of eternal salvation.

Everyone grants that a social community will not last forever. Those of us who are convinced that personality will last for eternity see that education must depend on man's last end and be subordinated to it. It is impossible to integrate personality and ignore the existence of the soul; and consequently we must train the child's inner life. To do that we must acknowledge that because of the disobedience of our First Parents human nature lacks the integration it possessed when in the state of original justice. The effects of the fall from grace must be overcome if the personality is actually to be unified; hence the necessity of making Christ rather than the child the center of education.

When Dewey revealed his belief he defined the supernatural as that which is beyond experience, beyond what the senses can know; and while he fulminates against expending effort in preparation for a future need, he defines growth as "as cumulative movement toward a later result." In that inconsistency we find the crux of his failure as leader.

To ignore the past, as Dewey does, is to destroy possibility of avoiding its errors. Communists were ignorant of Sparta's debacle and had to change their plans; Hitler ignored history and plunged the world into the violence which must be expected (intellectual as well as physical) when those in power, those who should be leaders, attempt to scrap the past, pretend that human nature has changed or that the elements of life are only temporal.

The Church has always adapted itself to the civilization

to which it brings Truth—not by changing the Gospel but by studying the pagan or the infiltrating barbarians and gradually absorbing them. Catholic educators act similarly —studying current problems, using whatever non-Catholic experiment reveals to be true, sharing our Catholic heritage with each generation who, basically, will always be the same. Theories not buttressed by sound philosophy will pass; Catholic education must stand four-square against the fads and blighting winds of false philosophies.

*   *   *

The best known outgrowth of Dewey's teachings we find in what is known as the child-centered school, the essence of which is an emphasis on creative activity. Put such activity in a Catholic environment and you have an admirable result, for creative expression is a reflection of God in us. However, unless humility underlies our training, pride will prevent our expressing ourselves truly as integrated characters. There is no attendant endeavor to make all personalities the same, because the relation between God and the individual soul is different in every case. As Newman warned: One's alma mater is not a foundry, a mint, a treadmill.

Our Creator gave us freedom of will; but in order that children be trained to choose the good unerringly there must be guidance of the freedom in the Dewey-type school. For self-activity we cannot accept the idea of mere matter moving. We insist that the animating principle which vivifies the child and his movements—the soul—be recognized. Dewey holds education and experience synonymous, an integrative process of organism and environment. He thinks the prime essential is the activity of the child. Here again we meet the fallacy which negates the value of his thinking. While Dewey would have silence periods, for instance, in which the child schemes the next step in his activity, we would not stop short. We use silence for meditation and contemplation in order that God may operate in our souls.

Learning "to do by doing" is not applicable to all branches, nor are all types of "*doing*" to be considered "*learning.*" Dewey puts awry the basic principle of sensory education by taking the extreme.

The happy mean is to be found in the school sponsored by the Catholic Church, because here due attention is also given to the religious aspects of training. The child becomes aware of St. Paul's ideal of putting on the new man, who has been created according to God in justice and holiness of truth. The child gradually grows to face its life work on earth wholesomely. By evaluating life moments within the correct perspective of its eternal happiness, the child strengthens its character.

The Catholic Reaction following the Council of Trent provides a stimulating chapter for Catholic education at this point; but in so far as public education in the United States is concerned, sense Realism (Instrumentalism, Experimentalism, "Progressive" education) is the important development in reaction to the deadening results of the Calvinistic influences on education.

* * *

The intimate relation between our survey of the history of education and sensory training is apparent when we look at such a volume as Martha Peck Porter's *The Teacher in the New School.* This experimenter in Lincoln School, a practice laboratory of Columbia University, where Dewey taught for almost forty years, emphasizes that only those activities which are genuinely educative are to be chosen. They may be dramatic plays, construction work, experimenting, investigating, school journeys or excursions—the varied types we have treated in *Sensory Training for Catholic Schools.* If it were the visit to a coal mine, for instance, Dewey would object to a mere "succession of disconnected activities" because his objective is the integration of the child's personality. There doing is not enough, no matter how active the child becomes. It is only through activities genuinely educative that learning conditions are best met and characteristics most needed for social adjustment best built. Rugg and Shumaker's *The Child-Centered School* demands experience in the intellectual and emotional as well as the physical sense; therein we have the basis of the new type of school. The child works rather than listens, a carrying out of Dewey's precept that the child be able to say not "I know" but "I have experienced."

There is nothing new here for the Catholic educator who knows the real history of education. The Church has always insisted on vitalization as opposed to passive learning. In his treatise on teaching, St. Thomas shows that the student cannot be passive; he must co-operate with the instruction as the sick do with medicine. Dr. John M. Cooper built his series of texts *Religion Outlines for Colleges* in such a way as to demand students' discussing their own life problems and thereby animating their spiritual activity. With "the freedom wherewith Christ has made us free," as St. Paul says, we keep our finger on the pulse of the present in order to recognize symptoms of human nature; the unity and totality of view which Catholic philosophy alone affords finds its synthesis not in the child but in his eternal destiny. Such a viewpoint sees the child not as a mere aggregate but as an entity.

Pope Pius XI's encyclical on *The Christian Education of Youth* makes clear that the child has been deprived of his primary integration by original sin. One of the chief functions of education must, then, be the redemption of fallen man. In his *Philosophy of Education*, Dr. Thomas Edward Shields discussed nature and grace and free will; to the last two of which nothing is impossible. Unfortunately, just as in the modern world we find numerous old Christian virtues gone mad because they are not united to other virtues and hence wander alone, we find a confusion resulting from the admixture of Christian principles with theories of education and of life diametrically opposed to the teachings of Christ.

In the field of sensory education, as in all education, we can, therefore, see the necessity for avoiding the errors of those who have been handicapped by the aftermath of the Protestant Revolt and of using whatever of the new that will help us the more effectively to achieve our goal. To us the most important phase of creative work—the goal of our educational activity—is the formation of good character, a position now being approached in non-Catholic schools, often quite futilely, under various forms of personnel work.

❖   ❖   ❖

To make concrete these ideas we might well turn to such a work as Dom Anscar Vonier's *The New and Eternal Covenant*, "Inside the ordinary setting of human life, room was found for infinite sanctity to act, to move, to learn obedience from the things Christ suffered. . . . The profound significance of His way lies in the inward possibilities of the ordinary human life." The school centered in Christ is best for the child because that type of school is the best preparation for life, for Christ is Life. Following Him is the best training for development of the moral, intellectual, and physical powers—it makes possible the accomplishment of our life work on earth and insures our eternal happiness.

In their histories of education (thoroughly annotated, with bibliographies included), such authorities as Bishop McCormick and William Terence Kane, S.J., survey the literature of the field and show that the First Renaissance came to grief because the unsettled state of the time made impossible a continuance. Education declined, and the tendency of accepting everything on authority reigned supreme. In the Second Renaissance, Scholasticism endeavored to make reason support authority in religion. Education finally degenerated into formalized reasoning on insignificant points; practical aspects of life did not receive due attention, and religion dominated. In the Third Renaissance, theorists ignored the Middle Ages and, returning to ancient Greek or Roman civilization, enjoyed fame and pleasure, thus overcoming the tendency to regard life as being concerned with other-worldliness. Overemphasis on Latin led to Ciceronianism, a formalism involving drill, memorization, drudgery, and authority.

In attempting to escape from the *eruditio,* the misnamed Reformation was supposed to stand for freedom in thinking but degenerated into a struggle for domination of thinking by the various sects which secured control of schools and the co-operation of states in confining thought to a straitjacket. Such a situation gave rise to the gloomy outgrowth of catechetical method, memorizing based usually on rote-memory, and so abstract a content of education that it threw out of focus ordinary experience and utilitarian aspects. In short, schooling did not dovetail with life since it overlooked or neglected to point out in the content and procedure the involved possibilities of transfer of learning to life situation.

Basis for Disapproval of "Progressive" Education

Dr. Miles McDonald, Principal of a large metropolitan high school for thirty years, pillories the idea as *Progressive Poison in Public Education.* In addition one might suggest:

1. It subscribes to the theory of biologic evolution of man's continuity with nature.

2. It confuses individuality with personality.

3. It rejects the doctrine of original sin and of man's elevation to a supernatural state.

4. It denies the existence of a spiritual soul and the duality of man's nature.

5. It regards education as having no other purpose than preparation for citizenship.

6. It considers education to be best effected by control of the child's environment and denies the teacher a positive function in directing the child's mind and will.

7. By insisting on education as a response to the felt need of the child, it robs education of all real ends and aims and neglects the training of the will.

8. Although rightly giving place to activities, it does not place sufficient value on knowledge which is properly intellectual.

9. It not only modified the balance between self-expression and control (a change badly needed), it shattered it explosively. (Mental hospitals are filled with young patients who insisted on radical short cuts to nonconformity. Complete independence and absolute freedom of emotional thought and behavior do not exist together. We must retain a small amount of emotional reliance on others, on teachers, on ideas and ideals. Children confused, unconsciously resent removal of teacher control.)

10. Complete elimination of competition is also a mistake. In life there are rewards for success, penalties for failures. The criterion for the former need not be money, but those who do not strive successfully need not be humiliated or pained by the knowledge that power, recognition, honor, and appreciation have been gained by their peers. The conditions in a class are similar, although the rating must be of the whole child—not the result of a single test or a few items.

11. Progressive education reached its peak about 1930; much of the psychoneuroses in the Armed Forces were blamed on it. Theoretically it seemed opposed to the principles and practices of over-protection (Mom-ism). In theory it aimed to promote a rapid flowering of maturity, advocated independent behavior, opposed emotional dependency, urged individual selection of interests, scoffed at rewards and punishments. It would seem to condemn the instruments and devices of weaning children emotionally

as well as physically. (See Philip Wylie's *Generation of Vipers* and Edward Strecker's *Their Mothers Sons*.) But "progressive" education produced a spurious maturity. It veiled authority heavily. Large behavior concessions were granted; but the more self-expressive a child's behavior becomes, the more he needs protection. The more protection is given, the tighter the leading strings are drawn. Behavior restrictions and penalities for misbehavior were largely removed and the self-expression would be favorably hastened. That procedure lent the appearance of unrestricted freedom of thought and conduct—almost unique, unhampered self-expression; but habits were being formed and passions getting the upper hand.

Some of the practices of progressive education, subject to reservations, can be recommended.

1. Modifications of school programs to meet the need of the individual child and the recognition of the preeminence of the child's place in the educational process.

2. The important role of activities and the significance of interest and motivation achieved through the integrated curriculum and expressed in unit and project methods.

3. The stress upon the social phases of the learning processes.

4. The introduction of the scientific method and sound testing policy.

5. Abolition of the brutal classroom competition some teachers stimulated; because of that teacher stupidity, some children felt inferior for life.

In *Secularism in American Education*, long out of print but now available in microfilm, we traced the history of the exclusion of training of the spirit from schools in the United States. What the public schools offer today is vastly different from what the American Colonists included in their cur-

ricula, especially as regards religious education. All but
one of the early universities were founded to train ministers
to Christianize the Indians, and if one examines the mottoes
of those schools he has no doubt left that education was
for God and country.

The exclusion of religious training from the school curriculum is called secularization, a process which has shifted
from a by-product to a conscious aim. So accustomed have
people become to this exclusion that many have not realized
that until the second quarter of the nineteenth century
such a procedure was unknown here. It was not long after
the process had a strangle grip on the public schools, however, until administrators were suggesting that religion is
unimportant. Today we have reached a stage where thoughtful teachers are trying not to include sectarian instruction
but to exclude atheism from the schools, to use the effort
which could be wasted condemning the secularizing process
into trying to save the world religiously.

Referring to schools as godless cannot prevent children
from getting some idea of God, no matter how erroneous
the concept may be. Further, when the non-religious element in instruction over-shadows or barefacedly opposes
the spiritual training, worldly ideals dominate; and the
child's personal life, family life, our national life, and even
our civilization suffers.

With the opening of the eighteenth century the arrival
of settlers whose religious beliefs destroyed the homogeneity
of the Massachusetts settlements raised the question as to
what extent the civil authorities might further religious
education. Baptists, Quakers, and Episcopalians so ques-
tioned the justice of taxing everyone for the support of
Congregational churches and schools that in 1702 legislation
attempted to meet the Friends' objection. (In the *Connecticut Gazette*, August 2, 1765, and in George Stewart's *History
of Religious Education in Connecticut to the Middle of the*

Nineteenth Century, pages 159 f., we meet objection to the Congregationalists' exclusive control of education in that colony.)

The charter of the Jamestown colony (1606) stated explicitly that the Church of England should be their state Church. The intention was that "so noble a work may by the Providence of the Almighty God hereafter tend to . . . the propagation of the Christian religion to such people as yet live in darkness." By this stipulation Catholics, alone, were excluded.

A primary source fixes the origin of secularism in public education; other influences are contributing causes. In an oration delivered before the Philomathian Society, of Mount St. Mary's College, Maryland, June 29, 1853, Orestes Brownson showed (*Works,* 19:442) that America's "godless" schools resulted not from force of law or from conviction that our public schools must be secularized in order to be American but because of the activities of atheists.

It is far easier to educate for evil than for good, for children since the Fall take to evil as naturally as ducks take to water. The enemies of religion and society understand this perfectly well, and hence whenever in their power they seize upon the schools, and seek to control the education of the young. To accomplish their purposes they have only to exclude religion from the schools, under the plea of excluding sectarianism, and instead of teaching religion teach, as Frances Wright was accustomed to say, know-ledge, and they may soon have a community whose thoughts and affections will be exclusively of the earth earthy.

It is not without design that I have mentioned the name of Frances Wright, the favorite pupil of Jeremy Bentham and famous infidel lecturer through our country some twenty years ago; for I happen to know, what may not be known to you all, that she and her friends were the great movers in the scheme of godless education, now the fashion in our country. I knew this remarkable woman well, and it was my shame to share, for a time, many of her views, for which I ask pardon of God and of my countrymen.

I was for a brief time in her confidence, and one of those selected to carry into execution her plans. The great object was to get rid of Christianity and to convert our churches into halls of science. The plan was not to make open attacks on religion, although we might belabor the clergy and bring them into contempt where we could, but to establish a system of state—we said national—schools, from which all religion was to be excluded, in which nothing was to be taught but such knowledge as is verifiable by the senses, and to which all parents were to be compelled by law to send their children.

Our complete plan was to take the children from their parents at the age of twelve or eighteen months and to have them nursed, fed, clothed and trained in these schools at the public expense; but at any rate, we were to have godless schools for all the children of the country, to which the parents would be compelled by law to send them.

The first thing to be done was to get this system established. For this purpose a secret society was formed, and the whole country was to be organized somewhat on the plan of the carbonari of Italy, or as were the revolutionists throughout Europe by Bazard preparatory to the revolutions of 1820 and 1830. This organization was commenced in 1829 in the city of New York, and to my own knowledge was effected throughout a considerable part of New York State. How far it was extended in other States or whether it is still kept up I know not, for I abandoned it in the latter part of the year 1830 and have since had no confidential relations with any engaged in it; but this much I can say, the plan has been successfully pursued, the views we put forth have gained great popularity, and the whole action of the country on the subject has taken the direction we sought to give it.

Elsie W. Clews Parsons' *Educational Legislation of the Colonial Governments* (1899), one of the first attempts to write our educational history from the sociological point of view, showed how important in understanding that history is knowledge of the interaction of various religious and social groups in a community. From time to time newspapers record tensions of this sort first in one part of the United States and then in another. Mrs. Parsons revealed the objections to Congregationalism's domination of civil affairs in Massachusetts and Connecticut, although the Congregationalists continued to maintain educational control of Harvard until 1843. In 1827, when it became lawful to offer any sort of sectarian training in the common schools of Massachusetts, the Unitarians grasped control of the educational policy and have not relinquished it. Another important phase of the secularization of the public schools through the jealousy of religious factions is the dispute over state support of denominational schools.

Immigration of Catholic families to the United States became observable in the 1830's and with their coming a new problem arose in Protestant communities. The state, recognizing the protection she might enjoy if her youth were properly trained, had permitted the various Protestant sects an important share in the control of the schools. The secularizing legislation, which reached its height after 1850 and brought us into the third period of our school history, reveals how customary religious instruction was in these common schools. With citizens as a whole no longer interested in preparing an educated ministry, with the rise of the factory system and the growth of cities and towns, the goal of public education became civic and industrial, the state merely assisted private and religious agencies in education; but when all men could vote, the state felt it could no longer entrust its civic and national welfare (dependent, it would seem, on standards and results in education) to any agents except its own. Thereafter, control of education brought on uniform texts and courses of study and state and county certification of teachers. Any group accepting federal or state aid today may expect to be controlled from a bureau in the national or state capital and in consequence the private and parochial school will be denied the right to teach their religion in their own schools.

In his *Annual Report* (1845-1848), 4:308 f., as Secretary of the Massachusetts State Board of Education, Horace Mann, who bears the onus of the secularization of the public schools, tells of the tremendous problem he faced when Catholic immigrants, then entering Massachusetts in great numbers, withdrew their children if sectarian teaching appeared. While he and Barnard, Secretary for Connecticut are condemned for the exclusion of religious instruction from the schools, their motives were political and conciliatory.

Mann says he believed that sectarian books and sectarian instruction, if their encroachment were not resisted, would prove the overthrow of the schools.

I believed then, as now, that religious instruction in our schools, to the extent which the Constitution and the laws of the State allowed and prescribed was indispensable to their highest welfare, and essential to the validity of moral education.

I avail myself of this, the last opportunity, which I may ever have, to say in regard to all affirmations or intimations that I have ever attempted to exclude religious instruction from the schools, or to exclude the Bible from our schools, or to impair the force of that volume, that they are now, and always have been, without substance or semblance of truth.

Our system earnestly inculcates all Christian morals; it welcomes the religion of the Bible; and in receiving the Bible it allows it to do what it is allowed to do in no other system, to speak for itself.

Even the Protestants (who might agree with the idea of private interpretation in religion) knew that, for example, one reading the Book of Job would come on the passage where the Voice of the Lord came out of the whirlwind in great anger because Job's "comforters" were attributing his punishment to wrong causes. The person who took to heart (for meditation and motivation to action) the words that made the Lord angry would hardly, in his private interpretation, be acting intelligently.

Mann concluded by saying that the education a child receives at school is imparted

for the purpose of enabling him to judge for himself, according to the dictates of his own reason and conscience, what his religious obligations are and whither they lead. But if a man is taxed to support a school where religious doctrines are inculcated which he believes to be false and which he believes God condemns, then he is excluded from the school by divine law, at the same time that he is compelled to support it by human law. This is a double wrong.

Catholics, however, cannot accept indifferentism in religious matters. If one religion were as good as another, why should anyone choose the hard way to salvation? Basic Christianity has hard sayings and not all can hear them.

Catholics were not alone in thinking that religious and moral training were not appendages to education which could be tacked on in an hour once a week—religion must inform (articulate, give skeleton to) all instruction.

Unfortunately, however, even today there are persons who, from time to time, resurrect the bogie of the double allegiance of Catholics—the implication being that since Catholic (meaning "universal") necessarily demands loyalty first to a ruler outside the United States, Catholics cannot be loyal Americans. In charity, suppose we grant this invincible ignorance of those unfortunates who fail to understand the relationship of the spiritual and temporal in life. Anyone who can read need not ignore the facts in a reading list on God and Government appended to this unit. Pope Innocent III and many writers before and since his time in the Christian Era have made clear the dominance of things of the spirit in man's living, but he did not say (nor do Catholics contend) that any one form of government is best for all people or that loyalty to the Vicar of Christ on earth (to one's spiritual leader) prevents the very best type of loyalty as citizens of a country. Out of our ideals come our attitudes and appreciations; from them burgeon our conduct; from it comes our behavior as citizens. The person with the highest ideal should, then, make the best citizen. The only ideal (because it alone of all goals is open to everyone) is "Seek ye first the Kingdom of God and His justice" and any right thinking individual should grant that. Moreover, among all the motives that move men's wills, the most impelling is reverence or love of God. (When one acts from that motive, nothing else matters—through it one gets the courage to endure martyrdom.) Not only do Catholic church and home training but Catholic education holds up the only ideal; and since in the Catholic school love of God may be mentioned, that ideal can be striven for continuously with the most impelling motivation.

The Founding Fathers of our country did not attend "public" schools, and we append Readings for this Unit to show the Christian roots of American democracy and the influence of Catholic thought on the Declaration of Independence. Luther Weigle shows (*American Idealism*, pages 212 ff.) that all but one of the early American colleges were founded for a religious purpose; and if there was any difficulty deciding whether Harvard was the child of church or state, the *Massachusetts Colonial Records* (1654, IV Part I, 285) records its religious purpose and civil grants of aid for it. Catholics are not unique or peculiar in wanting their own school since the curricula of public schools have been secularized. Protestant sects were the great protagonists of religious training in our colonial and early public schools. Further, many non-Catholics want their children to be educated in schools where the Catholic religion informs all training. Jefferson, for example, sent his daughter to a convent in Paris; and Dumont TV in connection with one of their programs distributed free copies of his letter to a Ursuline nun (1804) which endorses giving religion central

place in education. (The Sisters teaching in Louisiana Territory had inquired about their school's standing in the new
Republic when, after the Louisiana Purchase, the school's
location became part of the United States.)

Among the forms of secularism, we meet liberalism, a
democratic secularism which became impotent after World
War I and again after World War II. Facing the sordid
realities of devastating wars brings men to their senses,
but it does not eradicate that aspect of secularism which
is most pernicious because not detected. Where man fails
to center his life in God, his religious sensibilities become
obscured, his moral perceptions blunted, and the warning
cries of conscience are lulled.

When T. S. Eliot got the Nobel Prize for literature, his
writing attracted the attention of many who previously
had never read him. In "The Hollow Men," when pruning
affectations and obscurities, he emphasized the fact that
secularism has corrupted the whole of modern literature.
Writers have been unaware of or simply unable to understand the meaning of the primacy of the supernatural over
the natural—something he considers our primary concern.

Not only is the United States under the patronage of
Our Lady of the Immaculate Conception but at the close
of 1946, Pope Pius XII, moved by the threat inherent in
crass secularism and the encroachment which the totalitarian state has made on the freedom of the Church, consecrated the whole world to the Immaculate Heart of Mary.

In "The Tamworth Reading Room," Cardinal Newman
warned against secularism, and even some Catholic schools
have been accused of being mere imitators of secular universities, dominated by a frenzy of activity, publicity, productivity, and similar results of the absence of creative
imagination. A Protestant magazine, a citadel of secularism,
blasted Protestant churchmen. Educators at Catholic Uni-

versity charged that President Truman's Commission stressed secular philosophy. A Lutheran minister warred on the Church vs. State issue, averring that the threat of secularism must be regarded first. A cross for Christmas decoration was taken off the school building at Floral Park, Long Island (because a cross is "sectarian"). *Catholic Digest,* December 1948, reprinted 'I Went to Wellesley" (secularism which must be unlearned) and "What Does the Catholic Church Want?" (when writing up civics, in the temporal order the seeking of faith and freedom from absorption in that order exclusively).

While at Brooklyn College (supported by city taxes— and one-third the inhabitants of New York City are Catholics but ninety per cent of the City College's students are Jews) there are three rabbis and two ministers on the teaching staff, there is no priest-teacher. One practicing minister is chairman of curricular counseling. His point of view appeared in a public address in which he cited Luther and Calvin as examples that "no human progress is made without their kind of discontent." In New Mexico (November 1948) Brothers and Sisters who staffed schools no one else would take were tried in District Court for wearing religious garb while teaching in public schools.

We have not added to the chart which appeared in our *Secularism in American Education: A History* (now micro-filmed) because the McCollum Decision is being reversed from time to time; Religious forbidden by court decision to teach in religious garb in public schools of Catholic communities are implored to return to the schools; and denying incidental Federal aid to private schools (bus service, lower price on school lunches or milk, medical, dental, or other auxiliary service) is upheld and reversed and upheld.

In 1894 the Pennsylvania State Supreme Court held that employment of nuns as teachers was not sectarian teaching (164 Pa. S.R. 629), but later in the same year religious garb was declared to signify sectarian teaching (164 Pa.

652). On July 1, 1910, the same Court held that the right of an individual to clothe himself in religious garb "may be restrained by statute" (229 Pa. 132)—a continual see-saw.

During the Depression (1929) Michigan put on the ballot a bill denying certification to any teacher lacking cadet teaching in public schools and forbidding the wearing of religious garb while during such practice teaching. The parochial schools threatened to close. Realization of the enormous expense parochial schools saved the state and nation prevented passage.

In January, 1930, the Pennsylvania Department of Public Instruction refused to validate for the permanent form the college provisional certificates now held by teachers in approved Catholic high schools and has ruled that permanent teachers' certificates will not be granted unless a teacher has had three years of experience in public schools of the state. How nuns may gain certificates is not clear, although among non-Catholic citizens there is no parallel to the Catholic teaching Orders of men and women who devote themselves, without recompense, to the profession. In April, 1930, the State's Attorney General of Nebraska upheld the action of the State Superintendent of Schools in ruling a school in Cedar County off the state fund benefit list because the nuns taught public school classes while wearing their habits.

Such endeavors as those of Michigan and Oregon to make private schools unconstitutional, such questions as Tennessee's right to prohibit schools from teaching theories opposed to the religious beliefs of the majority, and such legislative action as that forbidding the teaching of religion in private schools for credit (Mount Vernon, New York) are not academic. The recurrence of efforts in public schools to force the reading of a version of the Bible forbidden to members of a particular church or the Zoning Law of Portland, Oregon, or the refusal of a position to a qualified teacher because of her religious belief (at Harriman, New York, 1930) affect our daily lives pertinently.

To realize how impossible it is for the prejudiced mind to comprehend the case for denominational schools, one needs but review the discussion at a National Educational Association Meeting, Nashville, 1889. Cardinal Gibbons and Bishop Keane (Rector of Catholic University) presented the argument. These remarks, with appendices revealing the bigotry of opponents, were made available in *Papers on School Issues of the Day* (published by C. W. Bardeen, Syracuse, N.Y., 1889). Abundant additional references bringing the matter up to date we included in "Our Secularized Public Schools," *Thought*, 5:482 ff., December 1930. That the benighted are not always illiterates from the backwoods may be inferred from the remark in the autobiography of an internationally known American artist of tremendous popularity for his posters during World Wars I and II. He says he hated "Catholics and all fanatics."

The State of Washington (1883 and 1890) excluded from school libraries "all books, papers, tracts, or catechisms of an infidel, sectarian, or partisan character"; and after World War II a specific exclusion got much notoriety.

A bigoted attack on the Church appeared in a series of articles in a magazine that had deteriorated sadly under current editorship. A metropolitan school system excluded the periodical from its libraries and the articles took book form as *American Principles and Catholic Power*. Terrific pressure was used unsuccessfully by a Committee of 107 "leading Americans" and by every other means available to force the Board of Education to rescind its order. George H. Dunne, S.J., answered the attack in *Religion and American Democracy* (America Press pamphlet).

A famous newspaper evidences its deterioration and anti-Catholic prejudice in 1951 (not its first unobjective reporting) by championing a sacrilegious motion picture most offensive "to the sacred feelings of both Catholic and non-Catholic" (as the Board of Regents expressed it when condemning unanimously the film). No New York paper (except the diocesan) printed the Board's findings; but the *Motion Picture Herald,* March 3, 1951, remarked the paper's lack of objectivity.

In March, 1951, the states of Montana and Washington and the city of Indianapolis refused to parochial school children permission to ride in busses which collect children in places where they are widely scattered. In the same week New Mexico permitted such children to use the busses, but banned the wearing of religious garb by teachers (in public schools no one else will teach) and made it unlawful to rent school buildings from religious groups except under unusual circumstances.

In taxing school property Los Angeles County has gone so far that all the tuition in one Catholic school must be given for taxes. In December 1950, it doubled the taxes on a school that had been condemned, declaring its value was four times as great as before the condemnation. These outrages caused so much public opposition that in 1951 all such taxes were removed.

Interestingly by 1951, five recent decisions of the United States Supreme Court had encouraged the growth of non-public education on elementary and secondary levels even among non-Catholics and a corresponding decline of enrollment in public schools. Secularism has substituted for Lincoln's famous words "This nation under God" to "this nation without God" and has become identified with Communism as the foe of faith. With World War III impending, national unity is imperative. The main issue is love vs. hate, and history has shown that only great love conquers hate. The Court decisions have guaranteed the rights of private schools, upheld the right of states to use public tax funds for certain auxiliary services for parochial school children and barred religious instruction in public schools during school sessions. The last decision has roused to greater activity the churches and parents in making available to children religious training. Futilely a bill was introduced in the Des Moines Legislature in the attempt to legalize the teaching of Christian philosophy in the public schools in such a way that it would not be offensive to any group.

In the Everson and McCollum cases the U.S. Supreme Court held that the "establishment of religion" clause in the First Amendment to our Constitution means: Neither a state nor the federal government can set up a church. Neither can pass laws which aid one religion, aid all religions, or prefer one to another. No tax in any amount, large or small, can be levied to support any religious activities or institutions. The First Amendment has erected a wall between Church and State. That wall must be kept high and impregnable. But from 1937-47 the Supreme Court has reversed its position in thirty-two cases. After the removal of the evil influences of Justices of the Supreme Court who publicly attested their interest in advancing in the State Department and a Communist traitor now imprisoned— and he is the only one in the gang really caught—the country will get fewer anti-God decisions.

Current interest in providing some kind of religious instruction for children in public schools involves "released time"—permitting pupils to leave school regularly and periodically Wednesday afternoon to attend denominational religious instruction. In 1921 the Board of Education of New York City was enjoined from doing so, but at present such dismissal is permitted. The opponents have not, however, given up.

Because of a ruling of the United States Supreme Court in favor of an atheist's objection to "released time" teaching of religion, the McCollum Case attracted much comment. A knowledge of the disrepute into which the Supreme Court fell as a result of President F. D. Roosevelt's packing it will help in understanding its peculiar rulings. Wilfred Parsons,

S.J., surveyed the McCollum Case in *The First Freedom*. (See also "Supreme Court as a National School Board," *Thought*, December, 1948.) A Supreme Court Justice of the State of New York gave an opposite opinion to the Federal Supreme Court ruling in November, 1948. In questioning the McCollum decision *America* offered an editorial (October 8, 1949) and follow-ups which cited articles in law reviews—the trend being to criticize the decision and express misgivings as to its possible consequences. The *Kentucky Law Journal* sees in the decision a threat to our basic traditions, an impingement on the right of society to pass its ideals down through successive generations, and a jeopardizing of the fundamental function of the educational system—the inculcation of moral and spiritual principles. By March, 1951, Attorney Generals for fourteen out of the seventeen states where the matter was brought up found that the McCollum ruling does not bar moral instruction. While upholding "released time" they excluded use of school equipment and classrooms.

In his *Religion and Education Under the Constitution*, J. M. O'Neill proved the wide misrepresentation of Jefferson and Madison, which was the only basis (aside from personal philosophy) for the McCollum decision. He pictured Madison as against the complete separation of Church and State because he had never found (or seen cited by anyone) any statement of Madison's endorsing that theory and knows of no action of his which indicates a belief in the theory. He cited a number of statements and actions of Madison which indicate the absence of that belief.

About seventy-five Catholic Sisters teach in North Dakota's public schools, mostly in predominantly Catholic communities. When the State passed a law, similar to those of New Mexico, forbidding any public school teacher from wearing a garb denoting membership in a religious order, the Bishops permitted Sisters to don respectable "secular dress." The law, sponsored by Protestants, got a majority of 10,000 votes in a primary election.

The diocesan paper will keep Catholics informed of places refusing or permitting to non-public schools medical or dental inspection, free transportation and non-sectarian texts, and so on. When the "second-class citizens" in the Vancouver parochial schools were legislated against, authorities closed the schools and flooded the public schools with thousands of extra pupils. That terrific additional expense makes concrete what the private school saves the public taxpayer in mere money alone.

The diocesan paper will report, too, American cities infiltrated by typical Communist procedures—pro-Communist speakers as part of the school program to sway public opinion in the battle of propaganda, pro-Communist books in the libraries and texts in the classrooms, disguised indoctrination to corrupt children's minds through art (even dancing). (A Russian proverb contends that what is put into a child's mind with a pen cannot be chipped out with an axe.) In contrast to Communist villainy, diocesan papers will announce Catholic schools opened annually to teach English (not birth prevention or anything else) to new immigrants.

CHAPTER NINE

Achieving the Catholic Heritage

Consideration of the psyche or soul life of Catholics in America is basic to an understanding of the history of our education in the United States. Such exposition will demand, however, delving into the Hebraic and classical sources of our inheritance. From the cultural spate that has flooded America past the middle of the current century, we must select only what has intrinsic value for us in the field of education. We must transmit to the next generation our Catholic heritage, aware of the fact that some Americans find the idea of "the one true Church absurd and unsatisfying" [1].*

Explaining pervasive, long-persisting continuities in the field of education may be of supreme import; and that we shall do in going back to our Biblical inheritance, convinced that only those to whom the spiritual are the supreme values can properly control our destinies as a nation.

The civilization of English-speaking peoples is the result of many dissimilar influences. The most fundamental, inherent, and decisive are: the Hebrew, spiritual heritage from the Bible and the classical-Patristic culture whence comes our modern framework of knowledge and experience, the fullness of personal life and total integration which is the core of the perennial tradition. Our Hebraic heritage

* See notes to this Chapter in the Appendix.

is not the history of Israel; it is only the sacred writers' interpretation of a particular phase of that history.

Before the time of the New Testament, Rome conquered the Grecian world. Hellenic and Hebraic ideals met and the Hellenic, which Rome had adopted, dominated. As Christianity grew in influence, Rome decayed. When the Council of Chalcedon defined clearly the Incarnation (451 A.D.), the Hellenic mind reached its zenith by submitting to Christ. What this complete adjustment of the Greek mind to the Jewish-Christian thinking signified staggers the imagination. By fulfillment, not rejection, tradition superseded the authority of the intellect. The known world became the City of God. Christian dogma reconciled Plato and Aristotle. Until the Renaissance (fourteenth to sixteenth centuries) the classical and the Hebraic interplayed; their fusion caused the re-birth of interest in ancient culture.

The objective of Hebrew education was to train their people to live under a theocracy (a burning question in Israel today) and we may recall here that the American Colonial governments were largely theocratic. The Hebrews were the Chosen People who had a covenant with God, their Creator; Jehovah was their supreme and mighty King, his earthly representatives, judges, kings, prophets, and priests. Their leaders were Moses, the Law-giver (1459 B.C.), who had received the Ten Commandments on Mount Sinai; Solomon (983 B.C.), the builder of the Temple; Elisha (900 B.C.) and Isaias (679 B.C.), the Prophet who gave posterity the first philosophy of history.

As in the American Colonies, among the Hebrews religion and education were inseparable. Hebrew patriots were devoutly religious. Their idea of civil government was exalted above that of any other ancient people. The position of women in their family life and of the family in national life surpassed that of any contemporaries. Most of their religious exercises took place in the home, for on parents rested the obligation of instructing children in the Law

(Deuteronomy VI:5-9). Intelligent Catholics follow admirably this Hebrew (and early Roman) tradition of emphasizing the importance of home training.

The voice of the Rabbi, as teacher, was to the Hebrews the voice of God—and we find the same sort of respect for the priest in early American communities. With the younger children the Rabbi was severe and in teaching depended principally on the catechetical method. With older students he disputed—not in the sense of disagreeing; rather discussing to discover the real meaning of the Law.

From the New Testament a reader can recall Jesus' asking the lawyer, "What says the Law?" and in the story of the Good Samaritan, "Who is my neighbor?" As a child of twelve, in the Temple He disputed with the Doctors. With the Pharisees He disputed over texts from the Old Testament. (The title of Raphael's marvelous painting of "The Dispute" used the word in the Biblical sense. The painting depicts not a quarrel about the Blessed Sacrament but a discussion.)

Hebrews memorized the Law; the Psalms and the Book of Proverbs were known by heart. Catholics store the memory with liturgical prayers, hymns, and glorious traditions and ejaculations ("My Lord and my God"). The content of Hebrew education attracts more favorable attention than the method, when they observed the letter rather than the spirit of the Law. (Recall our Lord's frequent criticism of the Pharisees because their strict observance led them—and Hebrew educators—to lose sight of the spiritual truths that had been their heritage. So formalized and externalized had Hebrew religion become that when their King appeared they did not recognize Him. "They received Him not." Catholic educators and parents have known these facts.)

Despite their failures, the Hebrews transmitted Revelation to succeeding centuries; they passed on the deposit of spiritual and moral truth which, in the form of Christianity, leavened the world, converted Europe, and gave Catholics in America much that is fundamental to their educational heritage. In every instance, the concept of man—what he, redeemed by Christ, is worth—should decide what shall constitute his training.

Today Bible stories tend to displace the reading of the Bible itself, and for that reason too many people are unacquainted with the literary, spiritual, and historical features of The Book, which is what the word "bible" means. Bible histories are histories, including nothing from the Psalms, Proverbs, and other Books of Wisdom. Practically all of Genesis can be read by children—and they should know the language of the Bible. Certainly they should read the Psalms in their proper literary form in English.

The Philistine boasts of his ignorance of liberal culture, deceived by the thought that a lack of intellectual interests suggest his freedom from the domination of tradition, of his ancestors' thinking, and of the heritage of the race. He reveals his handicap—that he lacks mooring. Without the support of roots he tends to abuse real freedom, and his acts tend to deteriorate into license. Without fundamental connection with the past, he fails to realize his obligation to the future. The stream of racial culture, the advancement of the ages, means for him concessions. His present privileges he accepts without thought of his membership in world movements. His ignorance in the cycles of history prevents his realizing that a renaissance makes the past the present and will continue to do so.

The Philistine's hampered thinking blinds him to the discovery that liberal studies can free him from the domination of overpowering passions and appetites and of the snares of centuries. Provided he has a Christian character, they could exempt him from repeating errors of the weak and of the vicious who have preceded him. Liberal studies do not always, we emphasize, free one from wrong thinking and doing and from future regrets, for only the Christian character is really free, because knowledge (a liberal edu-

cation) must precede freedom so that free acts will really
be independent of the domination of habit's scourge.

Such independence does not, however, mean isolation,
although the Philistine and the cultured pagan are unaware
of our integration with the children of the Father of us all.
Here again the man is severely handicapped because lack
of social consolidation of interests and responsibilities has
precluded spiritual solidarity. The result is that restlessness
overshadows his living; he is inclined to depression, despond-
ency, and even to suicide. Despite vast material possessions,
rudderless and uninfluential as a refining influence in the
lives of less prosperous contemporaries, such unfortunates
are often dominated in living and thinking by a chaos only
a rootless pagan can actually know.

Far different the lot of those who realize the force and
worth of their heritage from the Catholic stream of culture.
The Apostles, the Disciples, the early Christians, and most
of the great souls of the last nineteen centuries were not
college graduates, so that academic training is not pre-
requisite to membership in the Mystical Body of Christ. *The
New Testament,* hagiography, history, and biography reveal the lives of these people triumphant in their search
for the rewards of eternity, even though, in many cases, they
seemed failures in the eyes of the world or in their outer
as contrasted with their inner life.

Cardinal Wiseman's *Fabiola,* Newman's *Callista,* Myles
Keon's *Dion and the Sybils,* and Father Joseph Spellman's
Lucius Flavius reveal such lives, under the guise of fiction.
Conscious of their membership in the Mystical Body of
Christ, of which He is the Vine and we are the branches,
the early Christians fostered our Christian heritage, its
sympathies and admirations for the likenesses of God in
their fellow men.

The Christian of the twentieth century also must let
Christ and His teachings dominate his life and thinking;
he then leads others to a spiritual and mental regeneration,

so that Christian principles rise to domination in all branches of the life about us. The history of the Church is an in-spiriting record of man's rise to actual social equality and freedom. Unfortunately, since the mis-named Reformation, men have veered from the use of God's gifts "with right reason," as St. Thomas puts it; so it is the present duty of Catholics, having achieved their heritage, to regenerate the Catholic spirit and all thinking. Living a Catholic life is the best explanation of what a Catholic sense is. We must live in imitation of Christ. We must lead others to do likewise. We must defend mankind against the abuses of pagans and all others ignorant of Catholic teaching and practice.

Beginning with the spiritualizing of self, and doing all we can to revitalize the various ramifications of life around us by effecting a preponderance of Christian principles therein, is, of course, Catholic Action as defined by Pope Pius XI. We base it on the liturgy (our communal worship of God), the love of Christ (the most impelling force in life) motivates it, the Hierarchy directs it, and lay men and women contribute by cooperating with grace as naturally as a healthy arm cooperates with the body. Each one strives continuously to become a saint; and, except sin, everything he does can be offered for the honor and glory of God.

Charity, we realize—and not personal piety—is the basis for sanctity. We strive to become holy by meeting our obligations daily in the spirit of Christ and for the honor and glory of God. We seek not the fervor of a special occasion or circumstance; rather we elevate our daily life by the Morning Offering, with renewal as often as we think of it, and sanctify the contemplative part of our existence by uniting with the prayer life of the Church through the liturgy.

Catholic Action is the dynamic process by which old and young will be prepared for living the reconstructed culture of their generation. We must reunite ourselves with

the spiritual roots of our culture, and our culture (as the
root of the word shows) derives from our worship. The
Liturgical Movement is our greatest aid; through it we
shall re-possess our communal worship of God. Regaining
that possession is basic to combating the false philosophy
which dominates our social order, whether it be in the field
of economics, of politics, of international relations, of social
work, of education, or in any of the other phases of living
we discuss in *Social Studies* and *Catholic Action*. The liturgy
is the integrating and socializing force in that most perfect
of perfect societies, the Catholic Church. It effects our union
with the Head of the Mystical Body and is the only satisfactory solution to the evils which enmesh us because it
leads us back to our Lord Himself and to His principles.
Christian principles will give a solid basis for solving any
social problem. Fortunate, therefore, indeed is any one
who gains his Catholic heritage.

Far different the dislikes and disdains of pagans, ancient
or modern, whose small souls (misled by the superficial and
the unimportant) have narrowed their outlook on life. Turning away from the heritage of faith and culture which
civilization (or Catholicism, to substitute a more concrete
term) had preserved for them, they blighted the minds of
their descendants of succeeding generations. Fullness of
faith and riches of intellect known only to the devout
Catholic are denied these disinherited modern pagans. Fortunately, as our survey of the Catholic heritage will reveal,
there is at present a renaissance of Catholic culture and
hopeful signs that numbers whose ancestors repudiated the
Catholic tradition at the time of the mis-called Reformation
will enter the true Fold. More and more are those creative
spirits who build churches turning to the Catholic tradition
for inspiration. Poets (which means at root "creators") and
philosophers, too, must turn, if they would build on foundations more solid than sand, to the perennial Catholic art
and thought.

Consider the moral conditions of the world in which Jesus of Nazareth set the foundations of His kingdom. St. Paul in his usual graphic and forceful manner has told us of the pride, and selfishness, the cruelty, the sensuality that reigned therein. Lest St. Paul's description be rejected as too severe let us remember that he is no more condemnatory of existing conditions than are Tacitus, Suetonius, Juvenal, Seneca, and the other pagan historians of the day. Tacitus sums up the moral situation at that time by saying, "The spirit of the time is to corrupt and to be corrupted." The provinces were not much purer than the Capital. Each province poured its separate contribution of moral filth into the great store which the increasing centralization of the empire had accumulated in the main reservoir at Rome. Each province in turn received its share of this reciprocated corruption.

Antioch was a centre of moral putrefaction. Egypt was one of the most corrupt countries of the world. Practically the same account might be given of all these districts, cities, and countries into which Christianity first made its way—Greece, Asia Minor, Africa, Corinth, and Alexandria. Even historians who deny the divinity of Christ are very ready to admit that the middle of the first century was one of the worst periods in ancient history. Pride and intellectual cynicism, cruel selfishness, which made the rich and powerful tyrannize over the poor and weak, and degrading sensuality were the keynotes of Roman civilization. The situation was described by a historian not given to overestimating the accomplishments of Christianity by saying, "Rome was a school of immorality and cruelty, a very hell."

From the opened tomb of the crucified Jesus of Nazareth went twelve fishermen of Galilee to establish in that degraded and degrading world the kingdom of the Crucified. Recall Paul as he enters Rome—Rome the capital of the Empire; Rome, where the pride, selfishness and sensuality which dominated the lives of all were worshipped in its gods—Jupiter, Venus, and Mars; Rome whose houses were roofed with gold; Rome whose luxury, refinement and culture were surpassed only by the degradation of its men and women. It is the afternoon hour. The Romans of importance and social standing are gathered in the sumptuously furnished baths, the common loitering grounds. There are the subtle-minded Greek philosophers with their haughty Roman followers; there are the women of Rome, young and old, matrons and widows included, scantily garbed, painted and perfumed, glorying in their shame, boasting of the number of husbands that were theirs. In all Rome it was impossible to find twelve women willing to lead the life of virginity required of the vestal virgin. There are their lustful paramours; there are the lawmakers, the successful professional men, the men of wealth, basking in the sunshine and breathing the perfume of Italian roses.

Into their midst one afternoon there limped this little Jew; a little blear-eyed fellow, humpbacked from bending over his tents, calloused of hand, his nails broken and blackened. Into their midst he limped, as he himself tells us, "with much fear and trembling," but with a magnificent, a Divine contempt for the persuasive words of human wisdom. He knew only one thing; he could preach only one thing, "Jesus of Nazareth, God and man; Jesus of Nazareth crucified and risen from the dead; Jesus of Nazareth, whom all nations must believe, must love, must adore if they are to be saved." It is Paul, the converted Saul of Tarsus. He looks about him. His soul thrills with the vision of society, even that degraded society, regenerated and clad in the virtues of Jesus of Nazareth beautiful above the sons of men. Divine power goes forth from him. Into the midst of the startled loiterers he leaps. He cries out as his fellow disciples did to the cripple at the temple gate, "In the name of Jesus of Nazareth I say to you arise and walk. Walk in the paths of humility, purity, and charity. I preach Jesus of Nazareth and Him crucified. I bring you a new message. Away with your intellectual pride, you who are ever learning and never attaining to the knowledge of truth. Listen to the words of Him whose disciple and witness I am."

In all her teaching the Church has used the soundest psychological principles. For each Sacrament she uses symbols, outward signs of interior grace; in her ritual she appeals continually to the mind through the senses. In the liturgy she encourages imitation and emulation when following the liturgical year by re-living the life of Christ and of those who because of their imitation of Him have been raised to the altars of the Church as saints. She demands the co-operation of the faithful in prayer and ceremonies and the actual carrying out of her teachings in their daily living.

Catholic culture consists of the communal life of the Christian realized through the liturgy, and the end of the liturgical instruction is the full realization of one's life-work as Christian. Catholic life must be restored before we really can restore the Catholic spirit, and the life of the social group must be modeled on the Catholic spiritual life. Communal worship of God in the liturgy is the ideal corporate life; so it becomes imperative that we learn to unite ourselves to Christ in the Mass and that we re-live Christ's life with the Church in following the liturgical cycles.

The synthesis the Church aims at in the life of the individual is a Catholic sense, an ability to see eye to eye with her in all matters of faith and morals. Catholic philosophy must inform all the phases of training, for the Church insists that in Christ we have the only synthesis of truth. Man can arrive at that goal through natural reason and the illumination of supernatural faith. Once the Catholic achieves this unity and totality of view, he can continue the integration indefinitely.

In this regard a student expresses his experience thus:

The study of the Church's liturgy has made me appreciate more fully the beauty of the Mass, the Sacraments, the sacramentals, liturgical prayer, and the liturgical year; and therefore I derive greater benefit from them. To offer myself, my parents, friends, actions, and even my very shortcomings on the paten with Christ, the Victim, is to feel a new sense of cooperation in the Mass. I now experience great joy at knowing that these are consumed and transformed into a pleasing oblation for the glory of God the Father to atone for my sins and for the punishment due to them. Further, by uniting myself throughout the Mass with the priest, by use of the Missal, I become more conscious of my relation with other members of the Mystical Body of Christ. Then I am led to pray more earnestly for help from the Saints that I may partake of their merits and to assist the Church Suffering. . . . Because I realize now the dignity and honor of my recitation of such prayer as Compline, for instance, of representing all the Church Militant in adoration, thanksgiving and petition to God, I am more careful to perform it with all possible devotion.

In assisting my performance of these public offices of the Church, my academic courses have been extremely beneficial. But I appreciate the influence of a Catholic training still more because it has excited in me a desire to delve more deeply and to expand my present knowledge of all things Catholic. I now appreciate what a stupendous program Catholic Action really represents.

The first Christian schools were catechumenal, designed to prepare converts for entrance into the Church and to prevent apostasy and reversion to paganism after baptism. In the writings of St. Augustine we have preserved some of the lectures and catechetical interrogations—doctrinal, moral, and ascetical. Particularly did such detailed ceremonies as those of Holy Saturday (when the catechumens were baptized) impress upon the witnesses as well as upon the participants the Church's teachings. In the third and fourth centuries baptism was often deferred as late as the catechumen's thirtieth year. St. John Chrysostom was baptized at twenty-five and we have recorded instances of men remaining catechumens for twenty years after having attained the use of reason and of their falling away from the Church's teaching three or four times. St. Augustine felt that had his baptism not been deferred, he might not have fallen into heresy; but although while studying, one fasted on vigils of feasts and performed other good works to which Christians could be summoned, he received none of the Sacraments, sat in a part of the church reserved for the catechumens, and withdrew from the Mass before the Consecration. The graces derived from full participation, St. Augustine felt, would have strengthened his faith.

* * *

The Church taught effectively through art and literature; in fact, both media furnish dependable criteria for judging an age or the people who produced the specimens. In the highest sense, art is an expression of ideals; hence nobility of art evidences a high standard of morality.

In the Catacombs, the early Christians used symbols to teach religion because most of the catechumens were illiterate. The anchor represented hope; a dove with an olive branch, peace; the fish (*ichthus*) Jesus Christ, Son of God, Savior. Because they tried to teach the same lesson through repetition, the subjects were usually treated in the same way. Their object was to bear in the fact that God was the creator of both Testaments (a necessity for counteracting an early heresy), to show that Adam and Eve were doomed to a life of toil and that in the Church alone was the great opportunity for salvation, to represent Christ as a teacher and the Magi as the first to bring glad tidings to Christians.

Artistic effect was not their objective. The paintings decorated graves; and, symbolic of atonement, they were dominated and penetrated by the idea of eternal salvation. The paintings were not primarily didactic; they used incidents from the Old and New Testaments in so far as they related to death in the desire to exhort beholders to pray for the dead. Emblematic of the Evangelists, one of their purposes was, however, to convey doctrine, to teach men that they were not beasts. Christian art differed from that of the Greeks, which represented only corporal beauty, in that it did not flatter the passions and it lacked the patronage of the wealthy. The themes symbolized devotional truth. Favorite subjects included the Blessed Virgin, the Baptism of Jesus, the Adoration of the Magi, Christ as the Lamb (we are His lambs), the four gushing rivers under His throne, and, most important, the Eucharist as the Breaking of the Bread, the Loaves and Fishes, and so on.

So important was the work of the Church Fathers that we have a science of patrology, the study of the lives and writing of the Fathers of the Church. Those interested in Catholic Evidence or other apologetic work today are always pleased to discover that patrology was our first Christian literature and apologetics, the first struggle of the early Church. Manuals of patrology, which direct study about a Church Father or his work, have as authors at least two we should mention. Bishop Shahan translated Otto Bardenhewer's work, which contained biography, selections, and bibliography. Schmidt's Manual has also been translated from the German. While the latter is small, its introduction includes a fascinating sketch of the history of patrology, less technical than Bardenhewer's

A Father of the Church (1) lived when the Church was in her youth. [Pope Gregory the Great, who died in 604, was the last Father in the West; St. John Damascene, who died in 754, was the last in the East.] (2) He led a saintly life; (3) his writings were not only free from heresies but excel in the explanation and defense of Catholic doctrine. (4) These writings must bear the seal of the Church's approval. Such saintly writers of the first centuries of the Christian era the Church acknowledges as witnesses of the Faith. Doctors of the Church, by way of distinction, she extols not primarily as witnesses to the Faith but rather because of their brilliant exposition and skillful defense of Catholic doctrine—Saints Jerome, Ambrose, Augustine, Gregory, and Teresa of Avila, for example.

Julian the Apostate was a fellow student of St. Gregory Nazianzen. How can you have, in the same classroom, pupils whose later lives are so diametrically different?

There is such a thing as invincible ignorance, but there are reasons other than ignorance and prejudice which might explain a man's pagan philosophy or non-Catholic beliefs. A minister could hold off conversion because he had a family to support; so there are in England and the U.S. societies that get jobs for convert ministers. When the intelligent or well educated oppose the Church, their motives may not be self-interest or bad will, although many teachers at secular universities go along with (at least, raise no objection to) wrong philosophies because they feel they have to hold their positions and want advancement on the faculty.

One can mistakenly act badly from good motives. Facts and behavior are not the final criterion; it is the interpretation of the facts that is important. Two persons may see a man stagger, one thinking he is drunk. If he falls he may have a card in his pocket warning that he is diabetic. A cough can arise from many causes—cigarettes, whiskey, TB, heart affliction, or cold. When former President Conant of Harvard spoke against parochial schools and Catholic colleges, he may have thought he was encouraging democracy. St. Thomas says such a person may (and one should be slow to decide otherwise) be only using the wrong means. Attacks should distinguish the man from his deed—condemning the act, of course, if it is wrong.

St. Augustine, who knew what it was to be a heretic, said the same thing centuries before St. Thomas. A man's goodness (he taught) depends on what he loves (an act of will) rather than on what he believes (an act of the mind). When one lives in agnosticism and heresy, it is patent, he cannot comprehend as clearly, steadily, and wholly as if he had faith. Happily, in America, because nowadays the big cleavage is between Communism and its

chief opponent, difference in belief has shifted largely from
the field of religion to that of politics; but one cannot forget
that the Communists are anti-Christ.

Without, then, being so broadminded as to be flat (lacking depth) we should judge those outside the Fold to be
good until the evidence that they act in bad faith is in-
disputable. Scoundrels can be anti-Christ, rogues can act
viciously; so everyone should guard against being taken
in by them, his suspicions and rash judgments unexpressed.
The letters of St. Justin (martyr of the second century)
afford an excellent example of the Christian spirit in dealing with the opposition. Pagans killed him; but like the
other Church Fathers, through teaching and preaching, he
fought heroically anti-Christian beliefs and practices—it was
the sin and not the sinner he hated.

Never did heroic Christians compromise with pagan
practices; but they loved their enemies and gave such good
example that pagans exclaimed in awe, "See how they love
each other for the love of God." So deep was the impression
made, moreover, that when the Roman Empire fell, pagans
looked to Christians for help—for the corporal works of
mercy. Feeding the hungry, clothing the naked, and hos-
pitalizing the sick were most efficacious in winning Europe
to Christianity; and the same procedure will make Catholic
Action effective today. Without use of physical force, denied
political and social standing, gathering into their ranks
everyone who labored and was heavily burdened, with the
grace of God Christians animated by the spirit of Christ
triumphed. On his deathbed, Julian the Apostate (Roman
Emperor of the fourth century) who had once referred
sneeringly to our Lord as "Only a carpenter's son," muttered,
"Galilean, thou hast conquered."

The approach of the Church Fathers (as revealed in
their writings) was always cool, meeting the vilest charges
against the Church as if the opponents were intelligent and
meant well, with no reviling or accusations of bad faith.

Such an attitude was not cunning or planned strategy; St. John Chrysostom (golden tongued) and all Christian apologists separated men from their deeds. The reaction was, as it is today, the conviction among many bitter opponents that Christians really follow our Lord's teachings. When one hears "You are mistaken" but not "You are evil," he may examine his policy or way of life carefully and discover he is wrong. The fact that his opponent has shown sympathy and kindness for man, although continuing to oppose his opinions and acts, opens the ears and the mind of the misguided. Charity brings the teachings of Christ and His Church to fruition.

To realize the amazing change from Roman Empire to medieval Christendom one needs but read Newman's *Callista,* or, better, since he will be dealing not with fiction but with actual facts, study the life of St. Ambrose of Milan (337-395 A.D.). Curiously enough, in such studies of the fourth century we not only come across all the historical elements of fifteen centuries—including the century before Christ's birth and fourteen centuries after it.

St. Ambrose was an Empire official as was his father before him; indeed, from his headquarters at Trier, the father ruled practically all western Europe for the Emperor. Officially Christianity had been the state religion from about the middle of the fourth century when Ambrose, in his early thirties, was sent, as a civil official, to supervise the election of a bishop of Milan, second only to Rome in importance among Italian cities. Although his father and he were Christians, Ambrose had not been baptized; so we can imagine his astonishment when all factions insisted that he himself be Bishop. He reiterated his absolute unworthiness and unpreparedness, but the populace refused to excuse him. To be sure, he had the best education Rome afforded; he was thoroughly familiar with Greek and was well read. His ignorance of theology seemed to him an insurmountable obstacle, although when he was convinced that he must become Bishop he began his study of this science of God and of religion with his natural thoroughness and efficiency. In eight days he passed from Baptism and minor orders to his consecration as Bishop; and as a result of his persistence in his new vocation we have the copious writings of this Doctor of the Western Church revealing marvelously the distinction between the new structure of Catholic theology and the old foundations of Stoic philosophy which had been St. Ambrose's educational inheritance and that of every one of his social position among his contemporaries.

His biography is inspiring because of its revelation of the marked distinction between Christian ethics and the code of public service sanctioned by Romans in the imperial employ, with its grafting, sale of privileges, and suppression of inhabitants in the provinces. While bishops were at the time important local leaders with rather widely extended spheres of authority, during the Middle Ages they faced tasks undreamed of by St. Ambrose. However, possibly his best known treatise is that on the duties of priests, written with the Ciceronian treatment of duties as model. In adapting the best of the old Roman heritage to establish solidly the new Christian order, St. Ambrose was following the eminently successful policy of the Church throughout history. Instead of destroying, it has always builded on the known, on what the non-Catholic already had, relating the new to the old. Since the special characteristics of the Ambrosian Rite show the Oriental influence and St. Ambrose's predecessor as Bishop was an Oriental, instead of creating something new St. Ambrose may rather have confirmed liturgical customs with which the people were familiar.

In St. Ambrose after Baptism and consecration we see a symbol of the Roman Empire itself. His remarkably practical nature and his strong moral character brought unusual success to his concentrated devotion to his bishopric, impressing St. Augustine, even at a distance, deeply and lastingly. In contrast to the subservience of the Eastern Church to the Emperor, St. Ambrose formulated courageously the Church's right to discipline secular rulers, including the Emperor himself.

Early Christianity stimulated the production of literature remarkably because the Church Fathers realized how vitally reading material could help the material mission of the Church. We need but recall how Newman's *Callista* destroys the prestige of all that is classical to realize how effectively St. Augustine's *City of God* could develop the law of progress from Creation up to the fifth century, his period. The magnificence of his vision of a new empire in which brute strength would be of no avail and in which women could be as powerful as men in converting the world was arresting. The Romans, who had oppressed the weak and wallowed in luxury and decadence, complained that they were prosperous in pagan days, that Christianity had brought them bad luck. St. Augustine answered that Rome fell not because it was Christian but because it failed to be Christian—a city of God. The benefits of Christianity, moreover, were not essentially fatted calves but principally spiritual joys.

Clotilde converting the heathen Franks, Theodolind the Arian Lombards, and St. Patrick, St. Benedict, and St. Gregory heading the battle of civilization against barbarism made inspiring records.

As we recall, however, pagan literature retained its hold, preserved by St. Augustine, St. Jerome, and St. Basil until Christian poets learned to create. Abundant traces of the pagan masters lingered in Christian literature for a long time.

The universal use of Latin encouraged the dissemination of Christian writings. The hymns of St. Hilary, the preeminence of St. Ambrose as the greatest early Christian poet, and St. Augustine's prolific output all contributed

melody, imagery, feeling, and thought. St. Jerome taught
Biblical exegesis, St. Augustine dogmatic theology, and St.
Ambrose moral; while St. Anselm began Christian meta-
physics in his desire to explain the existence of God.

In the one hundred twenty-five letters, covering the last
fifty years of St. Jerome's life, that have been preserved
for us we find few short epistles. Addressed to St. Augustine,
the Pope, bishops, religious and lay people of various classes,
the many treatises of pamphlet length make a thesaurus of
varied knowledge from the fields of theology, Scripture,
religion, asceticism, philosophy, education, literature, monas-
ticism, Christian perfection, world politics, geography, ath-
letics, and social service. They treat sins of the aristocracy,
library science, elocution, oratory, debating, funerals, ban-
quets, heretics, mail carriers, secretaries, sweethearts, pious
frauds, storks, fleas, race horses, puling infants, maidens,
toothless old men, chemistry, physics, botany, barbarians,
saints, near-saints—in fact, all sorts of subjects from a skull
cap to a trip through the Holy Land.

The unalloyed delight one gets from these letters makes
'him realize that the reason they are not better known
must be that St. Jerome's reputation as the Church's greatest
Scriptural teacher over-shadows all other memories of him.
Dr. P. J. M'Cormick's *History of Education* includes a stimulating introduction to the Saint's letter-writing activities.

The letters are a pen-portrait of himself, the mind and
heart and soul of an immortal champion of Christianity
revealed as he dictates his messages to the world. We discover how the man and the saint combined to form the
literary artist. Here we have a gigantic intellect and volcanic heart, a Christian Delphic oracle of the fourth century, warring on heresy and sin and sham. This Demosthenes
of the desert, the St. John the Baptist of his age—with a
terrific punch added, was the Cardinal Newman of Latin
Letters; and letters were but a secondary item in his life
work.

Wherein lay St. Jerome's greatness? He was a thinker, because he was a great student, a keen observer, an omnivorous reader, and a philosopher. In Latin he rivalled Cicero; he was a master of Hebrew; and he was the greatest Greek scholar of his time. Success in study he owed to his genius for hard work, his wonderful mind, his prodigious memory, and the direction of the best teachers the world afforded. He observed himself; through introspection and meditation, he learned his own heart and the hearts of other men. As world-traveler and correspondent, he observed objects and events. He seems to have read everything worth while, sacred and profane, in the ancient and his contemporary world. He knew the Old and the New Testaments by heart and quoted from the works of Cicero, Caesar, Virgil, Horace, Tacitus, Quintilian, Livy, Sallust, Persius, Juvenal, Martial, and other classical authors. He was a philosopher by nature, by design a great debater and reasoner. He was familiar with the thinking of Socrates, Plato, Aristotle, the Stoics, the Epicureans, and the rest. He was indeed a great thinker, packing his sentences with meaning. His epigrams alone fill a good-sized volume.

Other phases of St. Jerome's personality which enriched his letters were those which may be integrated under his activity as teacher, reformer, and spiritual director. As scriptural scholar and authority he solved difficult questions of interpretation for the learned men and women of his time, including St. Augustine and Pope Damasus, whose secretary he was. Not only was he teacher of morality, prophet of the higher life, and reformer of corrupt society; he was spiritual father to the best and greatest souls of his time. He taught poverty, penance, fasting and abstinence, virginity and chastity. He emphasized hard work and ceaseless prayer, meditation and the joys of spiritual reading, particularly of the Scriptures. As teacher he was enthusiastic, fearless, absolutely sincere, and outspoken. Mercilessly he satirized and chastised cant and hypocrisy. Much admired,

he was hated by those strong enough to prevent his becoming Pope. He was noted for pugnacity and a temper
so irascible when aroused that he used to say, "Forgive me,
God. You know I'm a Dalmatian." Above all he was sane,
practical, and a teacher with common sense.

Naturally St. Jerome's sanctity illumined his letters. A
humble priest who never exercised his ministry, a monk
at Bethlehem, a warm-hearted, intense lover of liberty, a
hater of injustice, in the Syrian desert and in the monastery
heroically penitential in dominating his impetuous, rebellious
flesh, a severe saint with himself and others, he was cheerful, zealous, and glowingly chaste.

As a literary artist, he was a master of the written word;
his composition, full of thought, approaches perfection in
matter and manner. Devoid of padding, his expression is
always clear; though careful and painstaking, his style is
easy, fluent, smooth and elegant. He is as adept at saying
the beautiful and lovely as with the straightforward, harsh,
ugly, stinging, crushing, unadorned truth. His style is swift
and graceful as a dove, clever as a serpent. Conscious of
his great power, he strives heroically to reserve his force lest
it carry him off in the lava flow from his volcanic heart.
He is always delightfully entertaining, with a happy sur-
prise on nearly every page. Witty, sarcastic, at times he is
even outrageously funny, though unintentionally so. His
word pictures are vivid; he illustrates his thought constantly
with suitable examples, anecdotes, comparisons, and illustrations. His use of quotation is splendid.

In his translations he is as much the literary artist as in
his original composition. He knew all the rules and devices
and niceties of rhetoric and could use them tellingly. What
Johnson wrote for Goldsmith's epitaph, St. Jerome's letters
reveal true of him—he ornamented all he touched.

In addition to all Catholics know about principles of
education and method, they realize that the Third Person
of the Blessed Trinity can enter a mind and enlighten it

with far greater effectiveness than any of man's teaching. They believe that many devout persons have learned more by meditating in the presence of the Blessed Sacrament than they could have gained from teachers and books on a particular problem. Report on how St. Catherine of Siena learned to read by inspiration, or try to emulate this student's voluntary paper on "Education and the Holy Ghost."

Possession of the Holy Ghost is the possession of true Education—not only for time but for eternity. The Holy Ghost by means of His Gifts safeguards the teacher from error (for the Holy Ghost is the Spirit of Truth) and the mind of the one being taught from a mistaken interpretation of the teachings. Where a teacher is not guided by the Holy Ghost and His Gifts there is false education of intellect, of the body but not of the will (moral education), which is intended to guide the learner in achieving the salvation of his soul and the fulfillment of God's plan for him on earth. Christ promised that the Holy Spirit would sustain His Church so that the gates of Hell would not prevail against it and the Third Person of the Holy Trinity usually works through a human agency.

The Gifts enable men to reject erroneous doctrines. Fortitude especially enables them to teach God's law without fear of human criticism according to his Divine Law. Fear of God, which is a filial fear—fear without terror, is due to the love of God and will aid one to live courageously according to the Divine Law. Piety is necessary for the ability to recognize a true Christian, since this Gift is a characteristic trait of Christianity. Counsel may be joined by the Beatitude of the merciful. By the Gift of Knowledge the capacity of reason increases and faith is illumined. The purification of the heart is the proper work of the Gift of Understanding in this life. Wisdom is primarily an intellectual gift by which we accustom ourselves to judge everything from on high, in the light of eternity.

The third architectonic movement in surveying the

history of education includes what is usually referred to as "modern times"—following the Renaissance (which was implemented by a comparatively few literates) and the mis-named Reformation (like any revolution, a mob or mass movement). Our purpose in viewing modern times is to inculcate a Catholic sense—the seeing eye to eye with the Church in all matters of faith and morals. A careful student sees a concatenation linking the literary revolt of the fifteenth century, the upheaval in the field of religion in the sixteenth, the peculiar philosophical systems of the seventeenth, the political revolts of the eighteenth, the Oxford Movement of the nineteenth, and secularism's domination of life in the twentieth century. These upheavals were, naturally, felt in America and although the contemporaneous reflections of the Oxford Movement (for example) were pale, the influence has been deeply felt continuously through the Catholic Renascence.

Cardinal Newman stands out as a leader of that Movement in England; and, pertinently, again our Hebraic-Hellenic heritage is revived by him, some of whose ancestors were Jews and whose *Idea of a University* (the title Platonic) was a typical, effective answer to current hostility to the Greek culture of his time. His essay "The Gentleman" revealed a Periclean balance in the love of beauty without extravagance, cultivation of the mind without effeminacy, and use of wealth not for display but for proper ends. The Catholic *via media* which Newman exemplified, encourages a Periclean interest in public affairs, everyman's attempt to understand them, and public discussion of civic problems to gain proper insight into them.

Unfortunately most school editions of Newman's "Gentleman" give an impression directly opposed to the author's by omitting the closing paragraph which emphasizes that a man may have all the outward characteristics of a gentleman and at the same time be a pagan at heart—a whited sepulcher. Although Pope Leo XIII's encyclical in 1879 pronounced Christian Scholastic philosophy a continuation of that of Aristotle, the contrast between the pagan Greek and Hebraic Christian elements in our heritage is clear-cut.

Not only is the tradition in English, as well as in American, literature Protestant; but, as Newman made clear one cannot have a sinless literature about sinful man.

Since the Christian idea of life never penetrated Europe to its inner depth, although both the Latins and Nordics did meet under a pretended Christianity, the former really remained pagans—never did become Christians—and the Teutons always were savages. The older forms of pagan world-view persisted beneath the Christian surface. In the modern era they have increasingly penetrated upward, transforming what we still call our Christian civilization into an almost entirely pagan culture. The lay apostolate must strive zealously to penetrate from above down to the superstition or ignorance of the uninformed. If those who have had chance to learn what the liturgy is fail to deepen this penetration, the Liturgical Movement will not achieve in this century what people in the Ages of Faith had as part of their daily living. The Mass will be ignored as the center of daily life and Christian love.

In *The Salvation of Nations* Père Danielou presents the dynamism of outlook that should inform all phases of Catholicism, a recalling of St. Paul's missionary concept—directly opposed to parochial-mindedness. In keeping with this idea, the Te Deum Forums (in mid-western United States) are sponsored by the Te Deum International, a group of Catholic men concentrating effort to promote good will and better understanding among the people of their community regardless of race, color, or creed.

The primary purpose is education through the presentation of a Catholic viewpoint on current affairs. All Catholics, Protestants, Jews and others are invited to become members at any time during the course of the lecture series. A typical series included: "Around the Post-War World,"

"Has Britain a Future?" "Hollywood in Focus," "Can Christians Unite?" "The Catholic Intellectual Revival," and "Inside Spain: the Realities of Spain Today."

Moreover, although the Breton, Irish, and Polish peasant understood his relationship to his Creator, Christianity did not penetrate to the lowest European classes as a whole, and from them may come the Goths and Vandals of modern times striving continuously and most fiendishly to destroy Christian civilization. Such a scourge appeared in the French Revolution, in the spread of atheism and rationalism in the eighteenth century England, and in the loss to the Church of the working classes in the nineteenth century. The Socialists peddled *Twenty-five Reasons for Being an Atheist* among working men attending their lectures in Victorian England, and Communists continue that diabolical work today.

Pope Pius X issued an encyclical against Modernism and by excommunication lopped off from the Vine such well-known branches as Father Tyrrell (English Jesuit), Antonio Fogozarro (Italian novelist), and Alfred Loisy (editor of *L'Action Francaise*).

Liberalism, industrialism—the mechanization of Western civilization, and secularism nourished the gospel of Mammon. In his *Religion and the Rise of Capitalism,* Richard Tawney, a non-Catholic, has revealed how Calvinism, Presbyterianism, and similar sectarian "religions" played up the idea that God loved only the rich, that worldly success was the goal of life, that "religion" was respectable and no matter what your evil manner of life it "helped" business to be seen at church on Sunday. Newman attacked such hypocrisy in such sermons as "The World, Our Enemy," "Doing Glory to God in Pursuits of the World."

In the eighteenth century, Edmund Burke foresaw, as did Coleridge and Carlyle, and the leaders of the Oxford Movement in the nineteenth, that the secularism resulting from the empirical skepticism of the eighteenth century, the revolutionary democracy following the French Revolution, and the materialistic industrialism which grew out of the Industrial Revolution I aimed to kill the spiritual characteristics in man. The laissez-faire rugged individualism united with factory machinery to dissolve society and submerge individual personality.

Newman and his non-Catholic group at Oxford were publishing a series of tracts (hence their name Tractarians) in the attempt to introduce the traditional piety, spirituality, and authority of the Church Fathers and to show the direct line of succession in Episcopalian beliefs from the Apostles. Because of their claiming the teachings of St. Paul and St. Augustine they were not attracted by Victorian pantheism from belief in the supernatural order and the efficacy of grace in conjunction with man's free will. For them the Church, divinely established, was a perfect society thoroughly capable of providing a principle of order which safeguarded the minds of men against the skepticism which resulted from uncontrolled roving of the intellect in the field of faith and morals. Only a religion established by Christ, the Son of God, could with authority solve the problems presented to man who must live under a natural and supernatural order. Denial of the latter undermines belief in the Mystical Body of Christ, in the religious support for the power holding the peoples of the world in an organic unity. With that gone, the totalitarian state takes over, human personality loses significance, the individual soul has no value, and the secular state rules ruthlessly. When the Tractarians published their ninetieth tract, the world saw that these men were Roman Catholic in belief. No one was more surprised, however, than Newman when this fact became apparent.

After Newman became a Catholic—in fact, when he was accepting the Cardinalate in 1879—he exemplified the reasons literary critics have acclaimed him the ablest writer of exposition in the nineteenth century when defining Liberalism, man's exclusion of Christianity when attempting to solve the problem of life. "Liberalism in religion is the doctrine that there is no positive truth" in the field "but that one religion is as good as another. It is inconsistent with any recognition of any religion as *true*. It teaches that all are to be tolerated as all are matters of opinion. Revealed religion is not a truth, but a sentiment and a taste . . . and it is the right of each individual to make it say just what strikes his fancy. . . . It is as impertinent to think about a man's religion as about his sources of income or his management of his family. Religion is in no sense the bond of society. . . . Hitherto it has been considered that religion alone, with its supernatural sanctions, was strong enough to secure submission of the masses of our population to law and order; now the Philosophers and Politicians are bent on solving the problem without the aid of Christianity. . . . Instead of the Church's authority and teaching, they would submit first of all a universal and thoroughly secular education, calculated to bring home to every individual that to be orderly, industrious, and sober is his personal interest. . . . It would provide the broad fundamental ethical truths of justice, benevolence, veracity and the like; proud experience, . . . natural laws . . . or society, in social matters; whether physical or psychological . . . in government, trade, finance, sanitary experiments, and the intercourse of nations. As to Religion, it is a private luxury, which a man may have if he will; but which of course he must pay for, which he must not obtrude upon others, or indulge in to their annoyance."

In France, Felicité Robert de Lamennais had argued for authoritarian religion as a basis of social order and with the aid of such zealous helpers as Lacordaire, Montalambert, and Maurice de Guérin moulded an entire generation by spiritualizing Liberal teaching.

Nazism, rampant nationalism, racism, fascism, and Communism—all forms of totalitarianism, sprang luxuriantly from secular liberalism and nineteenth century middle-class industrialism. Christopher Dawson, the ablest current exponent of political philosophy (which must be based on religion) has shown that Communism, Nazism, Capitalism, and Liberal Democracy in Western civilization are actually three forms of the same theory, moving by different but parallel paths toward the same goal—mechanization of human life and complete subordination of the individual to the state and to the economic process. Christianity teaches that the State exists for the citizen. If the State becomes too totalitarian, the citizen has not been totalitarian enough. He has acquiesced in the secularization of life, allowed his own aims to be divided and his religion to become a sectarian affair—cut off from his real interests and real life.

Luther has been the evil genius of Germany and the source of Hitlerism and Nazism. Followers of Luther worshipped a god neither just nor merciful. The law of nature which should be the court of appeal against unjust authority is identified with the existing order of society, to which absolute obedience is due. Gloomy Dean Inge (*Time*, Nov. 6, 1944) hopes the next swing of the pendulum will end Luther's evil influence in Germany. To him may be attributed a contribution toward building and justifying the absolute state (Nazism) and toward building the modern capitalistic state in which man's energy is directed into a single channel of worldly achievement. Where the Renaissance had exalted the intellect, Luther attacked it as a vicious thing, where it had glorified free will, he had flatly denied it, and where the Renaissance had praised worldly human endeavor, he asserted that all human actions are essentially vicious. The completing of the so-called Reformation has been the depleting of religion and philosophy. Not until the great synthesis (broken in religion by Luther and in philosophy by Kant) is restored will philosophy and religion regain the democratic character both had before the Protestant Revolt.

The current anti-intellectualist shifting of the center of

human confidence from reason to sentiment began with the Reformation. The Nazi cult of violence which George Bernard Shaw encouraged pleads for dictatorship, the abolition of private property, and the right of government to exterminate recalcitrant minorities (anti-social elements so-called). Shaw was typical of the bourgeois intelligentsia that used to be standard bearers of Liberalism in the past but have not gone Communist. In Europe today Liberalism is a lost cause; in Germany Liberals have gone over to Communism; in other countries they drift to neo-paganism or tribal patriotism. The latest stand of "liberals" in our country was the signing of a round-robin protesting the ban against a magazine which had printed thoroughly false and defamatory statements about the Church. A metropolitan Board of Education refused to let such bigotry be fed to children in the schools. A senator, a rabbi, a judge, a Protestant bishop noted for bigotry, a novelist, the wife of a former President, the head of a school of education who had been pushed unsuccessfully for the superintendency of the school system, the "chancellor" of a university no longer in office—over a hundred in all lent their names to this charge of censorship and suppression of criticism. Later the magazine itself threw off all pretense of "liberalism" by suing another magazine for libel.

As a result of their training Catholics in America could learn from Columbus, in sharp contrast to the vagaries of the leaders of the Protestant Revolt and their spiritual descendants, to draw from a divine source strength of mind and constancy in bearing the sufferings which are man's lot—whether they be inflicted by the "learned" who have grasped power over their fellow men or result from religious persecution, infidelity of friends and companions, calumny, or perfidy. Like St. Francis, one becomes a troubadour of God by being bound irremovably to Christ. One would collapse under the daily struggle were he not buoyed up by an indelible consciousness of the purpose of his existence and the inspiration of a vivified slogan: the salvation of the multitude and greater glory of God.

Where religious leadership has failed, the Kingdom of Anti-Christ has flourished, re-introducing in harmful form the ideas it rejected in the teachings of the Catholic Church. Vicious dogmas, debasing moral standards, and will-to-world conquest have enslaved hundreds of millions of the world's inhabitants today. When a City of Man supplants The City of God, such horrors follow inevitably.

A Catholic sense makes clear-cut the distinction between right and wrong and helps its possessor to choose the right unerringly. The Ten Commandments, the Seven Capital Sins, and the Laws of the Church are unwavering criteria against which one can put his actions and know immediately whether, in the field of faith and morals, he is right or wrong. Such certitude convinces that the world's problems can be solved satisfactorily only on Christian principles.

CHAPTER TEN

Missionary Efforts

Knowledge of geography and past history can contribute greatly to current operation and future planning of Catholic education in America. The relation of education to history is close, for it is an educational problem to transmit the elements of culture and of institutional life found of value in the past. To that cultural heritage must be added the contribution of the present generation. While the problems of adjustment are perennial, the form differs.

Those who think the "American way of life" * something entirely new and vastly superior to that of any other people have been accused of wanting to make the entire world American. It would be a distinct handicap in dealing with other peoples to think that they (the Chinese, for example) grant that Western Civilization is superior to theirs; patently, it is comparatively young in comparison. Hindu youths remark the blunder in having them learn the language and other aspects of the heritage of the Occident if the Hindus or any other people are left ignorant of their own language and heritage. It would be short-sighted, too, were anyone to confuse what is ridiculed as America's missionic complex (wanting to make the world American) with the missionary spirit of Catholics, who know they have

* For added notes to this Chapter, see the Appendix.

the truth and want, in charity, to share it with less fortunate people.

If one Catholic made a convert a year and each made another in a year, in thirty-two years the world would be Catholic. If each Catholic made a convert a year and each convert acted likewise, the world would be Catholic in three years. Realization of that fact stimulated our Catholic College to sponsor a contest on "The Catholic College Student and the Post-war Mission of the Church."

The impact of soldiering and actual combat has made many young men think seriously about religion and about themselves, or, to put it another way, about God and about their souls. The chaplains testify to that.

In the camps many non-Catholic young men for the first time have been in close contact with real Catholics. By direct observation they have seen in many instances, the good example of Catholic boys. They have noted how much the Catholic religion means to their Catholic buddies. They have made the acquaintance of a Catholic priest—the chaplain.

In actual combat they have seen that chaplain at work —hearing confessions, giving Holy Communion, ministering to the wounded and the dying, saying Mass, when possible, up near the front. They have seen the Catholic faith stand up under fire. For they have witnessed its strengthening and consoling influences upon the Catholic lads in the midst of battle. They themselves have felt the need and sensed the value of prayer. They have come to a more personal appreciation of God because they have been so near to death.

In the post-war period, it seems safe to say, such men will present an opportunity for the grace of God and for our efforts to help them to become converts to the Catholic Church. In religion they will want to know the real thing. They will be in no mood for substitutes. They will be no challenge to God's grace. But they will be a challenge to our prayer, our example, and our knowledge of our faith. Conversion is a job for all Catholics; however, we know there are 900 counties in the United States without priests. Areas without priests take up about one fourth of our country particularly in the South. In all there are over five thousand villages, towns, cities without evidence of Catholicity.

Annually from January 18 (the Feast of St. Peter's Chair at Rome) until January 25 (the Feast of the Conversion of St. Paul) Catholics the world over unite in common supplication for the fulfillment of the Savior's prayer, "that they all may be one, as Thou, Father, in Me and I in Thee; that they also may be one in Us; that the world may believe that Thou hast sent Me."

The Holy Father has to support 97,758 missions in foreign fields, 42,000 elementary schools with 3,400,000 children, 4,000 high schools with six million students, 2,200 colleges and professional schools, 174 leprosaria with 33,000 lepers, 7,200 orphanages with 95,000 orphans, and 1,115 hospitals with 66,000 beds.

*　　*　　*

No soul is unimportant; so Americans must direct effort toward creating leadership for the minorities in our nation—Catholics, Negroes, Puerto Ricans, and Indians, for example. In the early Christian centuries lay men and women helped the Apostles, Saints (Sebastian, Agnes, Cecilia, Tiburtius, Tarcisius) inspirited their fellow men. Pope Pius X warned, "No one can be an Apostle who does not first possess the virtues of a Christian." Good example before all else will attract others to our religion, for persons are persuaded more by our daily living than by what we say. On the contrary, uncharitable actions can discourage those seeking the Faith and, as a deterrent, by that obstacle put off the conversion of the world. Attractive meeting places for recreation and social experiences must be provided for handicapped groups if they are to become good citizens. The light of inter-racial education can lead minority groups out of the darkness of bitterness and frustration.

Barriers between races in our country are deplorable and ugly. Catherine Cate Coblentz's *Sequoya* presents attractively for adolescents the biography of a great Indian who not only lent his name to our largest trees, but developed an alphabet for the Cherokee language and stood out from a minority group which struggled unsuccessfully against unfair aggression. Fortunately, legislation designed to end Federal supervision of Indian life has been introduced in Congress. Patently, before we are ready to handle subject peoples in Europe, Asia, we could practice long-overdue charity by improving conditions among the Indians. Forty thousand of them handled industrial war jobs, twenty-five thousand fought in the armed forces in World War II. Catholics particularly should carry on the tradition of the Religious who for two centuries have not only Christianized Indians but have taught on Reservations and ministered to these only Americans who are not descendants of immigrants.

News of the one hundred fiftieth anniversary of the founding of the Mission of San Fernando Rey (San Fernando, California, 1947) will help us realize how much longer the Indians have been Americans than we have.

In its century and a half of existence the mission has turned almost a complete cycle—development, ruin, decay, then almost complete restoration. The first Mass in the area was offered September 8, 1797, by a Franciscan, Father Lasuen. Another Franciscan, Father Dumetz, served. The same day Father Lasuen baptized ten Indian children. Only fourteen years later, the Franciscans had in their care 1,081 neophytes.

The first church, built four months after the missioners' arrival, was too small only two years later. A second church was built and served until 1806, when the present structure, seating five hundred, was dedicated. From every point of view the mission was a success. Spiritually, practically every Indian to the crest of the San Gabriel Mountains had been converted. In 1803 Chief Pirubit was converted and brought 361 with him.

After the revolt of Mexico from Spain in 1810, the repercussions hit the Mission hard. From 1811 to 1846 its story is one of tyranny and robbery on the part of the soldiers, spoliation, and enslavement of the Indians. The padre in charge at the time, Father Francisco Gonzales de Ibarra, protested again and again, but always in vain. The Indians escaped to the canyons and in 1834 only a hundred were left at the mission.

When the Americans came, in 1846, General Fremont restored the mission to the care of the padres, pending court action to determine its true ownership. In 1862 President Lincoln confirmed the findings of a Federal court and the property was restored to the Church.

Restoration of the buildings was undertaken by the Landmark Club and the monastery was repaired and a temporary roof placed on the church in time for the centennial in 1897. In 1923 the Oblates were given charge of the parish and the restoration progressed rapidly until today most of the buildings are again in full use.

D'Arcy McNickle's *They Came Here First* is a thoroughly documented manual, imperative reading for every student of American history because based on geological anthropological, archeological, and historical evidence. It avoids the romantic and is patiently objective in presenting the American spoliation of the Indians. Our courts are given full credit for protecting the Indian, as are the Spanish Court (despite some vacillation), the Popes (the papal pronouncement *Sublimis Deus*), Father La Casas, O.P., the Jesuits and their model republic in Paraguay, as well as the Franciscans and other missionaries.

Shirley Graham's *There Was Once a Slave* (the heroic

and romantic life of Frederick Douglass) etches like acid
our responsibility toward those descendants of slaves whom
some Americans abuse or take advantage of. Molders of
public opinion (writers, newspaper men and women, and
radio commentators) can help tremendously in channeling
the fact that racial segregation is unnecessary, stupid, and
thoroughly wrong.

Carnegie Corporation and the Rockefeller Foundation
have made possible a five-year program of education, training and research in race relations at the University of Chicago. The objectives are:

1. To organize a program of research designed to develop and
test significant theories concerning race relations; and to build
a scientific foundation for policies, programs, and methods of
operation in the field.

2. To infuse authentic knowledge concerning race relations
and minority problems into the curricula of general education
and of adult education, and to develop methods of effective
teachings and learning in the field.

3. To provide advanced professional training for leaders and
practitioners in the field of race relations and minority problems.

4. To establish a plan of co-operative training and research
with other universities and research agencies throughout the
country, to the end that the more important agencies will be
drawn into a more concerted program.

5. To institute pilot programs to test newly discovered knowledge and techniques in inter-group relation, and to develop
scientific procedures for evaluating existing programs.

The American Council on Race Relations, a national
service agency for organizations dealing with this subject,
is co-operating with the University's Committee on race relations.

Three other University units also are co-operating with
the committee: The Industrial Relations Center, which is
concerned with the problems of labor relations; the Com-

mittee on Communications, which is primarily concerned
with the analysis of public opinion and mass media of communication; and the Committee on Human Development,
which is studying the development of personality, the genesis
of attitudes in children and youth, and human behavior.
The Committee will seek the co-operation also of other
universities and research agencies throughout the country.

A feature of the committee's program will be publication
of a set of manuals, affecting the practice of public officials
and private groups on race relations and minority problems.

Catholic schools, which lack the funds for such studies,
can adopt the findings as recorded in the manuals and discover what the Catholic contribution can be to the solution
of those problems which seem insoluble because of a purely
material approach.

*   *   *

UNESCO, the United Nations Educational, Scientific,
and Cultural Organization, is reported as having secured the
following evidence in regard to race equality: (1) Mental
capacity in all races is pretty much the same. (2) The
mixture of the races produces no biologically bad results.
(3) Superiority of race to race is less a fact than a myth.
(4) Scientifically speaking, no large modern national or
religious group is a race. It looks as though we are all alike
under the skin.

Although only three per cent of the Negroes in the
United States are Catholic, in all parts of the country the
Colored look to the Church to solve the problems of racial
unity in the spirit of Christ's charity. Unfortunately, some
Negroes have been ensnared by the promises of Communism; but since Communism denies God, and there can be
no natural rights (of freedom and the dignity of the individual, for example) without God, as always Communist
promises are not kept. The Church, in contrast, teaches
today and forever the Divine principle that, despite colors
or races, we are all brothers in the Mystical Body of Christ.

When Latin-American fraternities in Catholic colleges celebrate Pan-American Day they may well recall that the first free schools in what is now the United States were founded in Florida by Spanish missionaries. The oldest university in America (St. Mark's, Lima, Peru) is Catholic, founded in 1551 (over a half century before the first English settlement at Jamestown and eighty-five years before Harvard College opened. The library of St. Mark's was famous, its parchment books and records worn with use, its graduates known on two continents for science, literature, theology, and medicine, and law centuries before the United States had a public school system. (A book in Latin on mining, with covers of iron, was chained to the altar in the cathedral at San Luis Potosi. The chain prevented the book's being lost; a priest read from the book to miners and the methods used in metallurgical working spread up through Mexico to the famous Comstock Lode, Nevada.)

Pope Pius V founded St. Mark's and its undergraduates were creating poetry in French and Spanish and writing Latin prose before New York City existed. The Library at Lima was the first public library in the New World. A catechism (still preserved in the Library) was the first book published from the first printing press set up in the New World. These publishers knew that Catholic principles were not only the foundation but the guarantee of the survival of western civilization. As an example of how well grounded we find that civilization in South America today, there are fewer divorces in the entire continent than in Chicago—and the family is the cell of Christianity.

No question about the zeal of Catholic missionaries in the New World—a Catholic made the first settlement in New England, a priest conducted the first religious services there, and the first Indian converts there were baptized in the Catholic faith. (Too many people associate the Pilgrims or the Puritans with "firsts" in New England.) Catholic priests conducted the first religious services (celebrating the Mass) in Alabama, Arizona, Florida, Kansas, Louisiana, Mississippi, New Mexico, and Virginia. And yet the Navajo Indians in the United States have no public school—two-thirds of the children are neglected.

Politicians have encouraged Puerto Ricans to swell the number of voters in a metropolis and, having put them on relief rolls, abandon them to the desperation with which these fellow citizens struggle to survive in the most wretched section of the city. A soft-voiced, well-mannered student, with a better economic chance than the rest of his family because of an uncle, a physician, who employs him part time, felt keenly the pushing around his people got. While many Puerto Ricans are Negroes, the American Negro is treated better than the Spanish Puerto Ricans with their clipped speech, a proud and sensitive people whose good points are presented attractively in *Readers' Digest*, January, 1949 ("Puerto Rico Fights Back"). They are thirsty for knowledge, try hard, pick up basic skills with unbelievable deftness, react marvelously to responsibility, repay an employer's good opinion of them, and fight back against what has long been accepted as an impossible dilemma—a prolific birthrate and a stagnant economy.

Like all Latin America the extractive economy of Puerto Rico tends to destroy subsistence while the death rate has been reduced sharply. Again, as in all Latin America (except Brazil and Argentina) the internal markets (the people's purchasing power) cannot increase much because of the land's low carrying capacity. Lack of coal prevents much industrialization and the sources of electric power are so far distant as to be almost unreachable.

The life story of a forgery spreading calumnies about the priesthood in South America was exposed in *Catholic Mind* (1912 volume, pp. 165 ff.). After two years' persistent correspondence the character laughingly acknowledged that although he was a well-to-do lawyer and member of decent family of social position, as a diversion he wrote such letters under a pen name. (Charitably he could be classed as paranoiac.)

The regime ruling Guatemala oppresses Catholics—about one priest for eighty thousand people; foreign priests (but not ministers) are barred. Marriage is lightly regarded. More than one and a half times as many children run wild as are in school. Church property has been confiscated.

Anti-Catholic politicians have been busy in the Philippines. Despite what Dominican and other Catholic missionaries did for those people centuries ago when they were benighted, all children in public high schools must read before graduation a specific anti-Catholic book (printed by a leading "reputable" New York publisher, and written by an anti-Catholic about a retracted Mason—his retraction denied but Church records prove it.) In February, 1951, new laws aimed at Catholic schools and other institutions were passed.

South of the border a criticism and hostility against us as exploiters ("dollar diplomacy") has not been softened by the stupid selection of most of the good-will representatives sent to Latin and South America. "The Colossus of the North" is now seen through Communist eyes as "imperialistic"—not because of desire for territorial extension to the south, but because USSR has been blocked in Korea or in Germany or on the Danube and in the Balkans. The Pan-Slav movement which Russia has encouraged officially in Chile, Argentina, Uruguay, Paraguay, and Brazil is analogous to a former Pan-German drive, which ended disastrously in World War II.

Anything which we can do to arouse a leadership in these countries which will raise the standard of living for the lower classes and overcome black markets and inflation will lessen the discontent Communism exploits wherever there is economic bankruptcy. We lack such leadership here at home; so we cannot be too successful in the matter abroad. However, Catholic missions—with no material gain in view—

can do heroic work in real education and training the exploited to carry their burdens more satisfactorily. Even in St. Paul's time, pricking against the goad was not helpful; but consciousness that after they had known Christ and Him crucified they lived through Him and He through them has given the heavily burdened new zeal in working for an eternal reward.

Realizing that, in order not to be irrelevant, material for background must be as pertinent to the matter at hand as are the specific facts enriching our thinking in a particular unit, we would not include material on South America, China, Japan, India, and Africa at this juncture merely because we excluded them when discussing ancient education. Since they bore no relation to our Hebraic and Hellenic heritage, they were omitted. We turn to them now principally because they are the fields of major missionary endeavor and we cannot succeed with them unless we make Christian what they have already. To attempt to force on them an occidental civilization is to waste effort. We have seen how Christianity elevated, purified, and absorbed the pagan customs of ancient Greece and Rome and the tribal procedures of the invaders, which were merely crude acceptances of natural law.

Centuries ago China's state system of education was rigidly uniform; in fact, this secular education trained pedantically for state purposes only. The competitive tests were the goal; the demands were regulated to the minutest detail. Free play of the mind was not worth anything. Aesthetic and spiritual ideas, the simplest elements of humanity, the possibility that a teacher or an inspector could err—all these were anathema. Even today with the Chinese character or letter meaning honest or good goes a sly suggestion of slow-wittedness.

Since literature and government were the only professions other than the army, unsound and unworthy motives for education fixed the objectives. Preparation for the examinations excluded all else. Any possibility of a resuscitation of the advancement of the very earliest Chinese was always killed by Confucius' influence through ancestor worship. Had it not been thought sacrilegious to advance farther than one's ancestor, the Chinese might well have taken on western civilization as rapidly as did the Japanese—even though we are appalled at the latter's assumption of every occidental unpleasant characteristic. Homely wisdom was characteristic of Confucius' philosophy even more markedly than it was of the Greek Epictetus and the Roman Marcus Aurelius. So great is Chinese veneration of Confucius that they never forgave the League of Nations for slicing off Shantung, the birthplace and shrine of Confucius, at the Peace Conference following World War I—and giving it to Japan.

Our chief concern in the educational interests and procedures in Africa, Latin America, China, Japan, and India lies in their possibilities as mission fields. Tragically, the United States has refused to help China's Government fight the Communists. The country was sacrificed because Communist sympathizers in our Government did a good job. We got Japan out of China only to stand by while Russia takes over. The calamity does, however, give opportunity for heroic missionaries.

The Catholic Church in China maintained the astounding total of 14,000 schools; not parochial schools, but Government schools, conforming fully to the regulations of the Chinese Minister of Education.

Because of the large number of men formerly in the United States Armed Forces who have asked to join the Maryknoll Society for the foreign missions, a specially adapted course of studies has been arranged for servicemen. Many applicants have written that they want to become missionaries after the work they have seen in Korean mission fields, where their war service has taken them. The prayer of the Catholics of the new China is: "God re-vitalize China and begin with me."

The foregoing paragraphs indicated only the Catholic educational achievements in China of the glorious past. What should and would the Catholic Mission in China do in matter of education after the conclusion of the present devastating war? Will it devote all its energy exclusively in relief work, in taking care of abandoned babies or orphanages, leper asylums, catechumenates, or be devoted to purely spiritual exercises?

The answer must be an emphatic NO. To justify this statement, there are the following reasons:

1. Teaching is one of the essential functions of the Catholic Church. Thus, so long as the Church exists or wherever she sets her foot, her responsibility in matters of education shall always remain. To some of the human society, certain programs or functions must come to an end because the war has ended, but the Catholic Church's function in education will not be terminated until the consummation of the world. So, it is evident that in postwar period the Catholic education in China which has had a well-recognized reputation in the prewar days should be continued.

2. China is not only the oldest nation in the world; she is also the only living and integral ancient civilization of today. To convert the primitive people in central Africa, an act of Christian charity or human understanding might be sufficient to serve as an effective motive or impulse; but to convert the Chinese, it is absolutely necessary to prove to them the different arguments concerning the existence of God, the existence of an immortal and spiritual soul, the soundness and truthfulness of the Catholic Church, and the divine Redemption of our Lord. To achieve these objectives, there is a definite need of education.

3. Enemies of the Church from many directions, taking full advantage of the present war condition, are seeking

every opportunity to minimize the Church's influence, to spread rumors against the Church, and to carry both the individual and society away from the truth, the principle of justice, and, above all, from the true light of faith and the spirit of Christ's charity. China is no exception. Thus, if the Catholic Church in China is going to be expanded and the four hundred fifty million souls be given the opportunity to know and worship their true God, educational work should, no doubt, be taken as one of the most effective means in achieving the Church's supreme goals in the post-war period. Ancient China once worshipped One Supreme Being whom they called "The King of Heaven." Later, ministering gods and hundreds of spirits were added and superstitions and cultism dominated. To bring China back to originally true knowledge and worship of God and to convince her people of the doctrine and grace of Redemption, Catholic education has the safe and fruitful way in this land of ancient culture and Oriental humanism.

Typical of how work among the colored thrives is an "Experiment in Understanding" which describes St. Peter Claver Center for children, in Seattle, Washington. Few are the Religious Orders who are not succeeding in such work; their stories may be located through the *Catholic Periodical Index*.

Baroness de Hueck continues to establish Friendship Houses. Following her initial successes in Harlem (New York City), on Highway 18, two miles beyond Victorville, California, the Murrays opened a summer camp for colored children, which has become the only Negro Dude Ranch.

On January 26, 1947, William Rose Benet wrote to the New York *Times* commending their editorial on the Segregation Number of the *Survey* but calling attention to the horrible conditions under which his family helper, a woman of highest character and respectability, of middle age and of a naturally cheerful disposition, has to live in Harlem. Such conditions breed intense and festering dissatisfaction and cynicism, if not lawlessness and crime. When, however, new housing units are erected, Catholic day nurseries and parochial schools (a high school too much to hope for?) became so crowded that waiting lists of 250 names line up for the twenty-four placed allowed by law. Nor is there a turn-over of twenty-five annually in that Harlem Day Nursery; the child who gets in may stay five years. All Catholic agencies should be eager to help in such a worthy cause—never to let red tape block any possible solution.

Because of his personal interest in the problem, particularly while under the editorship of Father La Farge, *America* championed the Negro cause. Commenting on a deplorable situation in southwest Chicago where two priests were pelted by ignorant Catholics and other vicious un-Americans, this Jesuit weekly reported they were heartened to read of the stand taken by Monsignor Reynold Hillenbrand and Father Daniel M. Cantwell in the tense situation which exists in Chicago as a result of the opposition of white tenants to the Chicago Housing Authority's inter-racial policy. Their insistence on a Christian attitude toward the houseless Negro is all the more welcome, since it is reported not only that Catholics were prominent in the opposition but that even a priest was found to be supporting them in their highly un-Catholic attitude. Similar reports came from Buffalo and Detroit, also centers of tension.

Catholic opposition to the equitable sharing of the nation's housing facilities with the colored race could come only from ignorance or disregard of the clearly expressed mind of the Pope and the hierarchy. In his very first encyclical Pope Pius XII pointed out racism as one of the two errors that most threaten the world today and "make peace among nations precarious, uncertain, and well-nigh impossible. It consists in losing sight of that kinship and love which ought to bind human beings to one another, in virtue of their common origin, their common nature and their common redemption in the blood of Christ. When speaking directly to the American Hierarchy, the Holy Father mentioned "a special paternal affection, which is certainly inspired of Heaven, for the Negro dwelling among you." What he would say to Catholics who violently exclude their Negro fellow citizens from a chance for decent housing— and what he would say to a priest should he aid and abet them—one can imagine.

These happenings in Chicago, Buffalo, and Detroit—and there are the potentialities of similar incidents in many other cities—show a deep and widespread ignorance among Catholics of the true nature of the racist heresy and its manifestations in America. While the Catholic Interracial Councils and other Catholic bodies are doing heroic work, there is need of much more, if a serious danger to the Church in America is to be avoided. The race question in the United States is intimately bound up with Catholic dogma and Catholic moral teaching; and it is complicated by human passions uncontrolled.

Diocesan papers reported papal honors for Eleanor N. Figaro of Lafayette, Louisiana, who has spent forty of her sixty years in the cause of religion for members of her race. What the colored have accomplished in that See city is remarkable. The first Catholic Negro woman has been appointed to the post of probation officer of Kings County Court, Brooklyn. Since entering the Church a few years ago, she has been a leader in social and youth activities at St. Peter Claver's Church, where she is director of the Claverettes, an organization of girls of sixteen to twenty-one years. She has also been head counselor of Camp Claver at Wading River, L.I., and for a year and a half was social worker with the Little Flower Institute there. One of the leaders in the social work program at St. Peter Claver's parish, Miss Dublin served for fifteen years with the Urban League, ten years of which she was engaged in court work. She is also active in the Big Sisters' Movement. Her appointment would please Booker T. Washington, the Apostle of

Goodwill, Walter White, and Lester B. Granger, Executive Secretary of the National Urban League, which is laboring heroically to further industrial training for the American Negro, a critical situation with no sign of improvement. In this educational area Catholic schools are needed tragically.

Newspaper reports of the first Negro to play with a white college (Duquesne U.—Catholic) team at Louisville, Kentucky, recall Jackie Robinson's entrance into Big League ball on the Brooklyn Dodgers line-up. But in the same week (and on Christmas Eve) we read of the University of Tennessee basketball team refusing, in the presence of twenty-six hundred fans, to play Duquesne if the colored player was included.

How displeasing to our Common Father it must be to see segregation within churches. A Protestant Federal Council of Churches appealed for an ending of this pattern. Putting it on a purely natural basis, the appeal emphasized that we cannot believe in a master race and at the same time uphold democratic principles of equality. The Soviet upcasts that we talk Four Freedoms and still have lynchings and riots, the Ku Klux Klan and political brigands looting public treasuries with unbelievable greed.

Christ's admonition that we love our neighbor (and even our enemy) will solve minority problems, but segregation will not—it arouses prejudice, hatred, and mob violence. To improve intergroup relations Americans must oppose movements and agencies that are divisive and foster an economy that will feed, clothe, and house every American, regardless of national origin, color, or religious beliefs. Paying equal wages to all who meet the requirements of character and skill and providing sufficient employment without discrimination is a national as well as a Christian must. This idea applies also to rulings of the United Nations Assembly in regard to colonial peoples.

Annually during the week which includes Lincoln's Birthday New York City celebrates Negro History Week. Hailing the oustanding contributions made by Negro Americans to the cultural, scientific, educational, political, and industrial life of the nation and their assistance in building a free post-war world, the Mayor's proclamation stresses the importance of these achievements in minimizing racial hatreds. Negro History Week is a period dedicated to celebrating the accomplishments of Negro Americans and of drawing nation-wide attention to their progress. Schools, libraries, and other public bodies and institutions are requested by the Mayor to conduct proper observances of Negro History Week through classroom lectures, displays, and other public functions.

The Schomburg Collection of Negro Literature is available at the New York Public Library with conducted tours and direction for individual students interested in race relations here or abroad. One of the largest and most important libraries on the Negro, it contains twelve thousand books, three thousand manuscripts, two thousand etchings, several thousand pamphlets, and is growing continuously. Newspapers from Africa, the West Indies, and all parts of the United States are available; and authors and specialists in Negro studies lecture publicly in the library.

This collection represents the life work of Arthur Alfonso Schomburg, a great American collector. Schomburg, of Negro descent, was born in San Juan, Puerto Rico, in 1874. He searched the book marts in Latin America, Western Europe, and the United States for materials on the Negro.

In 1926 the Carnegie Corporation presented the collection to the New York Public Library. It was placed at the 135th Street Branch in the heart of Harlem. Schomburg served as curator until his death, June 10, 1938.

The literature of the Schomburg Collection is devoted not only to the Negro in the United States but takes in every section of the globe where black folk have lived in considerable numbers. Thus Africa, the West Indies, Brazil, and other regions in South America are represented. The Haitian Collection is perhaps the best in this country.

The writings of European Negroes found in this library are distinguished by Alexander Pushkin's poems, Jacobus Capitein's Latin thesis, Dumas' novels and the various editions of the autobiography of Gustavus Vassa.

The work of many of the major and minor American Negro writers is here—treatments of war, peace, politics, labor, history, science and folklore. Some of the rare items include textbooks from the Republic of Liberia and grammars of the various African languages. The collection has recently been enriched by the acquisition of over three hundred scripts of radio programs: the eighty-one manuscript volumes of the field notes and memoranda used by Gunnar Myrdal in writing *An American Dilemma: The Negro Problem and Modern Democracy*, the Eric de Kolb collection of African arms and war weapons, and the extensive Harry A. Williamson library on the Negro in Masonry. On display are choice samples of African ivory, metal, and woodwork.

Catholics will enjoy particularly a biography of George W. Carver. Anne Parrish has presented Harriet Tubman sympathetically in *Clouded Star*. Martha Foley includes in *Best Short Stories for* 1946 Irwin Stark's "The Bridge," which presents the horrible conditions under which some of the colored attend public school in Harlem. Some compensation for the indifference to our colored brethren appears in authors' fascination with the problem. If the situation has improved little since the Emancipation Proclamation, our tears should be shed not for the Negro, but for ourselves and our children. We are responsible.

When announcing Holy Year (1950) Pope Pius XII listed as intentions (a) defense of the Church against renewed attacks of the enemy and (b) prayers for peace.

In preparation for the first, Catholics (a) sanctify their souls through prayer and penitence and unshakable faith in Christ and the Church, (b) defend the Church against attack and implore true faith for those who have lost faith, for those who have not received the Gift, and for the Godless, and (c) strive for social justice through assisting the humble and needy. The additional preparation demanded action for peace and the safeguarding of the Holy Places in Palestine.

Political machinations in the United Nations as regards the Holy Land and other parts of the globe will bear close attention. An editorial on their hypocritical stand on Spain emphasizes San Francisco's good fortune in missing election as home of the U.N. as it now is because it could bring little but contamination to the land of the Spanish missions and Franciscan padres, who came from Spain. Talk of a world superstate (the United States of Europe) or one in the western hemisphere (Pan-America and the United States) arouses hostility among the purely European nations, as it does in Argentina and Brazil. What is referred to as Pan-America is not a self-contained community of like-minded republics, nor would such a Union succeed those countries included because of geography and history join it. Unfortunately we cannot build from the Monroe Doctrine, a citadel of safety for the nations of the Western Hemisphere and for the liberty and democracy we cherish.

CHAPTER ELEVEN

Integration Through the Liturgy

The history of Catholic education in the United States reveals factors contributing to the advance of human development to a more balanced and complete life for everyone whose life is integrated through the liturgy and the interrelationship of those factors which regard the soul most highly and respect personality. The relationship between the Creator and the individual soul is different in every instance and ideally that creature who most perfectly mirrors God has the finest personality. Just as the sun shining through stained-glass windows reveals their meaning in every detail, so the Christ burgeoning from the *alter Christus*.

In making adjustments one must face his own day; so when our consideration reverts to the Ages of Faith it is not with wistful renunciation. It is to follow the colorful threads in the tapestry of current life which have come down to us directly from the twelfth and thirteenth centuries. At that time were founded religious orders of men and women teaching in many American cities today. Public education cannot hope to get back on the right course until it goes back to St. Thomas (thirteenth century) to pick up continuity with educators of that time (which will include all those the history of education records as having intrinsic interest for Catholic education in the United States today).

Public education must get the concept of training the child as the object not as the center of education.

The Protestant theologian de Rougemont acknowledges that all the culture of the West—music, painting, philosophy and literature—came out of the churches and convents. Non-Catholic writers, such as Arthur Machen, have declared that beauty finds its source in the liturgy; Augustine Birrell contended: "It is the Mass that matters." Today we still sing St. Bernard of Clairvaux's "Jesu Dulcis Memoria," Thomas of Celano's "Dies Irae" (the Sequence of the Requiem Mass) and Jacapone da Todi's "*Stabat Mater*" (the Sequence of the Mass for the Feast of the Seven Sorrows of the Blessed Mother). Every Friday during Lent students in Catholic schools sing the "Stabat Mater" as they make the Way of the Cross. (In their reading they are inspired by Helen C. White's exposition of the relationship between St. Francis of Assisi and Jacapone da Todi in *A Watch in the Night*. They are awed by reading that Jacapone da Todi's life was changed diametrically as was St. Francis from pursuit of pleasure to championing God by becoming the slave of Christ—when he discovered through his wife's death upon collapse of a platform from which she was viewing a spectacular Mardi Gras, that she wore a hairshirt. (Did he contribute in any way to her feeling of necessity for such penance?)

Richer is the students' association with five hymns in which St. Thomas Aquinas summarizes the theology of the Eucharist: "Adore Te Devote," "Pange Lingua" (two stanzas of which are the "Tantum Ergo" sung each time at Benediction of the Blessed Sacrament), "Lauda Sion" (Sequence for the Mass of Corpus Christi), "Sacris Solemniis" (of which part is "O Salutaris Hostia"—Benediction hymn, which with "Tantum Ergo Sacramentum" students are accustomed to sing at Vespers.

Sensory training the Church carried over objectively into liturgy and art as we do today. The finest specimens of ecclesiastical architecture bear this point out vividly. A study of the parish church often may serve as an introduction to the symbolism of Church art; it may be a source of deepened devotion; it may help to strengthen one's inner life, for everything within is planned to gather and focus the mind upon one's ultimate goal in life—the Beatific Vision (seeing God face to face).

Not only have some of the greatest composers used Gregorian Chant melodies in their compositions, in a popular motion picture ("Come to the Stable") the friend of young composer who has been antagonistic to displaced Sisters building a hospital near his estate points out that his most popular composition is a direct steal from a hymn the Sisters have been singing for ages.

The history of English literature acquaints students with the fact that our drama grew out of the "Quem quaeritis?" of the liturgy and that the drama moved first from the sanctuary to the church porch. Catholics know that St. Thomas' *Summa Theologica* is still used as a basic text in our seminaries. The history of education records that the fine arts held an important place in popular education more than eight centuries ago.

Reading and discussion, as well as lectures on history and biography, can reveal our rights and liberties and the accomplishments of spiritual ancestors who won them for us. Columbus' first name means Christ-bearer. The Dominican, Las Casas, was protector of the Indians. Charles Carroll of Carrollton (brother of the Archbishop) signed the Declaration of Independence with his address—so the King of England would have no difficulty locating him. Roger Taney, first Chief Justice of the Supreme Court, took his place in the line waiting for Confession and said to those who suggested that he step ahead of others, "Before this tribunal I have no more rights than any other person." Father Marquette, St. Isaac Jogues, and numerous others referred to help inspiringly to create and preserve American liberties the more zealously because they maintained our most precious treasure, the pearl of Faith.

When discussing the emotional life of Catholics we might have considered what lifts them out of the ordinary rut of human existence. Emotion suggests a strong feeling or impulse toward overt action, an implication of more forceful response than feeling, which may be merely appreciative recognition. Among the stoic or pagan philosophers such as Epictetus or Marcus Aurelius one finds devout meditations on life from the standpoint of purely natural virtue, and even today there are many good people who shun what they would call spiritual ebullience. (We know that Quietism was condemned as a heresy.) To them the intense inner life of the Catholic mystic is beyond comprehension, as are the affection and sympathetic response—even aesthetically—of Catholics to the Divine Romance. (Granted, with Gerard Groote, author of *The Imitation of Christ,* that it is better to feel compunction than to be able to define it; nevertheless this sensitivity we have been discussing does not mean an emotional intoxication—any more than one must *feel* sorrow for sin. The will is free, and students learn that God wants willingness to amend one's life. No matter what the imagination or the memory suggest, if the will is right, with the help of God's grace one can amend.)

Further interest in the Ages of Faith here lies in the fact that during the so-called Middle Ages (a term to be avoided because the exoteric think of the period as a gap between an ancient classical period and the revival of interest in the classics during the Renaissance) people's lives were integrated through the liturgy. The communal worship of God so regulated their living that such problems as shorter hours, a shorter week, and lay-off periods of seasonal unemployment were taken care of when one assisted at Mass daily (the center of daily life and Christian love) and celebrated the Holy Days and Sunday without servile work.

By avoiding the term "Middle Ages" and the trite divisions of history into ancient, medieval and modern, we evade the suggestion that the Ages of Faith were a dark, ugly, or chaotic pit or merely a narrow passageway through ignorance and superstition. From the conversion of St. Wilfred (680) to the Acts of Supremacy and Uniformity under Elizabeth (1557), the nine centuries between the acme of early Greek and Roman culture and the blight known as the modern age of Enlightenment, communal worship of God and religion as the dominating force of daily life, permeated family life, work, art, and group living, each century continuing the Catholic tradition and passing on the Catholic heritage.

As one phase of integrating life through the liturgy (our communal worship of God) in Catholic schools students learn that children of the Creator and members of the Mystical Body of Christ injure self if they harm one of their brethren. Christ is the Vine; His brethren the branches. By sharing the knowledge that the solution of social problems will be found in Christian principles, Catholic students learn an individual responsibility for spreading knowledge of these principles. Charity demands, just as it makes clear there are no superior races, that accidents of birth—color, race, social or economic position—affect no one's standing in the eyes of the Creator. Moreover, while the Church is trustee of absolute truth, not everyone who calls himself a Catholic is.

Divine life through participation is the liturgical goal. The peace that came on earth to men of good will on the first Christmas can return annually as the cycle of the liturgy unfolds. Consideration of the effects upon a pagan world of His coming inspirits us anew with the hope and courage that lent light to the world that first night of the Christian era. The fact that in the Mystical Body we are an integral part of Him and His mission, united with Him intimately and personally, would quicken our determination to help save our civilization and enliven our personal living.

By means of the liturgy all the year around the Church sets before us various aspects of Christ's life and the virtues of the Saints. That method of teaching is effective because when following the liturgy we are not mere spectators at this drama of salvation; we actually take part in it. The primary goal of our Apostolate is not, then, to bring to our minds, for instance, the historical life of Christ but to give us divine life through participation. Pursuing the cycle annually leads to our gaining the inspiration of Christ through our understanding of all He has done for us; and our Apostolate will reach its highest level and bear its richest fruit when we lead the Faithful as well as those outside the Fold to draw inspiration and strength from the mysteries of Christ as re-lived by the Church in her liturgical year—when Christ will have been found increasingly in their souls.

If those who should appreciate the liturgy remain ignorant of it and of its impact, a century may pass before the Movement will be successful; and yet the liturgical concept is not difficult to grasp. The creature should be able to see that praise, honor, and glory is due the Creator, that the liturgy is the Church—it is Christ, and that the chief function of Christ's Body (the Church) is to continue His life. The Church should direct all Christian activities; therein lies the essence of the liturgy, the means whereby continuance of Christ-life in us (His members) is developed and brought to function in a Catholic Apostolate.

To combat the paganism breaking in upon our civilization, there must be a renewal of Christianity; and it must come through Christ and be in and by Christ. The liturgy furnishes the means for accomplishing this restoration; therefore we must go back to the liturgy—to the comprehension of the mysteries it brings before us throughout the liturgical year, to the sacrifice of the Mass (which is its center and heart), to the doctrine of Christ which it preaches, to its prayers, and to the Sacraments, above all to Holy Com-

munion, which is Christ's way of communicating His divine
life to us and of renewing us in Him.

By their training of young women to turn the world to
Christian principles and ways of acting, the Grail School
(Loveland, Ohio), for example, are focusing one phase of
Catholic activity lest it be ineffective through scattered aims.
These women teachers include in their personal apostolate
such public places as night clubs and race tracks. The
Legion of Mary and the priest workmen in France and
Germany are doing the same type of channeling of serious
effort in a positive way—using love and justice (rather
than hate and oppression). These groups give no basis for
calling Catholic "anti." Those Catholics who contend that
Communism arose because Christians did not solve social
problems (the laissez-faire and rugged individualism of a
world dominated by Capitalism deprived the laboring classes
of a living wage) want the world to know the Church's
positive social program, which encourages individualism
without radicalism and put first things first. They are not
thinking of the dictators in the Kremlin and other countries
but of the hungry and the disillusioned, staggering under
want, intolerance, and injustice who turn to Communism
because it is new. Catholic schools avoid spreading hate of
Communists, train the young in practical ways of resisting
it and its spread, and arouse all students to overcome the
social lag which has brought about the dissatisfaction of
the poor, of those oppressed economically, politically, and
socially. Those who would overthrow our government, those
who would plunge the world into revolution will lack followers if the downtrodden see a democratic way of life
operating successfully and fairly, if Christianity is really
tried.

To give students a concrete concept of their role in society, of the meaning of divine life through participation,

in *Readings for Catholic Action* we included such ideas as follow: The purpose of Catholic training should not be to organize new societies to overcome prejudice, hatred, injustice, deprivation, insecurity, and fear; it should be to breathe a new Apostolic soul into units now existing or impart to them a new soul—the Apostolic ideal. "If one member of the Mystical Body suffer anything, all the members suffer it; if one member gain glory, all the members rejoice" (I Cor. 12:26).

Men must be attracted to Christ, if they are to be transformed in Him and renewed in Him. He must be made so attractive to them that they will turn to Him and adhere to Him. Specific illustrations of these truths may lose their point as time passes, but students can find new opportunities and instances daily.

When the liturgy had the heart taken out of it by the so-called Reformation, Protestant worship disintegrated. The more the ceremonies commemorative of the Incarnation and the Redemption are neglected or disappear, the more religion disintegrates and disappears. So long as they understand the liturgy, men will love it and Christ—nourished by all the expressive beauty of text and ceremony and song which the most ardent love of His most devoted disciples has woven about the commemorative act through the centuries. This act (the Mass and Holy Communion) is also a communicating of Himself to His disciples by giving His flesh to eat and His blood to drink. Their abiding in Him and He in them makes possible the constant renewal of man in Christ.

"Abide in Me and I in you. As the branch cannot bear fruit of itself unless it abide in the vine, so neither can you unless you abide in Me" (John 15:4). There is no difficulty in seeing that the human race is largely a unit in so far as common weaknesses, blindness in regard to the True Light, and futility in the pursuit of pleasure characterize it. Its needs and sufferings are common to all. The solution of its problems should, then, be that which can be applied to all. The liturgy is the only real solution for the social disunion which threatens civilization because it would bring all men back to Christ and His teachings; it is the most effective concrete system for uniting men.

A student-critic might break in here with cries of "Wake up"; but teachers must not think that because of his seeming impudence he is less worthy material for training in leadership than one who, on the surface, seems to conform, accepts offices, but is never seen receiving the Sacraments. The objector means to emphasize that one cannot be a mediocre Christian. ("Are you for Me or against Me?") Christianity is not something passive and inert, mean and mediocre, comfortable and compromising. It should be explosive, dynamic, revolutionary. If students do not integrate their lives through living the liturgy, sentimental piety will not give them strength. They must learn to see Christ in social institutions, economic structures, business establishments, and the whole pattern of modern civilization.

In the Ages of Faith a spirit of co-operation characterized Christian life. In the Crusades (to protect Holy Places from the infidel) as in the building of cathedrals, this working together in a common cause included wholesome social relations, great moral strength, and economic unity. Only the Faith in common could weld so many thousands of people, so disparate in language, customs, education, wealth, and social position into conviction of the justness of so great a cause. While the education of the time trained the young for their place in their social groups, its chief aim was to make them worthy members of the Kingdom of Christ. All men were conscious of the supreme privilege of citizenship in Christ's Kingdom; they knew that it profited a man nothing to gain the whole world but lose his soul. They were convinced they must so use their natural and supernatural talents (bestowed by their Creator) with right reason that

eternal reward would be theirs. Today in Catholic schools
the same ideal informs all training. Seek ye first the Kingdom
of God and His justice—nothing else counts in eternity.

Having brought Christian principles into domination of
their own lives, they must work them into all the ramifications of life around them. The integrated personality is constantly aware of the religious, cultural, and scientific values
of existence, to which they must respond by relating them
to their daily lives. They must achieve an understanding of
their heritage and its contribution to Western civilization.
Thus will they increase their knowledge and comprehension
of God and their fellow men and serve Him the more effi-
ciently through serving them.

Students can see that when co-operating with the in-
structor and with each other to get the greatest profit from
instruction their *esprit de corps* is evidencing concretely the
doctrine of the Mystical Body. When, in the smallest way,
they are helping the Church mold industries and institutions
according to Christian principles, when they think of the
Church in that role rather than as bureaus or members who
have top political or economic positions, they have become
conscious of the Church as the Living Christ and not as
real estate.

We emphasize this distinction between the externally
visible signs of the Church and her embodiment of the
Spirit of Christ, His continuation, endowed with His in-
visible supernatural powers. We smile at the naïvete of
one who thinks that by the external marks of the Catholic
Church is meant the cross on the steeple or the worn steps,
but there may be need of emphasizing that without her
inner soul (which is Christ) the Church would be nothing
more than any other corporation of men, a mere juridical
association. To correct outsiders' impression that the Church
is a business corporation which can exact payment of dues
from members or punish those who do not pay becomes

imperative whenever her inner supernatural reality is over-
shadowed by her external social constitution. In education
such a point of view encourages the slave mentality
Nietzsche talked about. The impression must be avoided
under any circumstance.

Realization that the liturgy activates the doctrine of
the Mystical Body makes our Lord a living, present reality
and His principles dynamic and most efficient and inclusive
in the liturgy's possibilities for good. With such a perfecting
force, a student can integrate his life with his studies. He is
the more dynamic because conscious that in him, as a human
being, the kingdoms of heaven and earth can unite, that to
form the whole man each of these elements must be complete—the material and the spiritual, the theoretical and
the practical, each in its fullness.

By applying these teachings to their own lives as
thoroughly as possible, students can avoid enthusiasm for
man-made cures for festering sores on the body politic. Such
efforts are commendable, to be sure; but their harm lies
in a stopping short of realizing the basic functions of Christ's
teachings in all lasting reform or in permitting artificialities
to supplant Christian principles. To heal the divisions, put
order into the confusions, and socialize the individualisms
which are destroying civilization, men follow the complete
livable procedure of internal worship of the Mystical Body
as expressed outwardly through the liturgy. Lest that statement be considered a half truth until amplified, the statement
will bear restatement—the liturgy is the only effective, all-
inclusive solution for our difficulties because it continues the
life and activity of Christ.

To concretize the preceding ideas, Catholic education
must build Christian character, evoke well-rounded personalities exercising leadership through what they are and
not through a superficial showmanship or propaganda technique. Leaders must be formed from within, unfold organ-

ically, and develop their inner lives so they can inspire others to lives of fulfillment and not mere spectatorship. The reverence of self they learn will contrast strongly with the blunted perception of those who contend their bodies are their own to do with them what they please, with the subjective morality of those who choose their own movies, reading, and companions in defiance of moral guidance, or violate their moral being with infidelity, treachery, disloyalty, or blasphemy.

In Benedictine schools in the United States today we still feel the influence of the Cluniac reform. Nothing exemplifies the directing guidance of Christianity from the ninth to the twelfth centuries better than the foundation and development of the Benedictine Abbey at Cluny; in fact, it marks the turning point in the history of education in the Middle Ages. By the twelfth century, the Cluny system included three hundred fourteen abbeys instead of the typical Benedictine arrangement of each abbey a separate unit—the abbot having the powers of a bishop as in the United States today. (Because of Cluny there were ten thousand monks directly under Papal jurisdiction.) This growing Cluny system changed the character of feudalism and of all medieval society—an amazing work in education. It did not impose the central government (modeled on the Roman idea); it got each abbey to accept it voluntarily: As a result we find revived the Christian spirit of living according to Christ's teachings, the clergy and monks influenced for the better (full ecclesiastical control over bestowal of bishoprics—the Medician Pope Leo X, a cardinal at fourteen; William of Croy, a cardinal at ten), the lot of the serfs improved (they could gain their freedom more easily), the restoration of a society ready for intellectual development, and the truce of God introduced. This last reform not only prevented clashes of arms over the week end; it reaffirmed the fact that the knight was a man dedicated and it christianized the institution of chivalry (resulting in the first Crusade). When Cluny decayed, St. Bernard of Citeaux took up the banner of reform, as Father M. Raymond, O.C.S.O., shows in *The Family That Overtook Christ*.

Four great popes of the eleventh and twelfth centuries came from Cluny—Gregory VII, Urban II, Paschal II, and Urban V. (It was Gregory VII—Hildebrand—who defied and won his dispute with Henry IV over the question of lay investiture—Henry made his submission at Canossa. Catholic students draw inspiration from recalling Bismarck's "Nach Canossa geh ich nicht" and wondering what has happened to him and his Prussian aggression.)

The motto of all scholars, poets, musicians, and craftsmen of the Ages of Faith can still be ours—in fact, Jesuit schools work under the aegis "All for the glory of God," the slogan of their Order. All intellectual and artistic achievement blossomed under supernatural inspiration and found its apotheosis in the superb pageantry of liturgical worship. Since *"Omnia Dei majorem gloriam"* impelled craftsmen to give their best in metal working, weaving tapestry, and carving wood, what they produced were worthy offerings of homage to God and His saints. Students in Catholic schools have borne in on their imaginations that these glories have been and will remain ours as long as we say the *Credo*.

Henry Adams' *Saint Michel and Chartres* reveals inspiringly a Protestant's reaction to the Catholicism of the eleventh century. *Chartres* he finds the perfect Notre Dame (Church of Our Lady). As his letters to his brother Brooks show, Henry Adams was searching for a philosophy of history. During the period of the First Crusade (eleventh century) Europe had a unity in living, in religion, in art, and in poetry never achieved since. Man's energy was expressed through religion. Since the eleventh and twelfth centuries frequently men have confounded themselves by failing to unite the finite and the Infinite, by not making human economy accord with the Divine Plan.

Henry Adams has the same tendency as Spengler (German pessimist) and as Toynbee (special pleader for Episcopalianism), who see human history as thermodynamics (under laws of the expenditure of energy) and apply the theory to human energy as well. In searching for this fixed principle through art (architecture) Adams discovered what he thought the highest point in history (the widespread veneration of the Blessed Virgin). In the architecture (the stress and strain of the medieval cathedral), Adams finds mankind bursting asunder in triumphant creation in the effort of the finite to burst into the Infinite.

The great economies that surrounded the abbeys solved the social problems of the day. These people knew our Lady as well as they knew their own mothers—and much more familiarly than they knew the reigning queens of the time.

It took an enormously popular movement to build the cathedral. The inhabitants of Chartres were inspired as a working group—for the honor and glory of God. More than a thousand persons (rich and poor, aristocrats and commoners) would haul the carts loaded with stone in great silence—repeating prayers.

Adams leaves open the question of whether man may recapture a unity through one common religious concept (as they did in the eleventh to the thirteenth centuries). He would have appreciated deeply being without skepticism, doubt, and bewilderment. "The philosophers could have built the cathedrals and the architects could have built the philosophy."

Through improving organization, with the aid of religious orders of teachers, preachers, and social workers, in these centuries the Church benefited endlessly the nations she had Christianized. Today thinking people (non-Catholic as well as Catholic) are searching for that unity of Christendom and of the world (Gandhi, Churchill). When Protestant churches are trying to merge their efforts, Catholics should appreciate the advantage of their own unity.

APPENDIX

Notes to Chapters 5, 9, 10

To Chapter Five

1. Irvin S. Cobb mentions those sent to Europe to watch military operations in 1918 (*Exit Laughing*, p. 310). There are, too, in the news, men born Catholic but unable to live the life; in death whatever they gained of the world will be valueless to them. No need to mention unfortunates, baptized as Catholics, but neglected by a parent and reared without a religion. Gene Fowler, a brilliant writer, records, "If I had a father, all confusions would be miraculously resolved." His wife and family became Catholics before he did.

2. The Church is the only institution open to all sorts and conditions of men. Arthur F. Mullen's autobiography (*Western Democrat*), Gene Fowler's *Beau James* (Mayor Walker of New York City) and *Good Night, Sweet Prince* (John Barrymore), Frederick G. Lieb's *Connie Mack* (baseball), *Bing Crosby Story*, Martin W. Dougherty's *House on Humility Street* (North American College in Rome, where many of the Catholic Hierarchy studied), and S. T. McGrath's *Catholic Policemen's and Firemen's Companion* illustrate.

3. Compare the first note in Wm. T. Kane's *Essay Toward a History of Education*, Chapter on Reformation. The fact

that Luther and other leaders of the so-called Reformation were diseased venereally explains in part, at least, why these men could not accept the Church's teaching. A check on American born no-longer-Catholics who violated marriage laws is revelatory.

In Isabel Leighton's *Aspirin Age*, "Konklave Is Kokomo" by Robert Coughlan tells how the Ku Klux Klan lost some of its strength but none of its evil when their Grand Dragon murdered a girl on a train (1923). No amount of political influence has got him a parole.

General Winfield Scott, who brought the War with Mexico to a successful close a century ago by his victorious march into Mexico City in 1847, was mixed up with the Native American movement, which brought outrageous attacks on Catholic churches, homes, and individuals. *Researches* prints a letter he wrote November 17, 1844. Scott, however, says he had advised that religion be excluded as an element in the Party, and that the name *American* be used without *Native* in order to drive away loyal naturalized citizens. He wanted a legal distinction made between "citizens" and "denizens." But later his Nativist views changed. Scott's daughter, Virginia, a brilliant girl, became a Visitation nun at Georgetown in 1828. Her mother witnessed the ceremony and wrote a letter describing it. "I hope that I love religion," she said, "but if I were a saint upon earth I should never hide my light in a monastery." Two of her granddaughters disagreed—Maria Mayo and Emily McTavish, both of whom became nuns.

Another daughter of the Scotts, Cornelia (also a convert) was such a beautiful girl that when she was in Rome she was often taken as a model by artists for the Madonna. Major General Scott himself, when in Mexico City, issued official orders that demanded respect for the Catholic religion of the people. "No civilized person," he wrote, "will ever wantonly do any act to hurt the religious feelings of others." He told Protestant Americans to keep out of the way or to pay the Catholic religion and its ceremonies every decent mark of respect and conference.

(General Scott was, of course, not a Catholic. The Whigs gave him their nomination for the Presidency in 1852; and to serve in that position was the great ambition of his life, but he was not elected. It has been written of him that he "was the associate of every President from Jefferson to Lincoln and the emissary in critical undertakings of most of them." He was called "Fuss and Feathers" because of his punctiliousness in dress and decorum. He was 80 years old, less 15 days, when he died. His wife, who died in Rome in 1862, is buried beside him at West Point. They had seven children. Three married daughters survived him. Two of his daughters became converts to the Catholic Church in Rome, according to the *Catholic Espositor* of June, 1843. Virginia, the one who became a Visitation nun, died August 29, 1845, in her twenty-fourth year. The *U.S. Catholic Magazine* reported that she was in failing health when she entered the convent.)

Our Sunday Visitor Press published the pamphlets: (a) *History of American Persecution*, (b) *Reformers of the Church—Their Characters*, (c) *The Anti-Catholic Motive* (7 classes), (d) *Record of Anti-Catholic Agitators* (biographies), (e) *Catholics Always Loyal to Their Country*, (f) *Catholic and Non-Catholic Quotations.*

In June 1946, jealous mentality toward the Catholic Church was seemingly displayed in the General Assembly of the Presbyterian Church in the U.S.A. by its Standing Committee on Social Education and Action. "Aggressiveness of the Hierarchy of the Roman Catholic Church in pressing for claims for a favored position for itself as a Church" was charged. This "aggressiveness," it was said, at times involves action and pressure on sources of public opinion and public policy. Just why it is wrong for Catholics to try to influence public policy, but right for Presbyterians, was not explained.

The report said the principles of religious liberty are

freedom of worship, equality of all religious bodies before the state, and adherence to the following:

a. That the true head and authority of the Christian Church is neither a state official nor an ecclesiastical hierarchy but Jesus Christ.

b. That no Church should seek for itself, or tolerate others seeking for themselves, a privileged political position or status.

c. That the government should put no discriminatory limitations upon the liberty of any one religious body or group.

In answer to this report a Catholic clergyman pointed out:

a. That Catholics have never held that a state official is the head of the Christian Church. This has been a Protestant doctrine in some European nations, not a Catholic one. Neither have Catholics ever held other than that Jesus Christ is the head of their Church. The Pope is the earthly head, but only as the Vicar of Jesus Christ, not in the same manner as Christ Himself. As for the Catholic Hierarchy, Christ founded it; that is His method of ruling His Church.

b. The Catholic Church in the United States has never sought a privileged political position. It does expect all the rights guaranteed by American constitutional law. It is the duty of any Christian denomination, if it believes it is God's true Church, to try, by decent means to bring others to its way of thinking.

c. Signs are increasing of a pugnacious spirit by some persons against Catholicity.

The Presbyterian Church in the U.S.A. protested the present relations between the U.S. government and the Vatican and urged further relations be based on the "American principle of separation of Church and State."

In Fairfield, Washington, recall of Myron C. Taylor as the President's representative to the Vatican was demanded by the Northwestern district of the American Lutheran Church. A committee of the Federation of the Churches of

Christ in America was to see President Truman June 6 to make a similar protest.

These actions followed similar ones by many other Protestant bodies. The movement's real motive may be suggested in Matthew xxvii, 18, where it is said of Pilate and Christ: "For he knew that they had delivered him up out of envy."

Anti-Catholic bigotry separated the United States and Canada politically in Revolutionary days more effectively than the three thousand mile geographical border—and that natural combination has never been united in the centuries since. Because the basis of the American Regular Army consisted of Catholic Canadians, but for bigotry that tremendously rich territory comprising the vast stretch of continent north of our country to Alaska would be part of our country. The Quebec Act (1774) made Canadian Catholics refuse assistance to the fanatic anti-Catholic American Colonists who showed so violently their animosity. To Washington's credit in his ending (November 5, 1775) anti-Catholic celebration of the "Pope's Day" in the Army, but the widespread attack on Catholics revolted the Catholic Canadians—and another queer quirk was added to American history.

The Catholic Truth Society (Brooklyn) has given maligners a crushing rebuke by making known to Americans the Catholic pages of their history—a greater record than that of any non-Catholics. The Church uses no reliance on the denunciation of assailants to continue or support her existence. A perfect society, it renews itself from within, and assaults of enemies through the ages have failed to daunt her in her divine mission. In 1840 Macaulay, the English Protestant historian, novelist, and essayist, epitomized what should be said in this connection.

The history of that Church joints together the two great ages of human civilization. No other institution is left standing which carries the mind back to the time when the smoke of sacrifice rose from the Pantheon, and when camelopards and tigers bounded in the Flavian amphitheatre. The proudest royal houses are but of yesterday when compared with the line of the Supreme Pontiffs. That line we trace back in an unbroken series from the Pope who crowned Napoleon, in the nineteenth century, to the Pope who crowned Pepin, in the eighth; and far beyond the time of Pepin the august dynasty extends, till it is lost in the twilight of fable. The republic of Venice came next in antiquity. But the republic of Venice was modern when compared with the Papacy; and the republic of Venice is gone, and the Papacy remains. The Papacy remains not in decay, not a mere antique; but full of life and youthful vigor. The Catholic Church is still sending forth, to the farthest ends of the world, missionaries as zealous as those who landed in Kent with Augustine, and is still confronting hostile kings with the same spirit with which she confronted Attila. The number of her children is greater than in any former age. Her acquisitions in the new world have more than compensated her for what she has lost in the old. Her spiritual ascendency extends over the vast countries which lie between the plains of the Missouri and Cape Horn— countries which, a century hence, may not improbably contain a population as large as that which now inhabits Europe. The members of her community are certainly no fewer than a hundred and fifty millions; and it will be difficult to show that all the other Christian sects united amount to a hundred and twenty millions. Nor do we see any sign which indicates that the term of her long dominion is approaching. She saw the commencement of all the governments and of all the ecclesiastical establishments that now exist in the world, and we feel no assurance that she is not destined to see the end of them all. She was great and respected before the Saxon had set foot on Britain, before the Frank has passed the Rhine, when Grecian eloquence still flourished at Antioch, when idols were still worshipped in the temple of Mecca. And she may still exist in undiminished vigor, when some traveler from New Zealand shall, in the midst of a vast solitude, take his stand on a broken arch of London bridge to sketch the ruins of St. Paul's.

Catholics may be just proud of their ancestors' contribution to the American historical record; so closely are their evidences of gallant devotion interwoven with the marvelous tapestry which has amazed an admiring world that to blur or attempt to obliterate the record of Catholic's self-sacrificing heroism and patriotic virtue is to dull the brightest pages of our national history.

See (1) Hilaire Belloc's "Ignorance among Catholics" (*Sign*, 18:611 ff., May, 1939) and (2) "Non-Catholics Don't Know Us" (*ibid.*, p. 537) amplify. (3) "Back to Epicureanism" (*Catholic Mind*, Vol. 26, No. 15). (4) F. J. Mueller's *Brains and Belief* handles tactfully the doubts of those who fail to see the role of reason in relation to faith.

4. Matthew Johnson exposed *The Robber Barons* and McConnell, Melby, and Arndt's *New Schools for a New Culture* (Chapter VII) mentions Frank and Jesse James, Flo Ziegfeld, Hearst, Charlie McCarthy (a ventriloquist's dummy); those authors stress people rather than movements because it is people (Barnum, for example) who actually influence our cultural development.

5. For sincere conformity with the mind of the church, see *Catholic Educational Review*, 38: 487-91; *Natl. Cath. Ed. Assn. Bulletin.* 17:354; "Thinking with the Church," *Month*, 173:164 ff.; E. T. Watkin's *The Catholic Centre;* B. Confrey's *Original Readings in Catholic Action*, pp. 179 and 269.

See also Burton Confrey's *Moral Mission of Literature*, pp. 63 ff., for discussion of Crashaw and the Cambridge Platonists; his "The Perennial Opposition to the Classics," pp. 14 ff., and Discourse VIII of *The Idea of a University* ("Knowledge Viewed in Relation to Religion").

6. The Catholic University Press has microfilmed a biography of Chief Justice Edward D. White of the U.S. Supreme Court by Sister Marie Carolyn Klinkhamer.

7. Consult these Chapters from Volume 1 of *Catholic Builders of the Nation;* (a) Religion and Citizenship, (b) Notes on Religious Liberty, (c) Religious Liberty in the Western Hemisphere, (d) Church and State in the U.S., (e) Catholics and American Politics, (f) Catholic Civic Ideals, (g) Catholic Contribution to the Colonial Period. (h) Franciscan Missions, (i) Catholics in Civil War and

Reconstruction, (j) Catholic Co-operation in Establishing the Seat of Government, (k) Catholic New England, (l) Catholicism in Boston, (m) Catholic New York, (n) Catholicism in Philadelphia, (o) Pioneer Catholics in the Illinois Country, (p) Some Catholic Leaders in Kentucky, (q) Leaders of Commerce and Industry in the Mississippi Valley, (r) Catholics of the South, (s) Catholic Leaders of the Southwest, (t) Catholics in the Development of the Northwest, (u) Catholicism in Alaska. There is possibility of making a telling contribution by bringing the record in each case to date. Only anti-Catholics nowadays would refuse parochial school children auxiliary services such as bus transportation.

8. Consider discussing possibilities of using: (a) J. M. Finotti's *Bibliographia Catholica Americana* and its supplement *Catholic Authorship in the American Colonies before 1784,*
(b) My Bookcase Series (Wagner),
(c) "100 Best Catholic Books," *America*. 31:381 ff., Feb. 2, 1924.

9. For Catholic influence on the Declaration of Independence: see (a) *America*, 49:321 ff., and (b) 67:351 ff., (c) Alleged Catholic Sources, *Fortnightly Review*, 38:27 and (d) 39:88; (e) rejoinder, *ibid.*, 39:51 or (f) *Catholic Mind*, 28:283 ff. (g) Bibliography, *Historical Record and Studies* 34:137. (h) "Did Bellarmine Influence Jefferson?" *Commonweal*, 42:284 ff. (i) John A. Ryan and M. F. X. Millar, *The State and the Church* (Hamilton and Suarez *De Legibus,* pp. 193 f.). Father Millar in *Thought*: (j) "Scholastic Philosophy and American Political Theory," 1:112 ff.; (k) "Suarez and Chief Justice Marshall," 7:588 ff.; (l) "Origin of Sound Democratic Principles in Catholic Tradition," 2:805 ff.; (m) "The Modern State and Catholic Principles," 12:46 ff.; (n) "Bellarmine and the American Constitution," *Irish Studies,* September, 1931. (o) James J. Walsh, *Education of the Founding Fathers of the Republic*

(Scholastician taught in Colonial Colleges). (p) M. J. Adler and W. Farrell, "The Theory of Democracy," *Thomist*, 3:397 and 588. (q) Theodore Maynard's *Orestes Brownson,* p. 352, cites Jefferson's annotated copy of Robert Filmer's *Patriarchs vs. The Natural Rights of Kings* in Library of Congress. (r) A. E. Hott's *Christian Roots of Democracy in America.*

10. Pope Leo XIII's encyclical *Human Liberty* discusses the fact that the type of tolerance taught by liberalism leads to the type of tolerance Liberals show the Church, the deadly vice of liberalism, the extreme and moderate views of liberals, refutation of many Liberals' wish to separate the church from the State wholly and entirely, refutation of the teaching that the church should rule with the consent of her subjects, what would follow if nature gave unlimited liberty to man, and the attitude of the Church on various forms of government and the Church's teachings on civic duty and civic liberty.

Political liberalism, rooted in naturalism, was a revolt against the idea of "divine right of kings." The Church opposed that idea, too, teaching that kings have no power in themselves—all authority comes from God. The naturalism we have discussed in its evil effects on education and religion. The power which Liberals held would be placed in people's hands did lodge at first with men of the middle class (later with women), but the working class got little if any.

By tradition Protestants were Liberals in politics (and laissez faire in economics). The Church works for a *via media*—a balance between individualism (liberalism) and sociality. Liberal societies are free but not organic; totalitarian societies organic but not free. The Church, a perfect society, is both perfectly free and perfectly organic in so far as she maintains her Catholic center. This central position the Mystical Body represents and the liturgy realizes— as does the individual Catholic directly in proportion to his living (and active participation of) the liturgy.

To Chapter Nine

1. For an introduction to the reading of the Bible, a stimulating procedure is that of beginning with Genesis and reading straight through. Speed is not a factor in this perusal although one should finish within a year. (In the continuous re-reading of the Bible annually one becomes intimately acquainted with those characters—from Father Abraham on—whose memory has survived through the centuries.)

2. The names of the books of the Old Testament come, like those of a Mass or a papal encyclical, from the initial word or words. "Genesis," for example, means beginning. Make a list.

3. The most cultured person is he who has read most often understandingly the five great literary bibles: The Bible, ancient Greek epic and classical drama, Dante (and Milton, in contrast, for the Protestant side of the Renaissance), Shakespeare, and the Faust story (What does it profit a man to gain the whole world and suffer the loss of his soul?"). How can Richard Green Moulton's *World Literature* serve as an excellent introduction to this idea?

4. Why do you think there is a philosophy of history. Only such a philosophy can give meaning to the facts—not mere chronology. By taking a long view—seeing what happens in the world in the light of eternity—one realizes that history began with the Fall of Man (whom Christ redeemed), that there is a purpose behind it; and that the goal is the restoration of Christian unity to the world God created. (See "The Reunion of Christendom, *Catholic Mind*, November 22, 1921.) By making human economy accord with the Divine Plan, finding the part all things play in that Plan, and seeing in man the image of his Creator, one discovers the only really unifying force in society, the one

satisfactory explanation giving organization and cohesion
to the flood of events down the centuries. Re-union with
God should be the goal of society if history is to reveal the
sense behind it. Each individual can achieve order and
harmony in his personal life only by using God's gifts with
right reason. Isaias made that clear ("The Rhapsody of
Zion Redeemed," Chapters 40-66), as did St. Augustine (in
his *City of God*), Bossuet's *Universal History*, Brooks Adams'
Law of Civilization and Decay, and Count du Plessis' *Human Caravan*. Those writers who contend there is no sense
to history and that discovering any philosophy of history is
special pleading (as, for example, Toynbee's is Episcopalian,
Friedrich von Schlegel's was romantic and valueless today)
or those seeing in the modern corporate state a glorification
of the medieval guild system—such writers are pessimists,
seeing no order or harmony in history. Spengler, for example,
did not suspect the possibilities of integrating life through
the liturgy, of solving political and social problems through
application of Christian principles. See *America,* 69:577 ff.,
August 28, 1943, for T. S. Eliot's contribution or "Aquinas
and the Missing Link in the Philosophy of History,"
Thought, March, 1934. As a prophetic climax to the whole
Bible and as its Epilogue we have in St. John revelation of
a new disclosure of the divine plan of history—the Kingdom
of the World becoming the Kingdom of Christ.

5. Should anyone have particular interest in philistinism,
Bible history will reveal that our Lord (and every child of
Light) had to try to overcome that spirit of an age or community which makes people adamant toward ideas. Dull
respectability, stuffiness, and worship of material success
dominate them. Their grossly exaggerated idea of their own
importance recalls the Forsytes. Whited sepulchres, they
parade (sometimes through public relations experts, for they
pretend to shun publicity) their cold philanthropy and public charities. See the charted contrast between Christian

234 *Notes to Chapter 9*

charity and philanthropy in B. Confrey's *Catholic Action,*
p. 239.

6. In the Gospel of St. John ("I am in my Father, and ye
in me, and I in you") and in St. Paul ("I live now, not I,
but Christ in me") the achievement of at-one-ment appears;
Divinity and humanity are united. That consummation is
best exemplified in the doctrine of the Mystical Body of
Christ: The Pere Plus's *In Christ Jesus* and Pope Pius XII's
Mystici Corporis Christi (America Press).

7. Because of the difficulty of suiting varied tastes, one
of the following: (a) Francis X. Connolly, *Literature—the
Channel of Culture* [its definite, consecutive pattern of
thought demonstrates the integration of life and literature
and education. Part 1 defines the aims and outcomes of
Christian education especially that provided by the Catholic
college or university]. (b) The Fathers of the Church [new
series]—*St. Augustine,* for example. (c) Ancient Christian
Writers series includes St. Augustine's commentary on the
Sermon on the Mount translated, with notes, by John J.
Jepson, S.S. (d) Anton Pegis, *Wisdom of Catholicism* [early
Fathers to modern times]. (e) Sister Agnes Alma, O.P.,
"Assimilation of Catholic Ideals through the Beatitudes,"
Catholic Educational Review, September, 1928, to June,
1929. (f) R. Garragou-Lagrange, O.P., *The Love of God
and the Cross of Jesus.* (The marvelous harmony between
the mystical doctrine of St. Thomas Aquinas and St. John of
the Cross leads this master of ascetical theology to develop
his theme based on two questions: "Thou shalt love the Lord
thy God with thy whole heart and with thy whole soul and
with thy whole mind" and "He who does not carry his cross
and follow me cannot be my disciple.")

8. B. Confrey's *Original Readings for Catholic Action*
(p. 3) discusses truth as the source of real freedom—not
license to range in the field of faith and morals but avoid-
ance of the enslaving domination of sensuality, of thinking

without solid foundation, of the falsities of pseudo-science. Because they can know the truth in every ramification of life, Catholics have no reason to skulk in the shadow of half-truth or to lead low lives.

9. There will be no difficulty in locating discussions of Catholic Action—books through a library catalogue or *Cumulative Book Index,* articles through *Catholic Periodical Index.* B. Confrey's *Catholic Action,* a text for college level and study clubs, discusses in detail methods of bringing Christian principles into all phases of living. The companion volumes *Original Readings for Catholic Action* and *Readings for Catholic Action* present the materials on which the Activities of the text are based. The same author's *Social Studies* presents, with *Readings,* an approach to the same ideas for senior high school. The material has been used successfully with teachers when introducing them to methods of teaching social science, for each text has a Teacher's Manual edition. The definition of Catholic Action is the participation by the laity in the Apostolate of the Hierarchy. We base Catholic Action on the liturgy, the love of God motivates it, the Hierarchy directs it, and lay men and women contribute most effectively by cooperation with grace as naturally as a healthy arm cooperates with the body.

10. *Social Studies* (Unit IV) and *Catholic Action* (Unit II make clear the fact that the saint is the norm. Anyone not trying to achieve an eternity with God is short-sighted, odd, and not normal. So important is the achievement of this point of view that these texts include many varied Activities leading to its comprehension.

To Chapter Ten

Just as the Peace Corps is a significant test of Americanism, so one phase of the effectiveness of Catholic education in America may be judged by the willingness of Catholics to share their achievements with the less fortunate.

Such are conditions in mission countries throughout the world and so subject are they to change that instead of numerous activities related to each country we might recall the projects for the missions on the elementary, secondary, and the college level. *Maryknoll* will issue an annual statement on "Present Conditions in China" or South America, for instance. The *Messenger of the Sacred Heart* will discuss the mission intention for each month—in India, Uganda, Kenya, and Tanganyika. Diocesan newspapers will carry NCWC reports on conditions in Korea, Japan, and our responsibility for the future; and the special section of the Society for the Propagation of the Faith will tell what other schools are doing. News Notes will report "Russian Orthodox Leader Tells Followers Never to Surrender to the Reds," "Medical Mission Aid Rising" (shipments of medicine increases 40%; more vocations needed), "Korean Soldiers Appreciate Help from the Home Front," and "Pope Says Companions of St. Isaac Jogues Examples of Lay Zeal."

In *Social Studies* we included several essays on Negroes (Nos. 207-213), one on the founding of a Newman Club (pp. 215 ff.) and another describing a Communion breakfast at Howard University (pp. 593 ff.). *Catholic Action* (pp. 308 ff.) carries another essay on the Negro. *Readings for Catholic Action* has "The Negro and Catholic Action" (pp. 1621 ff.) and "The Negro and Communism" (pp. 1620 ff.). See also John La Farge's *Interracial Justice;* Buell G. Gallagher's *Color and Conscience;* and John T. Gillard's *Christ, Color and Communism.* His *Colored Catholics in the U.S.*

and *The Catholic Church and the American Negro* are authoritative and include materials on education. Father Gillard is a Josephite, an order dedicated to work among the Negroes.

In *Social Studies* we include four essays on the Indian (Nos. 214, 215, 216, and 217); in *Catholic Action* (pp. 308 ff.); in *Readings for Catholic Action,* "Justice for Indians" (pp. 1633 ff.); and the Marquette League (pp. 1631 ff.)

To realize that in four centuries Christianity in our hemisphere has grown from not one church to what we have today, one might begin a project of "firsts" in Latin America. From them one could imagine what results when a strong, self-sustaining nucleus of Catholicism in a mission land gets its own native hierarchies, clergy, Sisters and Brothers—with thousands of schools, churches, orphanages and hospitals.

(a) First grammar school—Mexico City, 1524, erected in Mexico by the Franciscans under Bishop Zumarraga. Children were taught writing, music and Latin. The U.S. now has more than 8,000 grammar schools with more than 2,351,000 pupils. It is to the great credit of the missionaries that they have nearly as many under instruction—out of a population ten times that of the U.S.

(b) The first printing press in the New World—as early as 1535, the Franciscan Bishop Zumarraga printed the first catechisms in Mexico. In the U.S. alone there are over 400 Catholic publications. The mission fields have recognized the importance of a Catholic Press. There is hardly a region that does not have some kind of publication.

(c) The Hospital of Jesus of Nazareth—first hospital in the New World. This hospital was established by the Franciscans in Mexico City under the title of the Immaculate Conception [La Purissima Concepcion] and is still in operation. In the U.S. there are 731 Catholic general and 110 special hospitals, treating 4,200,000 patients annually. The missions boast 936 hospitals.

(d) First university in North America at Mexico City. [See James J. Walsh's *Education, How Old the New.*] Cross College was erected in Tlatelcleo, Mexico, in 1536; the Capuchin College in Nova Scotia, 1634, and the Jesuit College in Quebec City, 1635.

The Spanish colonial period from 1500 to 1800 was the longest era of unbroken peace over so large an area, in all history. Racial discrimination was unknown, religious strife absent; all men, noble or peasant, red or white, stood equal before the law. Indian slavery had been abolished in 1546. Every important colony and city had its university, many of them founded before Harvard. Church and Crown vied with each other in the furtherance of education. That these things are not known in English-speaking lands is due to the "Black Legend" of alleged Spanish cruelty, propagated by bigots and pirates, economic and political enemies of Spain, until they have attained the axiomatic status of a devil's gospel.

Just as Mexican politics killed the great missions of California, so Spanish political power ruined the famous Reductions of Paraguay, the most successful civilizing settlements in the New World. Three of the Jesuit priests who met martyrdom in this labor—Rocco Gonzales, Alphonso Rodriguez, and Juan del Castillo, all killed at the instigation of an Indian Medicine Man in 1628—were beatified in Rome, January 23, 1934. Even the sneering Voltaire referred to the Reductions as "the triumph of humanity."

In *This Is Spain* Richard Pattee exposes lies spread by Communists to deceive other nations. Religious worship by non-Catholics is permitted. Propaganda by non-Catholics, however, is prohibited because Spain is overwhelmingly Catholic and non-Catholic propaganda is regarded as offensive to the nation. Of 200,000 who enrolled in the army some time ago only 22 were not Catholic.

"Puerto Ricans Are People" (*Sign,* March, 1948) discusses American citizens who, after five centuries of Spanish and American tutelage, are now asking that they be recognized. To do them justice, we must try to understand them.

Etsu Suramoto's *Daughter of the Samurai* describes the life of a pagan schoolgirl in Japan. The *Magnificat* (80:714 ff., July, 1947) included a searching article on the futile visit of the President of a large state university as chairman of a commission to study education in Japan. In his report he betrayed a fondness for the phrase "freedom of inquiry." What do you think of these questions a Japanese might ask? And would she appreciate the answers from Catholics, whose Christianity had been referred to slightingly as "idolatrous," "outmoded," "antiquated," "dogma-bound," "superstitious"?

Is it true that in American schools some people are considered better than others, perhaps because of the accident of birth or color or race or religion? I have heard it told that there are special schools for Negroes and that there are schools and colleges that will not enroll Negro students. Is it true?

Is it true that in America colleges have quotas for Jews, and medical schools are loathe to accept even the most promising of them? Is it true that Jews are called "kikes," Italians are "wops," Frenchmen are "frogs," and Irishmen "micks"? Is it true that young men and women in colleges and even sometimes in high schools band themselves together into societies that are called "fraternities" and "sororities" and that these are nothing but breeding grounds for snobbery and conceit and contempt for those who do not belong?

Is it true that there are large physical areas of America where valleys are granite canyons and mountains are steel girded skyscrapers, and where children see but a ragged patch of the sky? What is a Dead End Kid? What is a Four Eff? Is it true that in colleges in America hired athletes compete in athletic contests for the delight and education of the American public? Is it true that the shepherd of these gladiators receives a greater stipend for his services than does the most famous don? Is it true that for most young American men and women athletic competition and physical training is vicarious?

Is it true that juvenile delinquency is now written in capital

letters in America and that the American school system must
take its share of the blame and censure for that achievement?

Is it true that in America there are many one-room schools,
with poorly paid and ill-trained teachers? Is it true that the teaching profession has been the refuge for many psychological misfits
and cranks and cowards?